Crafting the Witch

Studies in Medieval History and Culture

FRANCIS G. GENTRY, *General Editor*

Fair and Varied Forms
Visual Textuality in Medieval
Illustrated Manuscripts
Mary C. Olson

**The Contested Theological Authority
of Thomas Aquinas**
The Controversies between Hervaeus
Natalis and Durandis of St. Pourçain
Elizabeth Lowe

**Body and Sacred Place in Medieval
Europe, 1100–1389**
Dawn Marie Hayes

Women of the Humiliati
A Lay Religious Order in
Medieval Civic Life
Sally Mayall Brasher

Consuming Passions
The Uses of Cannibalism in Late
Medieval and Early Modern Europe
Merrall Llewelyn Price

Literary Hybrids
Crossdressing, Shapeshifting, and
Indeterminacy in Medieval and
Modern French Narrative
Erika E. Hess

The King's Two Maps
Cartography and Culture in
Thirteenth-Century England
Daniel Birkholz

**Pestilence in Medieval and Early
Modern English Literature**
Bryon Lee Grigsby

**Race and Ethnicity in
Anglo-Saxon Literature**
Stephen J. Harris

**Aspects of Love in John Gower's
Confessio Amantis**
Ellen Shaw Bakalian

The Medieval Tradition of Thebes
History and Narrative in the OF Roman
de Thèbes, Boccaccio, Chaucer,
and Lydgate
Dominique Battles

Worlds Made Flesh
Reading Medieval Manuscript Culture
Lauryn S. Mayer

Empowering Collaborations
Writing Partnerships between Religious
Women and Scribes in the Middle Ages
Kimberly M. Benedict

**The Water Supply System of
Siena, Italy**
The Medieval Roots of the Modern
Networked City
Michael P. Kucher

**The Epistemology of the Monstrous
in the Middle Ages**
Lisa Verner

Desiring Truth
The Process of Judgment in
Fourteenth-Century Art and Literature
Jeremy Lowe

The Preaching Fox
Festive Subversion in the Plays
of the Wakefield Master
Warren Edminster

**Non-Native Sources for the
Scandinavian Kings' Sagas**
Paul A. White

Kingship, Conquest, and *Patria*
Literary and Cultural Identities in
Medieval French and Welsh
Arthurian Romance
Kristen Lee Over

**Saracens and the Making of
English Identity**
The Auchinleck Manuscript
Siobhain Bly Calkin

Traveling through Text
Message and Method in Late
Medieval Pilgrimage Accounts
Elka Weber

**Between Courtly Literature and
Al-Andalus**
Matière d'Orient and the Importance of
Spain in the Romances of the Twelfth-
Century Writer Chrétien de Troyes
Michelle Reichert

**Maps and Monsters in Medieval
England**
Asa Simon Mittman

**Rooted in the Earth, Rooted in
the Sky**
Hildegard of Bingen and
Premodern Medicine
Victoria Sweet

"She, This in Blak"
Vision, Truth, and Will in Geoffrey
Chaucer's *Troilus and Criseyde*
T. E. Hill

Through the Daemon's Gate
Kepler's *Somnium*, Medieval Dream
Narratives, and the Polysemy of
Allegorical Motifs
Dean Swinford

**Conflict and Compromise in the
Late Medieval Countryside**
Lords and Peasants in Durham,
1349–1400
Peter L. Larson

**Illuminating the Borders of
Northern French and Flemish
Manuscripts, 1270–1310**
Elizabeth Moore Hunt

**Speculative Grammar and Stoic
Language Theory in Medieval
Allegorical Narrative**
From Prudentius to Alan of Lille
Jeffrey Bardzell

Crafting the Witch
Gendering Magic in Medieval and
Early Modern England
Heidi Breuer

Crafting the Witch

Gendering Magic in Medieval and
Early Modern England

Heidi Breuer

New York   London

First published 2009
by Routledge
711 Third Avenue, New York, NY 10017

Simultaneously published in the UK
by Routledge
2 Park Square, Milton Park, Abingdon, Oxfordshire OX14 4RN

Routledge is an imprint of the Taylor & Francis Group, an informa business

First issued in paperback 2011

© 2009 Taylor & Francis

Typeset in Sabon by IBT Global.

All rights reserved. No part of this book may be reprinted or reproduced or utilised in any form or by any electronic, mechanical, or other means, now known or hereafter invented, including photocopying and recording, or in any information storage or retrieval system, without permission in writing from the publishers.

Trademark Notice: Product or corporate names may be trademarks or registered trademarks, and are used only for identification and explanation without intent to infringe.

Library of Congress Cataloging in Publication Data
Breuer, Heidi, 1972-
 Crafting the witch : gendering magic in medieval and early modern England / by Heidi Breuer.
  p. cm.—(Studies in medieval history and culture)
 Includes bibliographical references and index.
 1. Literature, Medieval—History and criticism. 2. English literature—History and criticism. 3. Witches in literature. 4. Arthurian romances—History and criticism.
 5. Older women in literature. 6. Magic—England—History. 7. Magic in literature. 8. Witchcraft—England—History. 9. Witches in motion pictures.
 I. Title.
 PN671.B73 2009
 820'.9377—dc22
 2008050963

ISBN13: 978-0-415-97761-6 (hbk)
ISBN13: 978-0-415-69957-0 (pbk)
ISBN13: 978-0-203-87678-7 (ebk)

Contents

Preface	ix
Acknowledgments	xi

1. "Are You a Good Witch or a Bad Witch?": An Introduction to Medieval and Early Modern Magic — 1

2. Gender-Blending: Transformative Power in Twelfth- and Thirteenth-Century Arthurian Literature — 13

3. From Rags to Riches, Or the Step-Mother's Revenge: Transformative Power in Late Medieval Arthurian Romances — 52

4. The Lady is a Hag: Three Writers and the Transformation of Magic in Sixteenth-Century England — 96

5. Hags on Film: Contemporary Echoes of the Early Modern Wicked Witch — 137

Notes	163
Bibliography	175
Index	187

Preface

I suppose every writer feels that the writing is never done; there's always one more idea, one more thing to say, one more source to footnote. At some point, we must let go, offer our creations to the world, even if we know there's probably one more thing we could do. We have to take the risk.

Every time writers publish their ideas, they take risks—they expose themselves to criticism and praise, to challenge and support, to opportunities for (sometimes painful) growth. It's especially risky to write in ways that challenge the dominant disciplinary norms, a fact many great thinkers have encountered in their quests for knowledge and progressive change. My project endorses many norms in my discipline—like the importance of using direct textual evidence to support claims about literature and culture, the need for accurate, consistent systems of citation, the assertion that representations have a direct, but complicated relationship to lived existence, and the claim that creative, artistic production is both valuable and necessary to human life. I join with feminist writers working in various disciplines in revealing the operation of patriarchy in representation and culture, an approach which, while perhaps not universally accepted, is certainly routinely practiced and endorsed across disciplines and campuses nation-wide. These are not moments of great risk for me, I think. But there are two instances in which I do, perhaps, risk something.

The first is this: I believe that academic writing should be accessible to non-specialist readers. This is not to say that I dislike theory, because I find literary theory to be one of the most vibrant areas of research and scholarship within the discipline, a revitalizing force that imbues my own analyses in myriad ways. But I think that complex ideas can be communicated in accessible, understandable prose, and even more, that academic writing can be creative, humorous, autobiographical, and playful (in the Derridean sense). I have tried to embody my belief in the importance of accessible, playful language in my own writing throughout this book. Maybe my language-play has succeeded, and maybe it hasn't—you'll be the judge of that. But I hope you'll enjoy it, and see it as play, rather than irreverence, as an invitation to join with me in reading the stories we'll discuss together, a call to enjoy the interpretative act.

x *Preface*

The other risk I've taken is to move outside my primary field of expertise—medieval and early modern literature—to incorporate the ideas and research of scholars in fields like economics, history, philosophy, religion, and film studies. While I have made every effort to represent accurately their methodologies and conclusions, I know that my search for answers took me far beyond the comfortable lines of verse full of maidens and jousts to which I'm so accustomed. I beg your indulgence (and theirs) for any missteps I have made while I visited, and I offer in my defense only this: to understand the operation of representation in a culture, we must learn about many aspects of that culture, far too many to be encompassed in one discipline. It is a privilege to enter the conversation with such powerful voices. I anticipate, and expect, that conversation to continue the moment this book leaves the presses, and I hope that my work generates fruitful lines of inquiry and opens up new avenues of discussion. I am well aware of the way in which our own biases and assumptions appear transparent, no matter how we try to analyze them ourselves, until someone else points them out; I am therefore grateful for the uncomfortable, but necessary moments of intellectual growth which will surely arise as my project reaches readers and generates responses.

These risks seem small, however, when compared to the risk of not writing. Not only are there well-known and well-bemoaned occupational and institutional rewards for producing, but this project has personal importance for me. It matters to me how women are represented in the world, and not simply because I am a woman (though I'm sure that has a lot to do with it). It also matters to me how men are represented, how representations function, and how they impact lives. My book is about those things. I hope they matter to you.

Acknowledgments

I will always be grateful that there were so many people who so willingly contributed to my success on this project. The first person I wish to acknowledge is David Johnson, in whose "Middle English Romance" course I first conceived my interest in medieval witches. Naomi Miller was instrumental in helping me coax that small spark of interest into what became quite a wildfire, raging across centuries, and she, Meg Lota Brown, and Susan White all helped me contain the unruly beast long enough to tame it into a dissertation, assisted by the guidance and practical knowledge of Marcia Marma, Daniel Cooper-Alarcón, and Kari MacBride. The long years of gestation, during which my creation was groomed, nurtured, and transformed into a mature, contextualized argument, relied on the generous support of Wright State University's Department of English Language and Literatures and the Department of Literature and Writing Studies at California State University, San Marcos. I would especially like to thank Anita Nix, Sharon Lynette Jones, Lynn Morgan, Leanne Moeller, Jennifer Sheets, and Beckly Traxler, as well as the staff of the Dunbar Library at WSU and the Kellogg Library at CSUSM. To Routledge (and Taylor & Francis), who decided to release the efforts of my proud labor into the wild, I am deeply grateful, and I'm glad to acknowledge the assistance of Frank Gentry, Max Novick, and Erica Wetter in this regard. Throughout this process, two friends in particular endured more than their fair share of whining, frantic phone calls, and the repeated assertion that "it's almost done": Kristin Moss, whose help especially in the final stages was instrumental to the completion of the manuscript, and Shannon Lakanen, whose continued friendship, support, and encouragement has sustained me in moments of doubt and worry, and with whom I have celebrated many of the small victories along the way. To my friends and family, who probably no longer believe me anymore when I tell them I have a book coming out, thanks so much, and I hope it's worth the wait.

Special thanks to the publishers of the following editions of the primary texts considered here (from which all quotations are taken):

Chrétien de Troyes. *Arthurian Romances*. Trans. William W. Kibler and Carleton W. Carroll. London and New York: Penguin, 1991.

xii *Acknowledgments*

Chaucer, Geoffrey. *The Riverside Chaucer*. Ed. Larry D. Benson. 3rd ed. Boston: Houghton Mifflin, 1987.

Geoffrey of Monmouth. *The History of the Kings of Britain*. Trans. Lewis Thorpe. New York and London: Penguin, 1966.

Gower, John. *Confessio Amantis*. Ed. Russell A Peck. Toronto: U of Toronto P, 1980.

Hahn, Thomas, ed. and trans. *Sir Gawain: Eleven Romances and Tales*. Kalamazoo, MI: Medieval Institute P, 1995.

Laȝamon. *Brut, or Historia Brutonum*. Ed. and trans. W. R. J. Barron and S. C. Weinberg. Essex: Longman Group, 1995.

Marie de France. *The Lais of Marie de France*. Trans. Glyn S. Burgess and Keith Busby. New York and London: Penguin, 1986.

Malory, Thomas. *Morte Darthur. Malory Works*. Ed. Eugène Vinaver. 2nd ed. Oxford: Oxford UP, 1971.

Shakespeare, William. *The Riverside Shakespeare*. Ed. G. Blakemore Evans. Boston: Houghton Mifflin, 1974.

Spenser, Edmund. *The Faerie Queene*. Ed. Thomas P. Roche, Jr. London: Penguin, 1978.

1 "Are You a Good Witch or a Bad Witch?"
An Introduction to Medieval and Early Modern Magic

I don't know any witches.

Well, perhaps that's not completely accurate: a student recently stopped me on the stairwell, having just come from a class where the day's topic happened to involve medieval magic, and told me, "I really enjoyed your lecture. I'm Wiccan, you know."

"Thanks," I said, "I'm glad you liked it."

"Are you Wiccan?" she continued, peering shyly under her bangs.

I smiled at her, "No. I really just study medieval magic." Our conversation ended abruptly, and it wasn't until much later that I realized I was the one who killed it. With my casual dismissal, I created a division, a clear indication that I thought there was a big difference between what I do and what she does, between the scholar and the witch. I might as well have said, "I don't believe in magic, you silly girl." So though I met a witch, I didn't really get the chance to know her. Let me try again.

I don't know any witches very well.

Perhaps that's not completely accurate either. I do know some witches quite well: I know the Wicked Witch of the West so intimately that I can recite all her lines from *The Wizard of Oz*, and I know the familiar chant of the Weird sisters, "Double, double, toil and trouble"; I know Circe and *The Witches of Eastwick*, the mistress of the tempting gingerbread house and the nefarious Morgan le Fay; I know the pretend witches, the literary witches, the witches we create, control, and manage to suit our own desires. It's the real witches I don't know, the women and men who practice magic themselves.

And I am not alone. Though there are many scholars who interview and study people who perform magic, the vast majority don't discuss personal relationships with magic-users.[1] In fact, at the 2003 International Medieval Congress in Kalamazoo, the attitude towards the practice of magic in the panels I attended was one of affectionate tolerance, the kind of attitude one adopts towards children. In the academy, we are fascinated by fake witches, but we look down on "real" ones. We are not so unlike those European folks in the Renaissance whose love for the witch-figure resulted

2   *Crafting the Witch*

in her frequent appearance in drama and romance, but whose distaste for practicing witches led to the widespread slaughter of tens of thousands of people. In the U.S., we are no longer violent towards most of those who call themselves witches; instead, we prefer to roll our eyes and let them do as they will, as long as they don't happen to be members of an ethnic minority and don't do anything illegal. The literary space created for witches allows members of mainstream society to enjoy fully something that might otherwise be uncomfortable or embarrassing for them to admit an interest in. And the literary witch is certainly an enjoyable figure, as her frequent representation demonstrates.

The literary witch is so fascinating she's inspired millions of pages of scholarship, including the ones most dear to my heart, *my* pages here. When I was finishing my Masters' coursework, I asked myself a question, and this project is my attempt to answer it. My inquiry was simple: how did Morgan le Fay become a witch? Interested in witches and magic from childhood, I met Morgan during high school when I read *The Mists of Avalon*, and I developed a fondness for Marion Zimmer Bradley's strong, troubled character. She was a witch, but a twentieth-century witch, a figure reclaimed by feminists from the misogynist representation in the prose of the *Morte Darthur*. When I ran into her again, in the pages of Chrétien's romances and Laȝamon's *Brut* (dressed as Argante), I enjoyed these cameos by the healing, magical woman I remembered. But the next semester, when I finally saw her in her most popular starring role, the wicked Morgan le Fay of Malory's opus, I hardly knew her at all. This woman was a malicious, sexually-aggressive manipulator with an unmotivated hatred towards Arthur's court—a wicked witch. At the very end of the *Morte*, I saw a glimmer of Morgan's former self, the one Bradley worked to restore, when she makes her final appearance to take Arthur for healing on the magical island of Avalon. How did this woman, famous in early Arthurian tradition for her healing magic, become the vicious thorn lodged deep in Arthur's side?

This question led to other questions. Was Malory's representation idiosyncratic or did other authors treat Morgan similarly? When did she change? Were there other witches who weren't always bad women, villains who used to be heroines? Did Merlin undergo a similar transformation? Was this unique to the Arthurian genres or representative of a wider literary trend? What social factors may have affected the change in representation? What does the change mean for constructions of femininity and masculinity? Questions such as these led to this study, which documents and analyzes the gendered transformation of magical figures that occurred in Arthurian romance as it developed from its earliest continental manifestations in the twelfth century to its flowering in fifteenth- and sixteenth-century England.

To explain my project more fully, I need to tell you a story. Though I don't know any "real" witches, I've been fascinated with the fantasy of witches my whole life. When I was in fourth grade, my friend and I pretended to be magical, a game that allowed us to be free from the dictates of both gravity and societal convention—but in our game we were fairies, good fairies, not wicked witches. We thought witches were bad, despite the fact that we had both seen Glinda the Good Witch of the North in the annual airing of *The Wizard of Oz* on television. That same year, I gleefully dressed up as a wicked witch for Halloween. I remember that night vividly: after I put on a black dress, carefully tattered at the hem and the sleeve, green make-up complete with fake warts and blacked-out tooth, and a pointy black hat, my mother snapped a photo of my delighted, chesire-cat grin. I loved being a wicked witch!

It's easy for me to understand why a child raised on Disney and musicals might fantasize about having magical power. But there are two additional aspects of this childhood story that bear further investigation: the first is my choice to model my magical behavior exclusively on female figures, and the second is my division of magic into good and bad. Two kinds of binary division happened at once—I distinguished between male and female characters, choosing to identify myself with the female characters (rejecting one of the terms of the binary), and then I distinguished between good and bad magic, choosing to identify myself with both at different times (rejecting neither, but prioritizing good as normal and bad as "costume," as other). My investigation of the magical figures in Arthurian literature explores these two modes of binary division, analyzing the gendering of magical behaviors in tandem with the polarization of magical characters. This strategy allows me to investigate the relationship between the gendering of magic and the villainization of certain kinds of magical practices, including (and especially) witchcraft, in Arthurian texts from the twelfth century to the sixteenth.

THE GENDER BINARY, OR WHY I PICKED FEMALE MODELS

When I chose models for my magical behavior as a young child, my conception of gender was rooted in biological essentialism: because I had a vagina instead of a penis, I must be female. I don't remember being told I was a girl, I just remember knowing it—speaking and thinking about myself as a girl, even when I behaved, as I often did, like a tomboy. I had to be one or the other, didn't I? I didn't have a choice, right? Because I was a girl, I identified with female characters—with Princess Leia rather than Han Solo, with Guinivere rather than Arthur—and I performed those roles when playing with my friends. Gender was part of the performance.

As a child, my thinking about the relationship between sex and gender was strictly essentialist: vagina=female. Though the categories male and female do not adequately cover the range of sexual identities permitted by biology, when I learned to speak, I learned that I had to be either a girl or

4   Crafting the Witch

a boy, either male or female. Jacques Lacan explains how the operation of language translates anatomical difference—the physical markers on the body—into sexual difference—the binary system of classification designating persons as "male" or "female." As Lacan suggests, because we must use the binary terms that (always already) exist in language, we must participate in classifying ourselves according to its structure (or risk isolation and social censure). Language provides an external system of organization for the mind, one we are forced to internalize if we wish to communicate with other humans and participate in most social activities. Language and sexual difference are intimately connected, for the subject is subjected to both at the same time. The sexual relevance of the Oedipal metaphor (Lacan's "Name of the Father") is illustrated here; just as the language designates us "male" and "female," so must we designate ourselves. I did not remember learning to categorize myself as a girl because the moment I learned there was a category, "girl," was the very same moment I learned that I belonged to that category. My awareness of sexual difference was constructed through language itself.

Though psychoanalytical theory often finds itself mired in an almost inescapable biological determinism, Lacan's revision of Freud's Oedipal metaphor divorces sexual difference from anatomical difference. In Lacan's Oedipal model, the child's recognition of the mother's desire reveals the presence of the phallus, and all that it signifies. The display of desire demonstrates to the child that the mother does not have the phallus and the father does. The child then either feels afraid of being castrated (if it *perceives* that it has the phallus) or envious of the one who possesses the phallus (if it *perceives* that it does not have the phallus). The castrated subject is gendered feminine, and the subject possessed of the phallus is gendered masculine, but the stance a child adopts towards the phallus is not necessarily connected to anatomical difference. In fact, Lacan stresses the "constructedness" of the phallus and its tie to the penis, as Jacqueline Rose explains in her introduction to *Feminine Sexuality*:

> Sexual difference is then assigned according to whether individual subjects do or do not possess the phallus, which means not that anatomical difference is sexual difference (the one as strictly deducible from the other), but that anatomical difference comes to figure sexual difference, that is, it becomes the sole representative of what that difference is allowed to be. . . . The phallus thus indicates the reduction of difference to an instance of visible perception, a seeming value. (42)

For Lacan, then, when subjects allow anatomical difference (presence or absence of the penis) to signify sexual difference (presence or absence of the phallus), those subjects participate in the phallocentric order of the Symbolic, develop a normative (i.e., hetero-) sexuality, and engage in normative patriarchal interactions. When subjects do not allow sexual difference to be tied to anatomical difference, alternate sexualities emerge (some of which are extremely taboo and some of which are widely accepted) and behaviors develop which may exceed the allowances of hetero-normative society. Sexualities and behaviors organized by anatomical determinism become naturalized as normative under the patriarchal law of language; despite the arbitrary and false nature of the phallus (and thus, of the signifier), subjects are nonetheless subjected to the law of the Symbolic in order to interact with other humans through language. Language dictates that the subject adopt a particular stance towards the phallus, the marker of sexual difference. How the subject adopts that stance (and resolves the Oedipus complex) thus determines sexual difference. Implicit in Lacan's formulation of sexual difference, as outlined here, is the notion that participation in sexual difference is active, a set of behaviors, rather than a stable essence. The subject *adopts* a stance—the subject *acts out* sexual difference.

Judith Butler extrapolates this formulation in her theory of gender performativity, which positions gender difference as a discursive formation governing both anatomical difference and sexual difference. In other words, "the appearance of an abiding substance or gendered self" is maintained through "the regulation of attributes along culturally established lines of coherence" (24). We construct a gendered self "performatively," through the "regulatory practices" associated with male and female identities. Butler describes the situation as follows: "There is no gender identity behind the expressions of gender; that identity is performatively constituted by the very 'expressions' that are said to be its results" (25). For Butler, sexual difference derives not from anatomical difference, but from the performative construction of gender (through discourses and practices), which both establishes sexual difference and links its genesis to anatomy, simultaneously constructing and essentializing the binary sex/gender system. The implications for my story are clear: my choice to identify with female characters was part of what made me a girl. My performance of female roles created both my female identity and my belief in the connection between my female identity and my anatomy. As Butler puts it, "Gender is the repeated stylization of the body, a set of repeated acts within a highly rigid regulatory frame that congeal over time to produce the appearance of substance, of a natural sort of being" (33). Performing femininity both helps me be female and helps me to feel that my femaleness is not a performance at all, but an expression of a biological essence.

But what does all of this have to do with Morgan le Fay and the other witches cackling through this book? Simply put, it's this: representation shapes material existence. The representations of gender produced by culture—through language and literature, through film and art, through newscasts and advertisements, and so on—shape the notions of gender available to people within that culture. The relationship between representation and material existence is complex, reciprocal, and multi-faceted, expressed in never-ending variations, but the relationship is certain. Representation

6   *Crafting the Witch*

shapes material existence. This fact is expressed in different ways by different schools of thought: Marxists reveal how, via cultural representations, ideology masks material reality; post-structuralists argue that the operation of language defines the boundaries of epistemology; feminists, critical race theorists, and post-colonial theorists argue that cultural discourses reinforce patriarchal, racist, and imperialist ideologies and practices, respectively. We may disagree about how representation shapes culture, but we agree that it does. When I played games as a child, I modeled my performances on the representations most readily available to me—books, films, television shows, and biblical stories. The representations of femaleness and femininity surrounding me were an important part of my knowledge about my gender, though certainly not the only source.

In fact, representations of gender are intimately linked to its performative quality. Butler explains that "certain cultural configurations of gender take the place of 'the real' and consolidate and augment their hegemony through that felicitous self-naturalization" (32–3). Certain representations become normal; certain representations become "other." What I find especially provocative—what prompted this book—is the fact that modern American cultural representation still relies on medieval and early modern western models. The reason Morgan le Fay interests me is that she interests the culture in which I was raised. The reason the witch-hag attracts my attention is that she attracts the attention of writers, directors, artists, advertisers, and kids dressing up for Halloween. Representations of gender (especially those surrounding magical characters) in medieval and early modern literature form an important link in a chain of convention that stretches unbroken from the earliest extant manuscripts to the film edited only last week.

Though psychoanalytical models of sex and gender operate on notions refined throughout the nineteenth, twentieth, and twenty-first centuries, we would be making a great mistake to assume that because gender theory was developed after the medieval and early modern period it has no value in helping us understand the literary representations of gender prevalent in those periods. The reverse is true, in fact, as psychoanalytical models describe a logic internal to these texts: for example, the authors of a group of fourteenth-century Middle English romances invoke the question "what [do] alle women most desire?" centuries before Freud got around to asking.[2] The popularity of romances structured around the revelation of women's desire reveals a medieval interest in what we would now call sexual difference. It is especially important to view medieval and Renaissance texts with the lens of contemporary theory when the figures in these texts continue to appear in the most popular literary and cinematic modes of the twentieth- and twenty-first centuries. To do that, we need to ask (and answer) some questions: Why do medieval and early modern conventions of gender occupy similar spaces in contemporary literary fantasies in the U.S.? What are the effects of this gendered literary heritage on modern performances of gender identity? And just what is the connection between gender and magic?

GOOD OR BAD?: MAGIC AND TRANSFORMATIVE POWER

The allure of magic is that it gives power. It provides freedom from constraints of class or religion, from the limits of gender, race, or species, from political boundaries and physical obstacles. But it doesn't exist—at least according to mainstream science. As a former biologist, I follow the view of modern science here, along with most of the other academics who study the elusive force. Despite my personal disbelief in its physical efficacy, this study respects the power of magic as social force that operates in literary, dramatic, cinematic, imaginative, personal, and many other spaces in modern society. In medieval and Renaissance England, where a much higher percentage of people believed in magic than do twenty-first-century residents of the U.S., its social power must have been far greater. This is the paradox of magic—it has infinite power or no power at all. And this is precisely what makes it so fascinating, both for the world of imagination and for the world of literature, where it is freed from the boundaries of science and becomes exactly the kind of power we wish for in our dreams.

In my childhood game-playing, I accessed magic through the world of the literary, the imaginary. My appropriation of a magical identity was dependent upon the social representation of a particular figure, the witch. When I identified myself as a magic-user, playing myself in world transformed by imagination, I wanted to be "good," to remain within acceptable social standards even as I fantasized about having power over them. But when I wore the costume, transforming myself into an alternate persona, I wanted to be "bad," to play the role of the deviant, the acknowledged villain, to flout the Christian morality I grew up with in a safe social space. For me, good witches and bad witches served different functions at different times. The power of magic, channeled through my active imagination and a few cheap props, allowed me the freedom to transform myself—to idealize myself or villainize myself—to make myself the glorious center of society or marginalize myself in transgressive play. A similar polarization functions in medieval and Renaissance representations of magic use, where magic acts as a lens through which to read the response of chronicle and romance writers to social practices that threatened the maintenance of stable gendered identities. Magic is so useful precisely because of this polarization—it offers us a glance at what people see as extreme, as the best or the worst. Whether represented negatively or positively, magical figures are by definition different from the norm; they function as others against which normative conventions can be defined. In particular, describing and interpreting the gendering of magical figures allows us to configure normative gender conventions by delineating their boundaries, those liminal spaces where humanity fades into monstrosity.

So what exactly do I mean when I say magic? There are many different varieties of magic, from alchemy and astrology to necromancy and witchcraft, and they all carry with them the baggage of a long, long trip. The

8 *Crafting the Witch*

route of that trip can be traced through the etymology of that modern catch-all term for things supernatural and marvelous, "magic," which entered the English language by way of the Old French *magique*, a term borrowed from the Latin *magica*, a word itself taken from the Greek *magike*.[3] The large number of loan words in English referring to different types of magic demonstrates the influence of the French, Latin, and Greek linguistic and literary traditions on medieval English conceptions of magic: Old French (usually by way of Latin, by way of Greek), for example, provides English speakers with alchemy, astrology, necromancy, prophecy, and sorcery.[4] But English authors had a native tradition of magic available to them as well, as reflected in words such as Old English *elf* (elf), *wicca* (witch), *eotende* (giant), *witege* (wise man/advisor), and *læce* (healer/doctor). Sometimes Germanic and Mediterranean traditions coexisted: for instance, speakers of Middle English could choose a word derived from the Old English *feond* or *deofel* when they wanted to refer to a denizen of hell, or they could use a form of the Latin *daemon*. No matter which language they used, when medieval people spoke of magic in England, what exactly did they mean?

Ask a modern eight-year old what magic is, and you might get a bright smile and a list of Disney movies in response. Ask someone older, and you might hear about how magic is a mythical force that allows people to do seemingly impossible things. And if (magically) you could ask an average inhabitant of medieval or early modern England what magic is, you might get a surprising response. A country wife might define magic as the herbs she boils to heal her sick son; a cleric might speak of demons and their powers over earth-dwellers; a minstrel might speak of giants, witches, and enchanted castles. The answers would probably be as varied then as they are now, but as Bert Hansen notes: "Magic in the Middle Ages was not marginal to intellectual life, nor an activity of ignorant, credulous, or superstitious people—or at least not of these alone. Magic . . . formed an important part of medieval thought and experience" (483). Medieval dis-courses surrounding magic were similar to modern discourses surrounding science; they were a shared way of classifying, understanding, and manipu-lating the world. In the classical and early medieval periods, magic itself was neither good nor bad—it was simply a tool.

Scholars have often identified two major categories of magical practices present in medieval Europe, divine (or demonic) and natural (or occult), under which the various other types of magic can be classified.[5] Richard Kieckhefer delineates the two categories:

> Broadly speaking, intellectuals in medieval Europe recognized two forms of magic: natural and demonic. Natural magic was not distinct from science, but rather a branch of science. It was the science that dealt with "occult virtues" (or hidden powers) within nature. Demonic magic was not distinct from religion, but rather a perversion of reli-gion. It was religion that turned away from god and toward demons for their help in human affairs. (*Magic in the Middle Ages* 9)

Categories like these, while useful for analysis, cannot hope to describe completely the complex interrelationships that existed between different types of magical practices, religious beliefs, and scientific theories.

Despite the precise definitions provided by modern scholars, it is often difficult to distinguish between different kinds of magic. Just when is conjuring the result of Christian faith and when is it the result of Satan? How do we know if the power of an herb to heal is determined by "occult" properties that require special preparation to invoke or by the qualities of the herb known by all medieval herbalists? The problem confounds even those who support the categorization of magic into binaries like divine and natural: Kieckhefer, for example, acknowledges that "demonic and natural magic are not always as distinct in fact as they seem in principle" (1). If a magic-user takes a lizard, prepares it in a special way (say by drying it out and then rinsing it with milk and blood), chants prayers throughout the preparation of the lizard, and places it under the doorstep of the victim's home to cause illness, is that person practicing natural or divine magic?[6] The lizard must contain occult properties, as it requires particular preparation to be effective, but the prayers call on the power of Christianity. If the magician wants the victim to get ill, and she does get ill, is the magician also a prophet? Questions like these are impossible to answer, and in the end, the road down which they lead soon becomes a quagmire.

Whether magicians receive their power from religious faith, control over demonic spirits, or secret knowledge of nature, they operate because they have something special, a unique power that cannot be accessed by "just anyone." This special quality, no matter how we categorize it, gives the magician the power of transformation. It is not the preparation of the magic which makes it magic (as the processes by which various types of magic function are widely different), but the effect it should have on the object towards which it is directed. Magic is used to change the current state of a person or thing: an alchemist changes one metal into another, a love-potion changes a person's feelings, a healer transforms the body from sickness to health, an evil-eye transforms a healthy person into a sick person, a necromancer changes a dead spirit into an animated one, a demonologist changes the behavior of hell-fiends, and a prophet transforms the future by determining its course. The power to transform one thing into another is so important and so rare that it demands to be treated with the utmost reverence. Transformative power is what makes magic so useful to our understanding of medieval and early modern society, precisely because of its position as other. Because magic is unique, its representation tends to become polarized: magic-users are saviors or they are villains, saints or devils. Analyzing the gendering of transformative power (magic) reveals the sexual politics of this kind of ideological polarization. Which kind of power is admired, and which feared? Which kind of power gets naturalized as masculine, and which kind as feminine? How does the polarization of magic help define the possibilities for gender performance, for audiences then and now?

10 *Crafting the Witch*

THE ONCE AND FUTURE WITCH: ARTHURIAN LEGEND
AND THE PRESENCE AND ABSENCE OF WITCHES

Arthurian legend has been associated with magic since its Celtic conceptions, even before Geoffrey of Monmouth collected Welsh tales of a powerful king who managed to stave off the invasion of the Germanic tribes by
uniting the warring tribes of Britain for a brief and bloody span. During the
twelfth and thirteenth centuries, writers like Geoffrey of Monmouth and
Chrétien de Troyes helped establish an Arthurian tradition rife with magical elements, from club-wielding giants and damsels with magical rings to
wise prophets and potent healers. English romancers of the fourteenth and
fifteenth centuries followed in the footsteps of the French romances and
Latin chronicles, filling both the popular and literary versions of Arthurian
tales with enchanted people, magical underclothes, and even a few witches.
The sixteenth century saw the explosion of witches (and other female monsters) on the romance scene, accompanied by demons and sorcerers, a trend
whose echo we hear in Shakespeare's magical plays. The Arthurian tradition continues to be one of the spaces in which modern authors and directors utilize magical tropes.

In the following study, I explore the strategies used by writers of Arthurian literature to gender particular kinds of magic as masculine or feminine,
a process which results in the villianization of feminine magic, especially
as exemplified by the figure of the witch. While Arthurian texts from the
twelfth and thirteenth centuries featured the occasional witch, usually
practicing beneficial magic, texts produced during and after the fourteenth
century present witches more frequently, especially wicked witches who
practice forbidden forms of magic. Although the role of the villain was
played by masculine giants in the twelfth century, after two hundred years
the part began to go more and more often to the older lady with the throaty
cackle and black hat, and by the sixteenth century, writers were satisfied
with no one else.

Chapter Two, *Gender-Blending: Transformative Power in Twelfth- and
Thirteenth- Century Arthurian Literature*, surveys representations of magic
in the texts of four authors within the Arthurian canon: Geoffrey of Monmouth, Chrétien de Troyes, Marie de France, and Laȝamon. Though these
authors write in different languages and centuries, their representations
of magic share in a tradition inherited from Greek, Roman, and biblical
sources, a tradition including prophets, witches, giants, and magical objects.
While witches were clearly available, these writers rarely use them, favoring
prophets and giants instead. When witches do appear, it's mainly as extras,
background decorations with little importance. All four authors gender
magic similarly, representing prophecy and certain forms of transformative
magic as masculine and healing as feminine. In these texts, characters whose
behaviors conform to a set of normative gender conventions (i.e., masculinity
as aggressive action and femininity as passive inaction) practice beneficial

"Are You a Good Witch or a Bad Witch?" 11

magic without attracting a pesky stigma, whereas male characters whose masculinity is over-developed suffer not only condemnation but also death. Boasting extant manuscripts numbering more than 200 and 30, respectively, Geoffrey's chronicle (the *Historia Regum Britanniae*) and Chrétien's five romances are foundational examples of the two earliest Arthurian genres.[7] Laȝamon's *Brut*, on the other hand, remains in only two manuscripts, and Marie's *lais* appear in only five; these less frequently preserved texts offer perspectives which complicate the conventions developed within the work of Chrétien and Geoffrey. Despite their differences, the texts all work to explore and mitigate the threat of masculine power posed by the feudal patriarchy present in both England and France in the twelfth and thirteenth centuries. The witch nurtures and heals her way through these centuries, enjoying predominantly positive, though marginalized, characterizations.

The third chapter, *From Rags to Riches, or The Step-mother's Revenge: Transformative Power in Late Medieval Arthurian Romances*, analyzes representations of two magical characters who appear in a group of fourteenth- and fifteenth-century romances usually associated with Gawain: the churlish knight and the loathly lady. This chapter pays particular attention to the representation of a) the churlish knight in *Sir Gawain and the Green Knight*, *The Greene Knight*, *The Turke and Sir Gawain*, *Sir Gawain and the Carle of Carlisle*, and *The Carle of Carlisle* and b) the loathly lady as she appears in John Gower's "Tale of Florent," Geoffrey Chaucer's "Wife of Bath's Tale," *The Wedding of Sir Gawain and Dame Ragnelle*, and *The Marriage of Sir Gawain*. The authors of these romances appropriate transformative magic to structure gender conventions that depart radically from those developed in the works of their predecessors, curbing masculine excess with a submissive gentility situated within a decidedly aristocratic ideology and assuaging anxiety about land ownership. In addition to revamping constructions of gender, the authors of these romances conjure up a figure neglected by the earlier writers, the nefarious wicked witch. While a version of the murderous giant does appear here, the wicked witch replaces the giant as the villianized antagonist; what is especially revealing is that the witch shows up as a mother—a wicked step-mother, to be precise. The presence of the wicked step-mother, who appears only in the popular romances in this group, reflects an anxiety about expanding economic opportunities for women (especially young maidens and widows) in fourteenth- and fifteenth-century English society.

In the fourth chapter, *The Lady is a Hag: Three Writers and the Transformation of Magic in Sixteenth-Century England*, I follow the romance tradition into early modern England, punctuating the sixteenth century on either end with two monumental Arthurian romance-epics, Thomas Malory's *Morte Darthur* and Edmund Spenser's *The Faerie Queene*. Both authors characterize magic as a deceptive, illusory power reliant on control of demonic spirits, a representation William Shakespeare reinforces in *A Midsummer Night's Dream*, *Macbeth*, and *The Tempest*. As demonic

12   *Crafting the Witch*

magic widened its influence, so did one of the most infamous figures associated with demonology, the wicked witch. Two versions of the wicked witch populate the magical landscapes of these three authors, the beautiful temptress and the crone-hag. The juxtaposition of these two figures creates a construction of femininity that indicts both the overtly alluring and the grotesque. While Spenser expands his condemnation, representing maternity as abject and grotesque itself, Malory and Shakespeare both handle maternity by leaving it out, absenting its influence. The prevalence of villainized witches and the extreme anxiety over maternity in these texts reinforces a legal and social backlash against the changing gender roles precipitated by the economic changes of the previous two centuries, manifested especially in a widespread fascination with mothers and maternity during the sixteenth century in England.

Chapter Five, *Hags on Film: Contemporary Echoes of the Early Modern Wicked Witch*, traces briefly the legislative policy governing prosecution of witches in England. Heightened prosecution of witchcraft is reinforced by increasingly negative cultural representations, and these two mechanisms function together to implicate all women as potential witches. The conflation of witchcraft and maternity indicts women—if witches are anti-mothers, all women who are not mothers, or who are not good enough mothers, might be witches. In contemporary U.S. society, we do not usually prosecute magic-use, but the wicked witch endures. This suggests the ability of this cultural icon to satisfy modern western culture is rooted more in gender anxiety than its connection to magic. Wicked witches are still around because the gender crisis created by capitalism is still around. As long as women are able to gain power—even severely circumscribed forms—by participating in economic exchange outside the domestic realm, wicked witches will cackle over cauldrons, warning women of the consequences of maternity gone awry. The witch, I'm afraid, will be with us for a long time. Is the witch still wicked? You bet.

2 Gender-Blending
Transformative Power in Twelfth- and Thirteenth-Century Arthurian Literature

I. WHERE ARE THE WITCHES?: THE ABSENCE OF WICKED WITCHES IN EARLY ARTHURIAN LEGEND

Folks in the U.S. enjoy watching witches get killed on film—from classic films like *The Wizard of Oz* or *Snow White* to more recent flicks like *The Craft*, we happily attend cinematic screenings and replay DVDs in our homes where witches are melted, thrown off cliffs, or blown into bits. You've seen this happen, although you may not have responded as ambivalently as I did. You see, I never wanted the witch to die. Diane Purkiss writes of her early encounters with the film, *The Wizard of Oz* (1939): "I always cast my long-suffering mother as the Witch, as if in an early effort to prove the connections between witch-stories and images of maternity" (1).[1] Purkiss made her mother the Witch, but when I acted out scenes from the movie, I was the Witch. I screeched my favorite line, "I'm melting, melting," with empathetic abandon.[2] Really, what is so terribly wicked about this green-skinned woman? Sure, she looks a little different, and she has a crystal ball that gives her an edge on long-distance communications, but this is hardly grounds for execution. She tries in vain to acquire her sister's shoes (to which she is the rightful heiress), frightening Dorothy in an attempt to get them back, but doesn't actually harm the young girl. In fact, she doesn't kill anyone, preferring to incapacitate them, making her worst crime a series of (empty?) threats. The movie doesn't even try to present a case for her wickedness: the film instead marks her visually, inscribing "witch-ness" on her body through signifiers like her long, warty nose and dark (green) skin, so that her wickedness becomes a physiognomic fact. She's wicked because she looks wicked.

The Witch doesn't begin the film with visual markers as extreme as those she later gains. When she appears as Ms. Gulch, she looks prissy and conservative, but she is not physically inscribed with difference in the same way. Instead, it is her behavior that is aggressive and threatening, creating sympathy for Dorothy's situation and making herself look wicked. In Dorothy's world, things may not be what they seem, but in the magical world of Oz, good witches are beautiful and wicked ones ugly. If it looks like a witch and smells like a witch, it must be a witch. Mustn't it?

14 *Crafting the Witch*

Let us not forget that the head of this land of munchkins, friendly neighborhood lions, and creepy flying monkeys is the imposing patriarch, the Wizard of Oz. Toto reveals the Wizard's magic to be a grand illusion, a result of his ability to disguise (and thus transform) his identity by creating a new one. L. Frank Baum's book, *The Wonderful Wizard of Oz* (from which the movie took its story), emphasizes the polyvalent nature of this transformative magic, an element the movie downplays by presenting only one of the Wizard's guises: in the book, the Wizard appears to each of the four travelers separately, presenting a unique persona to each of them by transforming himself into a large head, a beautiful lady, an enormous beast, and a ball of fire (Baum 110–118). The film version, on the other hand, presents the ball of fire behind a massive head, combining the two images and emphasizing the illusion more than the transformation. Nevertheless, in both film and book, magic is connected to shifting identity, to the power of transformation.

In both versions, the Wizard's transformative illusions contrast with the power possessed by the witches: both good and bad witches can appear and disappear at will, but they cannot change their outward appearances. In these texts, magic divides along gendered lines—magical women look like what they are, whereas magical men have the ability to change their appearances. The film, in particular, inscribes magic visually onto the female body, as with the beauty of Glinda, the Good Witch of the North, and the ugly namelessness of the Wicked Witch of the West. The sight of their bodies reveals the nature of their magic. The male body disappears behind a curtain—his ability to hide his physical appearance allows the Wizard to maintain his position, and the revelation of his body diminishes his magical cachet.

In the 1939 film, the body is the nexus between magic and gender, situating gendered signifiers within a visual matrix. Witches and wizards both possess magic, but it differs along gendered lines. The age-old system of binary gender, described and analyzed by an army of scholars wielding tools from a variety of disciplines, obtains here. That gender markers are bodily in this text is not unusual: theorists have long argued that we inscribe gendered signifiers on the body. What is significant here is the result of that binary system: ridding the Wicked Witch of her power involves forcibly melting her body away to nothing, turning her latent feminine fluidity into real fluidity (a puddle on the floor), whereas ridding the Wizard of his power involves restoring his voice to his body and allowing him to return to the "real" world. First we witness the execution of malignant femininity and dissolution of the female body, which then allows the male body to resume ascendancy.

The Wicked Witch of the West is reminiscent, in certain ways, of her early modern grand-dames. In many of the infamous European Renaissance witch-trials, the woman accused is a covetous neighbor who has threatened a valued child, a description particularly suited to Oz's resident hag.[3] Oz's

Wicked Witch of the West is perhaps the most easily recognizable example of the wicked witches existing in twentieth-century film and literature, a clear icon of the witch as she has come down to us from the early modern period. As Glinda informs Dorothy, however, not all witches are wicked.

When we look at classical literature in conjunction with English Renaissance texts, a long tradition of witchcraft emerges: witches are the most common kind of female magician, and the majority of witches are of the wicked variety. A majority is not all, we must remember, and some witches are more like Glinda than her green-skinned counterpart. Calypso and Circe, from Homer's *Odyssey*, are examples of two witchy women who are not evil enough to warrant execution. Classical literature provides models of both the "good witch" and the "bad witch," but Arthurian romances and chronicles circulating in England during the twelfth and early thirteenth centuries, in particular, lack wicked witches. Why? Though romance-writers drew freely on classical material, they chose to present only one of these figures, the good witch. This raises some questions. If there are no wicked witches, what magical villains are present in the texts? What narrative and cultural forces motivated their development? When are men or women wicked in these texts, and how does that wickedness relate to the link between gender and magical practices? Who has access to what kind of magic in these texts, and how does that access help define a particular kind of gendered identity? The following chapter is an attempt to answer these questions by exploring the notable absence of wicked witches in the early Arthurian romance and chronicle traditions. Instead of wicked witches, we find three other figures in these texts, the healer, the giant, and the prophet, whose representations variously support or subvert a binary set of normative gender conventions not unlike those described by Lacanian psychoanalytical theory. The first two figures are polarized—feminine healers are "good" and masculine giants are "bad"—but representations of the prophet figure explore the more nebulous spaces in between.

II. WHEN IS A KNIGHT NOT A KNIGHT?: GENDER MUTABILITY IN THE ROMANCES

After Cligés rescues his beloved in Chrétien's romance of the same name, the narrator interjects a comment about the appropriateness of their behavior as lovers.[4] This passage reflects a widespread interest within the Arthurian romance genre, namely, the exploration of gender conventions through the forces of love and magic. Fenice, the heroine, and Cligés, the hero, have fallen in love, but their feelings remain secret. Both lovers "were so fearful of being rejected that they dared not open their hearts," and though the narrator finds Fenice's behavior quite acceptable, as "a maiden should be reticent and shy" (169), when Cligés behaves in exactly the same fashion, the narrator seems disappointed (if perhaps a bit ironic): "But why

16   *Crafting the Witch*

did Cligés hesitate? What was he waiting for? He, whose every deed was emboldened by her, afraid of her alone? God! What was the source of his fear, that caused him to cower only before a maiden, a weak and fearful creature, simple and shy?" (169). The narrator describes Fenice's behavior as normal: because she is a maiden, she behaves as a maiden should. But Cligés is acting against his gender; he is passive when he should be active, silent when he should speak. Chrétien's narrator expresses shock at Cligés's hesitation, using zoological and sociological metaphors to naturalize the gender conventions being developed:

> This was as if I had seen the hounds fleeing before the hare and the trout chase the beaver, the lamb the wolf, and the dove the eagle. Or imagine the peasant abandoning his hoe, with which he labours and earns his livelihood, the falcon fleeing from the duck, the gyrfalcon from the heron, and the mighty pike from the minnow; the stag would chase the lion, and everything would be reversed. (169)

His departure from normative masculine behavior is just as unnerving as if the very world itself had turned topsy-turvy—predators turned prey, peasants leaving their fields. Comments like these, where the narrator addresses the issue of gender difference directly, are so frequent in Arthurian romances (especially those of Chrétien de Troyes), that Arthurian romance has developed a reputation for gender-bending. Gender is commonly an explicit concern for the authors of Arthurian romance, which provides a literary space for exploration of gender roles while still constructing (and endorsing) a normative set of gender conventions. This discussion of normative masculinity and femininity provides the foundation for my analysis of magic, one of the few forces responsible for gender mutability in early Arthurian material.

Much recent Arthurian scholarship analyzes the role of romance writers in exploring the relationship between masculinity and femininity.[5] For example, Friedrich Wolfzettel edited a collection of essays, entitled *Arthurian Romance and Gender*, all of which build on the foundation of the connection made by the title. Lee Tobin McClain asserts that Arthurian material, in particular, is "about gender anxiety, and interest in it peaks when questions of how to define gender roles especially occupy our mass psyche" (193), and Matilda Tomaryn Bruckner sees lyrics, romances, and *lais* as sites for dealing with "the issue of male/female relationships" (32). Scholars have debated what this concern with gender means, some arguing that the romances reinforce a binary system of gender based on masculine aggressive activity and feminine submissive passivity, and others arguing that they provide space, however temporary, for dissolving, collapsing, or questioning the binary gender system.[6] Roberta Krueger explains how chivalric literature could provide a space for gender play while still endorsing normative gender conventions.[7] Krueger notes: "Courtly romance opened

Gender-Blending 17

up a discursive space for male and female readers in which boundaries could be temporarily confused, subverted or resisted—at least in the space of a fiction—even as they were maintained" ("Questions of Gender" 146). Krueger argues that the Old French romances examined women's paradoxical role in chivalric culture—simultaneously deprived and possessed of power—and represented the transgressive behaviors of both knights and ladies, calling attention to the "ways that gender identities are constructed within language" and exploring "the transformative possibilities of fiction" (146). Romances, then, may feature gender transgression, but only when it's carefully situated within the framework of a narrative otherworld.

The binary construction of normative gender in the romances and chronicles of Chrétien de Troyes, Marie de France, Geoffrey of Monmouth, and Laȝamon is plainly evident.[8] There are a few specific instances in which we can see most clearly the strategies used in early Arthurian literature to inscribe characters within a system of binary opposition. The initial descriptions of the heroes and heroines, for example, enact a characterization of femininity as static beauty and masculinity as valiant activity. Below, I offer a reading of the representations of normative masculinity and femininity, followed by an analysis of love's power to blur gender binaries.

All four authors represent their leading ladies—their heroines—as very beautiful, often the most beautiful in the land, and frequently provide extended descriptions of the heroines when they initially appear.[9] Their descriptions focus attention on the body, and more specifically, those parts of the female body which come to signify femininity, such as (long) hair, (smooth) face, or (high and round) breasts. We know our heroines are feminine women because the narrator lingers on this fact—it's what makes them desirable as lovers. The sexuality of the female body peeks through the clothes meant to contain it. Chrétien's Enide, for example, is dressed in a worn shift, but Erec can immediately see that "the body beneath was lovely" (*Erec and Enide* 42). The fairy-lady of Marie's "Lanval" wears a simple shift as well, which reveals her "well formed and handsome" body as "her side . . . was uncovered, as well as her face, neck, and breast" (74). The bodies described here are dangerously unprotected, revealed, and vulnerable to attack—completely unlike the masculine bodies which, as we'll see, are well-protected and strong, though not immune to suffering. The descriptions construct a female body that is beautiful because it is vulnerable—it is because her limbs are so delicate and her face so rosy that she demands the hero's attention.[10]

In addition to gendering the heroine's body as vulnerable, the romances visually mark the women by including details such as blond hair, light-colored (grey) eyes, or light skin, which privilege a white body.[11] Fairness or whiteness certainly connotes a racial designation, but it also carries a class signification. A person who had the luxury to stay out of the sun—an aristocrat or noble—would have a lighter complexion than a person forced to labor daily in sun, rain, wind, and snow—the peasantry. Both romance and

18   *Crafting the Witch*

chronicle heroes generally prefer ladies from noble families, women who are dressed well (as is Blancheflor in the above excerpt) and versed in the courtly art of graciousness.[12] When the beloved damsel belongs to a family less noble than desired, as is the case with Enide, our hero promptly grants her father two castles, elevating her family's social status with the precious gift of land and its accompanying revenue (60). The feminine aesthetic constructed here is very selective—only white, upper-class ladies need apply.

A final aspect of the initial descriptions of the heroines contributes to the construction of normative femininity as receptively passive—this is the narrative positioning of the male gaze. Though there are many other ways in which the introductory depictions of the heroines reinforce the gender binary, the heroines' cheerful and patient acceptance of the gaze in these descriptions is most revealing.[13] Heroines are most commonly presented in tableau—they stand, sit, or lie quietly while the heroes examine them. In Chrétien's *The Story of the Grail*, Blancheflor comes to greet Perceval when he arrives at her castle. After entering, she stands motionless while the hero gazes at her, besotted by her beauty and her willingness to be the object of the gaze (404). Similar scenes precede descriptions of Enide and Fenice in tableaux as well: arriving in the hero's presence, the maiden stands demurely and allows herself to be observed, occasionally stealing a peek from under lowered lashes (42, 156). In Marie's "Lanval," the heroine lies on a bed while the knight observes her body (74). In both chronicles, Ygerna is the passive recipient not only of Uther's gaze, but of the best plates at the table and the most delicious wines, which he sends her at a feast because he is obsessed with her beauty (Geoffrey 205, Laʒamon ll. 9245–9254). The lady allows herself to be observed, capitulating to the author's demand for conventionally passive behavior.

If the elements I have discussed combine to locate ideal femininity on the static body of the white, upper-class woman, a similar set of features work to characterize ideal masculinity as located on the active body of the white, upper-class man. The descriptions of female characters focus on the body in stasis, whereas the descriptions of the male characters center on the body in action. Few of Chrétien's introductory descriptions of the heroic knights take longer than a sentence or two. Instead, brief accounts of action characterize the descriptions of heroes in the romances, a trend continued in the chronicles: Lancelot first appears on a tired horse, madly chasing after the abducted Queen Guinevere (Chrétien, *The Knight of the Cart* 210); Yvain is introduced through his boast to avenge Calogrenant, followed by his immediate departure (*The Knight with the Lion* 332–3); Perceval's first mention involves his mounting a horse to go riding (*The Story of the Grail* 382); as soon as Marie's Guigemar is introduced, he "left the court, dispensing lavish gifts before he departed, and went off to Flanders, where one could always find war and strife" ("Guigemar" 44); and Geoffrey's initial description of Arthur includes his age, his reputation for

Gender-Blending 19

courage, his generous gift-giving, and his decision to "harry the Saxons" (212). Deeds are definitive in these examples.

Not only are the knights introduced through their aggressive actions, but their descriptions also commonly mention their already-existing reputations for valiant deeds and noble behavior.[14] Whereas the authors frequently remind us of the heroine's passive beauty, they prefer to call our attention to the men's active performance. In Chrétien's *Erec and Enide*, Erec "had received great honour at the court" and was more "highly praised" than any other knight (38), and Cligés (titular character of *Cligés*) "knew more about fencing and archery than did King Mark's nephew Tristan, and more about birds and hounds" (156). Marie's Bisclavret is described as "a good and handsome knight who conducted himself nobly" ("Bisclavret" 68), and her introduction to "Milun" notes, "From the day he was dubbed a knight he did not encounter a single knight who could unhorse him" (97). In the *Historia*, Brutus's unfortunate deeds are forecast before he's born—we learn that he will kill both his parents, but "after he had wandered in exile through many lands this boy would eventually rise to the highest honor" (54). Laȝamon's text features a group of counselors deciding to bring "bezst alre cnihten" [the best of all warriors] to court to be crowned king—that warrior is Arthur Pendragon (l. 9900). Deeds of war, in fact, are what distinguish femininity from masculinity in these descriptions: feminine women *are* (beautiful), masculine men *act* (nobly).

Unlike the heroine's body, which features prominently in her physical descriptions, the body of the knight is mentioned almost exclusively within the context of battle. Scenes of arming present the knight's body as it prepares for battle, girding male fortitude with strong leather and metal, a protected body constructed in opposition to the exposed female body.[15] These descriptions of battle-gear perform a similar function for masculinity as the description of the heroine's body does for femininity—gender definition. The narrator typically emphasizes those parts of the body which signify masculinity, like the (broad) chest, (thick) legs, and head, and provides the heroes with powerful phallic weapons like the sword, the spear, and the war-horse. Weapons and armor do not appear in descriptions of ladies—this is uniquely masculine equipment, guaranteeing the bearer a better position in the hierarchical social system dictated by feudalism.

The exquisite weaponry in many passages also indicates the tremendous wealth of the hero figures. Just as the heroine's rich furs reveal her to be aristocratic, so the hero's jewel-encrusted (sometimes magically-forged) battle-gear reflects his position at the top of the economic ladder. Armor, swords, and horses were expensive, and ideal masculinity relies therefore on wealth and high social standing to obtain the high-priced necessaries of knighthood. Fully armed and mounted on his charger, the hero is the fairest knight in the land, the epitome of masculine beauty, aggressive action poised for release.

20   *Crafting the Witch*

It is not only the initial descriptions of idealized masculine and feminine characters that support a binary system of gender based on activity and passivity. Their behaviors also characteristically conform to a chivalric construction of masculinity as aggressive action and femininity as passive endurance. In early Arthurian literature, knights fight to save victimized ladies, a fact which shall become evident throughout the rest of this chapter. Despite what appears to be an oppressively rigid set of gender conventions, the behaviors of the characters in the romances do not always conform neatly to the accepted mold.

In the scene I discuss at the beginning of this section, the narrator questions Cligés's lack of aggressiveness towards Fenice. His masculinity should propel him to pursue her, to confess his love, but instead he is afraid. There are other instances in the romances where knights behave passively, failing to act or speak when they should, submitting to the demands of a physically weaker person, or fainting when they see a sign of their beloved.[16] Though they must often submit to horrific torture, ladies and damsels don't always behave passively, as in one striking example where "more than a thousand ladies" rush in to a room where Fenice is being tortured by doctors and throw the cruel men out the window (196–7). Chrétien tells us, "No ladies ever did better!" Elsewhere, ladies manipulate their lovers or order them directly, rescue trapped knights, and organize tournaments for themselves to attend.[17] There are a number of critics who see romantic love as a dominating force linked to this type of gender transgression in the romances: for example, Gary Ferguson uses Chrétien's *The Knight of the Cart* to argue that male knights take on feminine characteristics when in love, and Vern L. Bullough notes that medieval writers inherited from Greek medicine a view of lovesickness as a form of madness which feminizes men (38–9). Indeed, this is precisely what seems to have happened to Cligés, whose great love for Fenice causes him to fear her. Chrétien's narrator explains Cligés's unmanly behavior by claiming that "Whoever wishes to love must feel fear; if he does not, he cannot love," being careful to note that a man "must fear only the one he loves, and be emboldened for her sake in all else" (170). As long as the beloved inspires aggressive action in all matters except the romantic relationship, masculine submission to the force of love is perfectly understandable. Likewise, it is love that motivates Enide to repeatedly disobey Erec's order to be silent, enduring Erec's increasingly abusive tirades each time she breaks the rule, until she finally earns his respect towards the end of their adventures (69–97). Scholars like Sandy Feinstein and Flora Alexander have made arguments which explore the ability of love to provide otherwise passive heroines with motivation to become aggressive.[18] Love not only provides an excuse for gender transgression, but causes it, and love cannot be avoided or predicted.

Love does not account for all gender transgression in the Arthurian tradition, however. The chronicle writers largely ignore romantic love in their accounts of Arthur's life, but many of their characters blur the boundaries of normative gender conventions nonetheless. There is another force present in Arthurian literature within both romance and chronicle traditions, a force which destabilizes convention, which blurs the division between masculine and feminine, creating what I call gender-blending or gender mutability—an ability to appropriate gendered behaviors to consolidate or generate transformative power. That force is magic. While these authors represent both magic and love as forces that allow gender mutability, magical power is distinct from the power of love in its specificity: magic enables gender mutability only in male characters. Female figures who utilize magic do so without challenging the normative conventions of gender described above, but male characters with access to magical power are able to exploit behaviors associated with both masculinity and femininity in pursuit of their goals.

III. HEALING FOR LOVE: ARTHURIAN WOMEN TRANSFORM THE WOUNDED BODY

If you are a bloody, partially dismembered knight, and you're looking to find some help in the bizarre otherworld of medieval romance, you'd do well to find yourself an ointment-toting damsel. You could look for another knight with a healing herb, but it would take you much longer, and you might bleed to death. Luckily (for you and any other knights-errant), romances usually blend a heaping dose of feminine healing magic with generous portions of masculine aggression to produce the captivating cycle of assault, battery, and healing central to the romance tradition. Without the remarkable ability of magic and medicine to heal the human body, romance as we know it would not be possible. Interspersed with riotous adventure and fighting with giants and dragons are scenes of the knights' ever-too-slow convalescence in the doting care of a lovely maiden. Without the healing women of romance, not only would there be more dead knights, but there would be no space for unmarried women (young or old) to participate in chivalric culture. Through their healing of the wandering knights, female characters can join the team, although they don't often get to play in the game of "whose lance is bigger?" Early Arthurian romance and chronicle traditions represent healing as an appropriately feminine behavior.

The healing women in the Arthurian texts considered here are an example of the polarization of magical figures which characterizes the romances. Though female healers are not always magical, they are usually good. By "good," I mean simply that the four authors unanimously represent feminine healing as a positive, beneficial force within the narrative world. Healing has traditionally been associated with women, especially domestic and folk remedies with quasi-magical (if not overtly magical) elements. Though it is often hard to determine whether or not a particular act of healing involves magic, female healing (known for its magical and quasi-magical elements) exists in an acute tension with the male, "scientific" study of

22 Crafting the Witch

medicine popularized by the rise of universities and widespread translation of Arabic scientific texts in the twelfth century. Nestled within this intertwined matrix of magic and medicine, we find the best example of the early Arthurian version of the witch, a domestic "good witch" whose magic helps the heroine maintain appropriate femininity through a series of challenges. Chrétien's good witch, Thessela, from *Cligés*, reflects the tension between feminine healing and masculine medicine. Her character is the culmination of a variety of literary trends that conflate healing, domesticity, and community with feminine access to transformative power.

There are many healing ladies in Arthurian stories, especially in the works of Chrétien and Marie. Healing women are a necessary part of the cycle of violence comprising the action of the romances. Heather Arden documents the cyclical nature of the romances, arguing that the emergent pattern involves the hero undertaking combat, enduring a test, and obtaining aid or information as a reward (85–88). A woman is often the distributor of the reward, dispensing healing, revealing information, or offering her love. Healing of flesh wounds is thus one of the many services the anonymous damsels and ladies of romance are happy to provide for the wandering knights. Though these women have significant transformative power (they change wounded bodies into sound ones, after all), this power is limited by the strict subordination of female healers to the male figures who dominate the texts.

Healing in the Middle Ages was a notoriously gendered set of practices. In *Woman as Healer*, Jeanne Achterberg documents the presence of female healing throughout western history. Domestic healing, she argues, or medicine practiced in the home by women, tends to be informal in training, is experience-oriented and orally transmitted, and focuses on preventing and healing common illnesses, easing pregnancy and childbirth, and first aid (often with botanical supplements and/or rituals that I suggest give it a quasi-magical quality). This kind of feminine knowledge has a history of subordination to the officially sanctioned, formalized, and overwhelmingly male medical practice. Doctors and surgeons undertook some form of scholastic training with authoritative medical texts, and they usually charged for their services, which often included bleeding. Achterberg argues that women have been closely associated with the practice of domestic healing throughout western history, moving in and out of mainstream medicine in varying degrees at different times. She describes the situation for European women practicing healing in the early Middle Ages as follows:

> The eleventh, twelfth, and thirteenth centuries were times of excitement and diversity for women healers. Domestic medicine continued to be practiced, even though the methods that survived the Dark Ages were of questionable value. The sociopolitical developments and the still-fluid religious tone allowed women to practice the healing arts with extraordinary freedom compared to the immediate past and future. The culture allowed an unheard-of emergence of women as physicians and ecclesiastics. (58)

Gender-Blending 23

Though at other times women have been banned from attending medical school, one center in Salerno, Italy, in operation from 1000 until 1811, had female faculty members during the early Middle Ages (48). Achterberg notes that though a domestic form of healing was commonly associated with women, the twelfth century in particular saw women participate in traditionally male medical practices.[19] The early medieval acceptance of both domestic and medical healing by women documented by Achterberg is reflected in Arthurian literature, which presents healing as a normative, acceptable feminine activity.

The representation of domestic healing in the romances and chronicles makes little distinction between practices that involve magical elements and those that don't. Some healing women use simple medicine, the kind familiar to most people these days, such as dressing and bandaging wounds—a mundane form of healing which does not approach the slippery edges of the magical. For example, Enide tends Erec's wounds personally until they reach Guivret's castle, where his two sisters meticulously cut the "dead flesh" away before they bandage him with an ointment (Chrétien 100–101). Others rely on powerful ointments, potions, and herbs: in Geoffrey's *History*, for example, Merlin prophesies that the foster-daughter of the Scourger will bring "a saucer of medicine" to restore the land after a huge calamity has destroyed it (183); Guivret's two "charming and cheerful sisters who know much about healing wounds" apply "ointment and dressing" to Erec's injuries in Chrétien's *Erec and Enide* (100–101); and in Marie's "Le Deus Amanz," the damsel's aunt, who is "well-versed in medicines," having practiced the "art of physic" for thirty years, gives the damsel's young suitor a potion which would "restore all his strength to him" no matter how "weary, afflicted, or burdened he might be" (83–84). In each of these instances, the author refers to the healing as a medical procedure requiring an ointment or potion.

It is often hard to determine precisely where medicine leaves off and magic picks up, as the effects of medicinal potions are frequently exactly the same as those of potions that seem more magical. The medicine of Guivret's sisters heals Erec as well as Arthur does when he uses Morgan le Fay's magical ointment, which is "so wonderfully effective that the wound to which it was applied, whether on a nerve or on a joint, could not fail to be completely cured and healed within a week, provided it was treated with the ointment once a day" (89). In the case of Marie's "Eliduc," the "bright-red" flower used by Guildelüec to heal Guilliadun possesses healing properties, but Marie does not designate it as magical. It's merely a "beautiful flower," which nevertheless has a quasi-magical ability to restore life to the dead (124). Magic and medicine are so closely linked in these representations of domestic healing as to be nearly indistinguishable.[20]

Women are so frequently associated with quasi-magical domestic healing in the romances and chronicles that damsels with healing magic become a part of the landscape, like the parade of castles, knights, and

24 *Crafting the Witch*

dwarves found in romance or the never-ending supply of invading armies within chronicle tradition. Arthurian women who bandage wounds and nurse knights to health come from both the servant and the aristocratic classes, and their labor is often anonymous. The fact that most of the damsels who heal lack names reflects the banality of their presence: female domestic healing is so commonplace that the briefest of descriptions suffices. Though they have power, their social position subverts that power, as they are economically dispossessed, performing their services for free (often in the name of love). It is because these damsels use domestic healing magic, accepted as the usual fare of average women, that they can play such an important role in the narratives without threatening the privileged position of patriarchy therein.

Morgan le Fay, on the other hand, is anything but mundane. The one named healer who appears in both the romance and chronicle traditions, she appears only as a name—an invocation of mysterious (but non-threatening) feminine healing magic. Borrowing from her reputation in Geoffrey's *Vita Merlini*, where she and her sisters on the Isle of Avalon are known for healing, Chrétien mentions her twice as the maker of powerful ointments: Arthur uses her ointment to heal Erec's physical injuries, and an unnamed lady uses an ointment "Morgan the Wise" gave her to heal Yvain's madness (*Erec and Enide* 89, *The Knight with the Lion* 332). Here, Morgan functions as a place-holder, a signifier of magical healing power. Her absence diffuses the latent threat of her transformative (healing) magic—though she may know much, her ointments circulate freely for the benefit of the masculine aggressive ethos. She herself is outside of society, but the fruits of her labor are available within it. Here we see evidence of a trend I describe more fully in a later section, the marginalization of overtly magical characters.

Laȝamon's version of Morgan, called Argante in the *Brut*, provides the best example of this trend. Laȝamon situates Argante even more securely outside the chivalric court than does Geoffrey or Chrétien. In the *Brut*, Arthur describes Argante while mortally wounded after the battle of Camelford:

> And ich wulle uaren to Aualun, to uairest alre maidene,
> to Argante þere quene, aluen swiðe sceone;
> and heo scal mine wunden makeien alle isunde,
> al hal me makeien mid halewieȝe drenchen.
> And seoðe ich cumen wulle to mine kineriche
> and wunien mid Brutten mid muchelere wunne. (14276–82)

> And I will go to Avalon, to the loveliest of all maidens, to the queen Argante, fairest of elven women; and she shall make well all my wounds, make me all whole with healing draughts. And afterwards I will return to my kingdom and dwell with the Britons in great contentment.

Laȝamon not only places Argante in an otherworldly realm, Avalon, but also calls her "aluen" (lit. "elven"). He writes her as not human, a creature of fairy-world who stars in Briton yarns about the once and future king. Laȝamon notes a few lines later that "Bruttes ileueð ȝete þat he bon on liue, / and wunnien in Aualun mid fairest alre aluen; / and lokieð euere Bruttes ȝete whan Arður cumen liðe" [The Britons yet believe that he is alive, and dwells in Avalon with the fairest of all fairy women; and the Britons still await the time when Arthur will come again] (14290–92). Laȝamon indulges the reader's curiosity about this absent figure with a glimpse of two beautifully-dressed women in a boat who come to carry Arthur's body away, but they quickly disappear with Arthur, who does not return in the *Brut* (14283–7). Here, Argante acts as a screen against which hope can be projected: because of her mysterious healing power, her elven magic, she provides an avenue for Arthur's death to be prevented. She exists only on the outside, to reinforce the inside.

Morgan/Argante has only a name, but her healing power is famous, whereas the mundane, ointment-toting damsels are anonymous. These two kinds of figures reveal a paradox common to representations of femininity: "woman" can be both a free-floating signifier of mysterious otherness or an integral, under-appreciated participant in daily life; she can be simultaneously exalted and subordinated. This trend is epitomized by the character of Thessela, in Chrétien's *Cligés*, a servant who is also a (good) witch. Though she is limited to the domestic sphere, Thessela uses those feminine resources to enable not only the protection of her mistress's virginity, but also the restoration of the rightful heir to the throne. Her magical practices are domestic rather than exotic, but the consequences of her power are monumental.

Thessela is the witchiest of all Chrétien's women. Though she compares herself to Medea, a notorious wicked witch, Thessela's not wicked (159). In fact, she's quite the opposite. Named for her homeland, Thessaly, "where diabolical enchantments flourish and are taught," Thessela was born in a land where the women, in particular, "practice magic spells and bewitchments" (159). She comes from a land where a community of women collect and distribute magical knowledge, and she uses her extensive knowledge to accomplish some amazing feats: she prevents the usurper Alis from consummating his marriage to Fenice by crafting a potion which makes him dream of sex (161), she provides a concoction for Fenice that makes her body simulate death (193), and when they are running away from Alis's army, "Thessela, their guide, kept them so secure by her enchantments and magic that they felt no fear or dread of all the emperor's forces" (204). She's a good witch, and a powerful one too.

Thessela's main function in *Cligés* is to help her mistress, Fenice, by facilitating the relationship between Fenice and Cligés, the rightful heir to the throne. She employs her magic only at Fenice's behest, though she offers her magical assistance without solicitation from the heroine. Each of

26   *Crafting the Witch*

the tasks Thessela performs helps to balance the scales for Fenice, as the narrative weights them heavily on the side of the male aristocracy. As long as Alis is emperor of "Greece and Constantinople," he may not marry, so that Cligés, his dead brother's son, will stay his heir. Despite his promise, Alis decides to marry Fenice, and Cligés and Fenice fall deeply in love when Cligés arrives to collect her for Alis. Though Fenice and Cligés are obviously the more well-suited couple, she must marry Alis. Fenice is therefore the victim of Alis's treachery, and the situation demands action. This is the first time Thessela performs magic. Fenice's only recourse in this situation is magical deception, as she has no legal right to refuse Alis and no physical means for preventing the union. Thessela's magic is thus justified as a means of self-defense, in that it allows Fenice to protect her virginity, an important aspect of her ideal femininity.

Thessela accomplishes this by making Fenice a potion that will make Alis believe he is consummating his marriage to his virginal wife when actually he is merely dreaming. The following description of Thessela demonstrates the explicit connection between feminine magic and domesticity in *Cligés*:

> I wish rather to speak of Thessela, who was ever intent on mixing and preparing her potions. Thessela ground her potion, adding spices in abundance to sweeten and temper it. She ground it and mixed it well, and filtered it until it was perfectly clear without a trace of bitterness, for the spices she used made it sweet and aromatic. By the time the potion was ready, the day was drawing to an end. (162)

Thessela prepares the potion carefully and thoroughly, like a cook fussing over a large meal, spending her whole day in pursuit of the right mixture. Both the reason for the potion (to protect Fenice's virginity) and the site of its preparation (the kitchen) involve conventionally feminine spaces—the body, the hearth. This is characteristic: when Arthurian women practice non-healing magic, it's domestic magic they use. The firm circumscription of magic within the domestic sphere diffuses the potential threat to rigid gender conventions posed by this kind of magic.

The next time Thessela uses her magic demonstrates the type of transformative magic available to female magic-users when they are not using their healing power. To help Fenice escape her marriage to the unbearable Alis, Thessela offers to provide a potion (a ploy later made famous by its appearance in Shakespeare's *Romeo and Juliet*) that will make Fenice appear dead. Fenice agrees to feign death, saying to Thessela, "I am in your hands; take care of me" (190): she expresses willingness to erase herself (if only temporarily) for the sake of the relationship, and the result is an extreme loss of bodily control. Thessela's potion makes Fenice "cold, colourless, pale and stiff" and masks "her power of speech and breathing" (189). This transformation is the obverse of that in healing: rather than

Gender-Blending   27

reactiving her body, the potion plunges Fenice into acute passivity, the perfect tableau, the extreme version of the pale, silent heroine.

The extreme passivity of Fenice's body does not convince the local doctors that she's actually dead. Even though Thessela's magic creates a Fenice who conforms most fully with the romance notion of femininity as passivity, the doctors find the situation threatening. They suspect magic—female magic—and this motivates their attempts to reveal that magic. Here, domestic magic directly opposes male medicine, pitting feminine magic against masculine science. The head doctor examines Fenice's "corpse" and feels "beyond any doubt, that life was still in her body" (195). The irony here is of course that the doctor is correct—Fenice is alive, and Thessela is trying to deceive them. But the doctor exceeds the boundaries of masculine aggression when he and the other physicians torture Fenice to prove that she lives, devising increasingly cruel torments, moving from lying and threatening Fenice to beating and scalding her with hot lead (196). Fenice endures it all silently, without revealing the truth, until "more than a thousand ladies" discover what's happening, break down the doors, and toss the doctors out the window, rescuing Fenice from this display of unchecked masculine aggression (196–7). Fenice's passive suffering is characteristic of heroines throughout the romances considered here: the leading ladies commonly endure cruelty from enemies and beloveds, and often inflict violence on themselves.[21] Fenice's situation is a mixture of victimization and self-destruction—she volunteers to crystallize her passivity for her beloved, but her enemies torture her. The actions of the thousand ladies, however, are decidedly unfeminine.

As I mentioned above, when the women throw the cruel doctors out the window, Chrétien says, "No ladies ever did better!" (197). The characterization of the male doctors as brutally suspicious of women marks masculine medicine as largely responsible for the medieval tension between domestic healers and licensed doctors. In this narrative, the doctors' representation implicates masculine healing and valorizes the feminine practitioner. The male healers do the opposite of healing: they inflict deadly wounds and cause great suffering. Though these women may not be domestic healers, they join together to help one another and save at least one woman from torture. The community of women here recalls the community of magical women in Thessely, as their combined effort results in the appropriation of a transformative power usually available only to men in these texts, the power to fatally wound and kill. This episode stands out as an indictment of the abuse of masculine power, a theme we will see reprised often in my discussion of masculine magic below.

If masculine healing magic is destructive, feminine healing magic is excessively generative. After her tortures have finally ceased, the mere sight of Thessela inspires Fenice: "When Fenice saw her nurse she felt she was already fully recovered, so much did she love, believe, and trust in her" (200). In Thessely, it seems the recipe for domestic power calls for a healthy

28   *Crafting the Witch*

portion of essentialist representations of women as nurturers mixed with a heaping tablespoon of herbalist earth-mother. Thessela's domestic magic helps Fenice achieve what she wants, marriage to Cligés and restoration of his throne, but in a way that does not challenge or threaten gender norms. Fenice does not take direct action or confront her foes: her character conforms to an ideal femininity that finds non-aggressive, circuitous routes to specific objectives. Thessela's solutions for Fenice involve deception, rather than fighting, and require absolute secrecy, rather than confrontation. Generally, domestic magic in these texts reinforces an essentialized notion of feminine behavior: feminine magic works best when female characters operate within the existing conventions of femininity.[22] The authors of these early romances and chronicles ratify the conventions associated with ideal femininity, stressing conformity in their representations of female characters and granting transformative agency only to those women who act in service of the feudal, patriarchal hierarchy.

Why didn't these authors find it necessary to villainize women performing magic (as did their counterparts in the fourteenth, fifteenth, and sixteenth centuries), instead opting to represent them with magical agency (albeit limited)? What social factors encouraged a cultural representation that offered female magical characters a chance to participate in the feudal hierarchy in limited, but overwhelmingly positive, ways? There is evidence that aristocratic women (about and for whom the romances and chronicles are written) experienced a decrease in relative freedom under feudal Norman Britain as compared to their Anglo-Saxon predecessors. As Judith Weiss puts it, "Noblewomen in post-Conquest Britain appear to have enjoyed less political and economic power than either Anglo-Saxon women or their counterparts in France" (7). In Anglo-Saxon England, for example, the law demanded that a woman who had borne a child to her husband receive possession of one half of his property upon his death, whereas Anglo-Norman wives could expect to receive usufruct of only one third of the husband's property (unless he had designated a specific or "nominated" set of holdings).[23] Likewise, whereas an Anglo-Saxon wife could expect her *morgengifu* to remain in the hands of her extended family upon her death or if she chose to end her marriage, the dower of an Anglo-Norman wife would revert to her husband's heir once she died.[24] In fact, the possibility of Anglo-Norman wives ending a marriage seems outside the imagination of many historians, and such a move would surely prohibit them from access to any of their husbands' holdings. Both French and Anglo-Norman women suffered under feudal rule with regard to property ownership. As S. F. C. Milsom notes, women under feudal rule had no laws to ensure receipt of their dower upon a husband's death, as the feudal contract bound a lord to grant land to the heir of his homage-paying tenant, not to a woman who had no role in the service-oriented land tenure system (60–61, 77). This meant that it was often up to the inheriting son to provide for his widowed mother, and Claire de Trafford argues this often created tension, as some

Gender-Blending 29

sons appropriated their mother's dower for themselves (40–45). The shift from Anglo-Saxon partible inheritance to feudal primogeniture made it increasingly difficult for female inheritors, as families worked to consolidate their holdings and preserve familial land dynasties.

It was not only in the areas of inheritance that Anglo-Norman and French aristocratic women found themselves less empowered than their Anglo-Saxon sisters. Paulette L'Hermite-Leclercq argues that rigid gender division and strictly enforced segregation marked feudal culture. Women and men received separate educations, and young noblewomen had little recourse when forced into politically or economically advantageous marriages at young ages; Cnut's law, which specifies that a woman shouldn't be forced to marry a man she didn't like, no longer applied. Whereas men were often fostered outside their natal households, women usually stayed within theirs until engaged or married. L'Hermite-Leclercq provides evidence that feudal gendered socialization was so effective that some women, like Christina of Markygate, felt intense "shame" when "forced to dress like a man and ride a horse like a man" (212). The well-marked gender binary apparent in the romances and chronicles considered here was clearly one of the many cultural mechanisms for enforcing the gendered separation documented by L'Hermite-Leclercq and others. Perhaps because an individual woman's potential to present a threat to the feudal order was so strictly curtailed in the social sphere, there was no need to villainize women who deviated from this model. Instead, writers could rely on positive models of women contributing to the feudal hierarchy. In other words, they did not need wicked witches, so they didn't use them.

There is one apparent exception in the works considered here to the trend of strictly circumscribed feminine magic, found perhaps unsurprisingly in the work of Marie de France: the fairy maiden of "Lanval." Though Lanval's fairy mistress does not heal the bodies of any knights, she does possess a unique form of magic that is active and succeeds in challenging the feudal status quo. At the beginning of the story, King Arthur forgets Lanval when he is distributing "wives and land" to his knights; as Lanval is still "far from his inheritance," the king's omission places him in a bad position, without monetary support (73). The feudal hierarchy has failed Lanval, and it is at this point that the beautiful fairy woman appears to rescue Lanval from his dire straits. In a reversal of the usual romance structure, where the knight performs some task to obtain the love of a lady, this lady seeks out Lanval. She drives the entire relationship: she offers him her love (without requiring him to perform any tasks or quests), she possesses the magic that allows her to appear to him whenever he wishes to see her (and sets the terms of her appearances), and to correct the situation caused by Arthur's failure, she provides him with unmatched wealth (74–75). The climax of the story finds the fairy lady rescuing Lanval from imminent death—riding up on a white horse, no less!—in a last reversal of the conventional romance moment (perhaps most famously represented by Lancelot's rescuing of Guinevere

30   *Crafting the Witch*

in *Morte Dathur*). In this story, Marie offers a picture of feudal tradition gone wrong—a woman must intervene when the patriarchal system fails a good knight, leaving him without resources. Joan Ferrante suggests that authors writing for female patrons and female audiences commonly create heroines with special power or attributes who help heroes by raising their social status or solving their problems.[25] Certainly Marie's work appealed to female audience members, prompting one of her contemporaries, Denis Piramus, to note that her "lays are accustomed to please the ladies: they listen to them joyfully and willingly, for they are just what they desire" (qtd. in Burgess and Busby 11). While the importance of appealing to a female audience cannot be denied, comparison of Marie's work with that of the other authors in this study suggests an additional interpretive possibility.

Marie's text represents the feudal world as an imperfect one, a move repeated by all of the authors considered here. In Marie's narrative, a lord's omission almost ruins one of his knights, someone who has played the feudal game correctly—Lanval grants Arthur his military service, represented by his physical presence in Arthur's court, but Arthur does not reciprocate properly. This state of affairs cannot be rectified by the men in the court; in fact, it is only the power of the otherworld, Avalon, that can rescue Lanval. Avalon appears to be a topsy-turvy world, where women have the wealth and power, evinced by the fairy-lady and her special abilities. She can fix what the feudal world cannot, but there's a catch—no one can know that she's the power behind the man. No one else can even see her, as if it is entirely beyond patriarchal imagination that a woman could fill the same role as a lord or king. As soon as her power is revealed, she must leave the feudal world, and the only way Lanval can be with her is to abandon the feudal world as well. On one level, then, this story operates as a critique of the feudal mode and its exclusive reliance on fallible male power.

The fallibility of male power is a theme taken up by Chrétien, Geoffrey, and Laȝamon, though they take a much different approach than Marie's. These writers seem less concerned with the potential threat posed by women to the feudal hierarchy than they do with the possibility for male power to spin out of control, threatening the order it should preserve. Indeed, the biggest threat to the questing knights and battling kings of these early romances and chronicles is a masculine one. Now that we have explored the construction of feminine magic, it is time to turn our attention to the other side of this binary, masculine magic. It's time to meet the giant.

IV. WHO NEEDS WITCHES ANYWAY?: GIANTS OF THE ARTHURIAN OTHERWORLD

If the magical women of early Arthurian romances are remarkably non-witchy healers working to restore knights' wounded bodies to health or to restore patrilineal succession, what role do the magical men play? And if villainous women are conspicuously absent, then who does offer the threat? What kinds of characters act as villains for the legions of questing knights wandering through romance? These questions find their answers when we consider the most prevalent element associated with Arthurian legend, the thing that makes a knight a knight, namely, battle.

Both the romances and the chronicles are characterized by the prevalence of fighting, battle, and war sequences, which contribute to the development of a masculine *ethos* of aggression. In both the romance and the chronicle traditions, ideal masculinity is expressed through aggressive fighting tempered by elaborate codes of honor, and these codes govern not only relationships between knights, as we've seen, but those between men and women and between different social classes. In fact, scenes of battle are the most common feature of three of the four authors' works considered in this chapter.[26] Chrétien, Geoffrey, and Laȝamon continuously engage their knights in some form of battle: for Chrétien, individual jousts are most frequent, whereas for both chroniclers, pitched battles fill the folios. Just as the knights pose a real threat to their foes, often killing them, they are a danger to the non-military men of lower classes and to nearly all women. Kings and knights have power in large part because they are lethally violent, and violence of this caliber must be controlled if it is not to destroy all societal bonds and institutions. The authors considered here provide a multitude of examples of "bad" kings and knights—and more insidious foes such as giants, dragons, or demons—behaving outrageously, murderously rampaging through the countryside, using their strength to inflict all manner of tortures on the people living there. These are the bad guys, the foes against whom our heroes so valiantly toil, those who should be punished for their crimes against humanity. They demonstrate by negative example exactly what makes the knights different, what makes their aggressive action heroic. They are male figures who are so masculine as to require execution: bad, evil, *wicked* men. We've finally found our wicked witches.

The giants are by far the most populous group of non-human foes in both the romance and chronicle traditions. Semi-human figures drawn from classical, biblical, and Celtic models, the giants populated Britain before Brutus arrived, according to the chronicles.[27] The narrative is a colonizing one: when Brutus and his people are done exploring Albion, they force "the giants whom they had discovered into the caves in the mountains" and thus take over the rich land (72). Later, the giants try to stage a comeback, but Brutus and his folks kill all but one, whom they save so he can wrestle one of Brutus's leaders, Corineas. Corineas "enjoyed beyond all reason matching himself against such monsters" (73). There is something special about fighting giants.

What makes giants so different from their knightly counterparts? Most knights follow a strict policy of "joust first, ask questions later," and the kings of the chronicles are ur-cowboys, forcibly expanding the range of their control and making their own justice. Fighting is so prevalent among kings

32   *Crafting the Witch*

and knights that at first glance it's difficult to tell the difference between our heroes and their foes. Both the titular knights of romance and their large adversaries fight with little provocation, both knights and giants take women as the prize of battle, and both fall down when hit hard enough with a blunt instrument. British soldiers in the chronicles exterminate an entire community of giants to gain control of the island, and both the British kings and giants fight to the death. We cannot tell friend from foe by observing how often or with what intensity a knight or king displays aggression, as the feudal system calls for swift and brutal defense of one's lands, if necessary. Instead, it is to the chivalric code that we must look to make sense of what kind of aggression reflects appropriate masculinity and what kind of aggression will get you killed—we must examine the reason for the fight and the manner in which it is precipitated, carried out, and ended.

One fight from *The Knight with the Lion* (*Yvain*) demonstrates well many of the details of chivalric honor. To summarize, Gawain agrees to fight on a damsel's behalf, but that damsel turns out to be an older sister who wants to dispossess her younger sister of her rightful share of lands inherited from their father (354–5). Yvain agrees to champion the younger daughter, and before the fight begins, we learn that Arthur favors the younger sister's position: "The king saw the maiden [the younger sister] and recognized her immediately; he was pleased and delighted to see her, for he sided with her in this dispute, as he wished to do what was right" (369). When the fight begins, Gawain and Yvain do not know whom they are fighting because their armor obscures their identities. The knights clash and "their lances [shatter], though they were stout and made of ash" (371). They continue the fight with their swords until they are bruised and bloody, take a quick breather, and fight again, until finally "the two ceased fighting, for each realized that, although it had been a long time coming, he had finally met his match" (372). They exchange compliments, each saying that the other is better than any foe, and eventually reveal their identities, which leads to rejoicing and embracing, and both knights concede the fight. Chivalric fights are thus motivated by issues of social importance (the position of women, property-rights, building a social support network, and so on), and the convention of fair fighting (agreeing to rest, conceding the match to the superior opponent) ensures that individual men won't be slaughtered outright.

The conventions which govern the most common form of romance fighting, the joust, also help prevent unnecessary death or dismemberment. Typically, knights begin the battle with a formal challenge or some kind of verbal aggression, move into a high-powered joust with lances (which shatter), fall or leap off their horses to continue the fight with swords, and trade blows until they are bloody or maimed. At this point, the fight can end when a knight asks for mercy or falls down (dead or unconscious). If a knight asks for mercy, the winner usually grants it, and the losing knight must take an oath to present himself as a prisoner to whomever the winner designates. The fight between Yvain and Gawain follows this pattern until

Gender-Blending 33

the end, when both knights realize that they are evenly matched. This is a quintessentially chivalric moment—after proving their aggressive masculinity through vicious battle, the two knights grant to each other the victory, refusing to take it for themselves because of mutual respect for one another. The representation of chivalric heroism thus provides a grammar of jousting which stresses the importance of the following things: solid justification for the fight, a formal challenge, fair combat conditions, use of protective equipment, and an opportunity for non-fatal resolution of physical conflict.[28] Each of these elements, if integrated into a culture of masculine aggression, could potentially help to channel (and thus limit) the most extreme violent behaviors.

If this is an example of a chivalric fight, then how is a fight with a giant different?

Let's begin by taking a close look at another fight in *Knight with the Lion*, Yvain versus the giant Harpin. Physically, the giant is marked by his appearance on foot, with a large club, which distinguishes him from the knights who ride a war-horse and carry lance and sword. Harpin's cruelty is emphasized by the ratty appearance of the men he has enslaved and his inappropriate sexual appetite: he wants to give the local lord's daughter to his lackeys, so that "she would have a thousand knaves with her constantly, all covered with lice and naked like tramps and scullery-boys, and all abusing her shamefully" (346). We don't get a good look at Harpin's body until the fight proper begins, but once it starts we zoom in closely.

Chrétien describes Harpin's great mass bit by bit: as Yvain slices off bits of flesh, we hear their descriptions. First, "Yvain struck him such a blow to the breast that it ripped his bearskin; he moistened the tip of his lance in his blood, the body's sauce" (347). We see the chest as immediately marked—by the bearskin (which should be armor) and then by the bleeding wound. The giant displays excessive pride (always a danger to the brave) by daring not to wear armor, as knights always do, a point which Chrétien emphasizes, saying "he had so much confidence in his brute strength that he refused to wear any armor" (347). His punishment for relying too confidently on masculine strength is to endure feminization; the blood over which Chrétien lingers is the signal of his hidden feminine fluidity, the weakness beneath the façade of strength. Yvain moves in with his sword, slicing "from his cheek enough flesh for grilling" (347); this description further develops the cannibalistic trope. From meat, the giant's flesh turns into a tree, as the lion enters the action by clawing off the bearskin, "like bark," and ripping away "both nerves and flesh" from Harpin's thigh. Yvain chops off Harpin's arm, and runs him through, finishing him. Harpin's fall is as loud as that of "a mighty oak" (348). The description of his huge body comes piecemeal, as if the enormity is too great to reveal all at once, and the final image, of a beast as towering and imposing as a mighty oak, is provided only after the giant is already done for, while taking his dying fall. The danger of such a large and imposing foe is mitigated by this description—by the time we realize

34   Crafting the Witch

Harpin's true size, he is already dead, an empty threat. That Chrétien takes such pains to diffuse the threat in this way suggests the high level of anxiety precipitated by the presence of such a gigantic creature.

Elsewhere, it is also the giants' physical differences that most immediately separate them from the ideal representatives of masculinity, the knights. Of the nine giants who appear in Geoffrey's *Historia*, five bear descriptions lavishing special attention on their physical characteristics. Gogamog is "particularly repulsive" and "twelve feet tall," so strong that he could tear up an oak tree easily after giving it one shake (72–3). The Giant of Wickedness terrifies everyone with the "piercing glance of his eyes" and later rides naked upon the back of the Dragon of Worchester (181). The Michel's Mont giant is of "monstrous size," a "foul" and "inhuman" monster (238–9). When Arthur first meets him, his face is smeared in pig's blood, and when the giant is finally defeated, he falls "like some oak torn from its roots by the fury of the winds" (240). The visible difference of the giants signals their social difference, their refusal to bow to the laws of chivalric social interaction, their inevitable display of egregiously inappropriate behavior.

Laʒamon, in particular, pays special attention to the excessive appetites of the Michel's Mont giant, providing ample evidence for the giant's wickedness. The "eotende" [giant] abducts Eleine, Arthur's kinswoman, and her old nurse, for which Arthur personally seeks revenge. Laʒamon expands considerably the scene just before Arthur arrives, which took only a few lines in the *Historia*. The giant returns to his fire, where Eleine's nurse remains bound, with "twælf swine iteied tosomne" [twelve swine tied together], and prepares to cook them (12962). The whole time, "he to þan wiue loh; / and sone umbe while he laid bi þan wife" [he looked at the woman, and almost immediately he laid with the woman] (12966–7). His rapacious desires are so excessive that the sight of an abused old woman excites him enough to abandon food for the chance to rape her again. Laʒamon's adaptation emphasizes the sexual nature of the giant's threat: unchecked aggression leads to sexual predation.

In early Arthurian literature, the giants function as examples of extreme masculine excess—their bodies, their appetites, the violent battles required to kill them. They reproduce the gazes, behaviors, and *ethos* of the knight-heroes, but with a difference: they behave without restraints. My analysis of the giant figure in early chronicle and romance agrees with Jeffrey Jerome Cohen's, who argues that "the defeat of the monster is an oneiric fantasy of the triumph of order and a vindication of the tight channeling of violent drives into socially beneficial expression over the usurpation of authority and status by transgressive individualism" (178). In other words, the giants represent what would happen to feudal order if knights were not restrained by a set of rigidly enforced laws. Those laws are especially important to contain male sexual desire, Cohen suggests; the giant's defeat "inscribes the romance compulsion to restraint, especially to sexual restraint" (181).

At the same time, if an ideal masculinity exists, then other, non-ideal masculinities must also be available: "The display of the severed head is at once an assertion of masculinity and an admission of its constructed nature—of the possibility of other masculinities, of a different gendering of behaviors" (181). For all the writers considered here, ideal masculinity is different from the excessive, hyper-masculinity of the giant because ideal masculinity isn't always masculine. Knights are not only subject to the chivalric system of honor, but also to the feminizing forces of love and magic. Rather than suffer condemnation when they submit to these forces, knights tempered by femininity receive rewards—women, kingdoms, healed bodies, and most importantly, respect. The gender mutability caused by love and magic is not simply desirable, it is necessary to prevent the kind of masculine excess represented by the giants. The giants are monstrous precisely because their magical, semi-human existence places them beyond the margins of normative masculine behavior, which requires the gender-blending provided by chivalric love and magical power. Both the romances and the chronicles participate together in using the giant figure to examine what the loss of mutability means for masculinity—extreme violent aggression. The giants, the magical, essential manifestation of hyper-masculinization, embody an extrapolation of the aggressive urges so valued and so carefully regulated by chivalry. Killing the giants removes the problem of unrestrained masculine power from society.

Arthurian giants function to contain and assuage anxiety about violent masculinity in feudal society, the other side of the chivalric coin. If giants tell knights how not to behave, it is chivalry which tells them what they should be doing. Richard Kaeuper argues that the chivalry in the romances was "an active social force" organizing the massive male violence that pervaded twelfth- and thirteenth-century medieval culture: "Chivalry was a code of violence in defense of a prickly sense of honor (and the honorable acquisition of loot to be distributed in open-handed largess) just as thoroughly as it was a code of restraint" (99–100). Chivalry thus determines which battles are acceptable to fight, and which aren't. Within the patriarchal feudal system, even men found their options limited, especially younger sons: as Frances and Joseph Gies argue, younger sons throughout Europe were often "disfranchised by primogeniture" and in England they were "not even classed as noble" (142). Because of their precarious situations, "young knights led a life in which pleasure mingled with violence, death was a commonplace, and turbulence reigned" (143). Though violence and masculinity were inextricably entangled, chivalry provided a means of managing that violence (although certainly not exterminating it). In fact, Georges Duby has argued that romances occupied an important place in the formal education of knights, which included a large number of single men: "in the 12th century, the majority of knights—the men the writers of chansons and romances most wanted to please—were *jeunes*, unmarried adult males, frustrated and jealous of men with wives" (259). To curb the

36 *Crafting the Witch*

violence of these young men (especially the sexual violence), romances promoted a code of self-restraint and friendship. Single men should not take anything they want, like the giants who inevitably end up dead, but follow the path of the chivalric heroes, who work to strengthen and maintain the feudal order.

The necessity for ordering the chaotic world of male violence results in literary representations, like those we have seen in this discussion, which privilege those men who allow forces like love or magic temporarily to feminize them. Normative masculinity is characterized by occasional gender mutability, as demanded by chivalry and enabled by forces like love and magic, and giantism seems to be the result of an inability or unwillingness to engage in submissive behavior. But is there a boundary in the other direction? Can someone have too much mutability, too much access to transformative power? To answer that, we must ask the prophet.

V. TRANSFORMING THE FUTURE: PROPHECY AND LIMINALITY

To prophesy is to speak the future into existence. The prophet says, "this will be," and for the prophecy to be true—that is, for it to be prophecy at all—it must "be." The prophet, like a mother, births the prophetic utterance from the womb of the mind, and in turn generates the events which will transpire.[29] The prophet, like God, speaks ("let there be light") and it is so ("and there was light").[30] Prophetic speech transforms the world, determines the future by narrating it. The power of prophetic magic is the power of transformation.

A glimpse into antiquity reveals that representation of prophecy's transformative influence evolved within a complex literary tradition. Writers in Greece and Rome commonly represented prophetic knowledge as determining the future, rather than merely predicting it.[31] Both pagan and Christian theologians attempted to solve the paradox of fate (or divine foreknowledge) and free will: to predict the future is to dictate it, and thus foreclose the possibility for human agency.[32] By the time Geoffrey wrote the *Historia*, prophetic writing had developed a tradition of ambiguity which lent itself to myriad political (re)interpretations over the course of many generations. Because Galfridian prophecy involved animal imagery and vague genealogical references, almost any group could find a way to use the *Prophetie* to validate a range of political positions.[33] As prophecy transforms the future, so readers of prophetic writing transform its meaning; transformative power seeps magically out of the narrative and into the hermeneutic space.

We can observe the effect of the transformative process of prophetic interpretation by tracing the development of the figure most commonly associated with prophecy in the Arthurian legend, Merlin. Though the French writers of Arthuriana in the twelfth century show little interest in Merlin, his notoriety in the English chronicles is unparalleled. Merlin makes only the briefest of appearances in Chrétien de Troyes's influential Arthurian romances. In *Erec and Enide*, Chrétien refers to the time of Merlin (119), implying that his day had long passed by the time Arthur and his knights roamed England. Chrétien's Merlin is a name only; we don't learn anything else about him from the descriptions in the romances, as he is merely part of the magical landscape, a decorative addition to the fantastical environment of the knights' quests borrowed from the *Historia Regum Brtanniæ*. Marie de France neglects Merlin entirely. He appears not once in her *lais*, not even as decoration. Merlin is an English obsession.

Scholars usually credit Geoffrey of Monmouth with developing the figure of Merlin from oral Welsh tradition and popularizing him in the *Historia*, the *Prophetie Merlini*, and the *Vita Merlini*.[34] Geoffrey's *Historia*, in particular, is the earliest text to collect all the elements historically associated with Merlin (such as his association with the birth of Arthur, his magical power, his mysterious father, his precocious childhood, his frequent disappearances, and so on). Merlin receives more attention in both the *Historia* and the *Brut* than any figure but Arthur. The enigmatic prophet is unique in his representation; nowhere in either text does another magician play such a critical role in the country's governance, nor does any other prophet occupy a position of such esteem and influence. Merlin is the premier prophet of the chronicles, and Arthur's reign is indebted to him.

In his extremely popular Latin chronicle, Geoffrey represents Merlin's prophetic power as linked to his ability to control his reputation through manipulation of his own body. Laȝamon's text develops the connection more fully, emphasizing the relationship between prophetic utterance and the body. Through the figure of the prophet, both the chronicles and (to a lesser degree) the romances offer alternative constructions of gender which subvert the boundary between masculinity and femininity. In the chronicles (particularly the *Brut*), Merlin's control over his physical appearance manifests in at least two main areas: a) the strategic appropriation of visual gender markers of both masculinity and femininity and b) the transformation of his body into the physical likeness of another. Merlin's ability to transform his body to best suit the current situation provides the foundation for his immense prophetic power, but that same ability forces him into a perpetual state of liminality as well. Because Merlin is so extreme, his gendered behaviors do not really function as plausible reconfigurations of gender difference, and thus the space for gender play, while present, is limited.

Transforming Gender: The Prophet as Androgyne

Nicole Loraux's *The Experiences of Tiresias* employs the figure of the titular androgynous prophet to suggest that ancient Greece privileged male knowledge of both masculinity and femininity. When Tiresias, "whose

38   *Crafting the Witch*

experience of both sexes gives him knowledge about feminine pleasure," reveals the privileged knowledge he gained while transformed into a woman, two things happen: first Hera blinds him, and then Zeus grants him the power of prophecy (11). Though the female figure in this myth is enraged at male possession of female secrets, the male figure endorses the knowledge, even increasing Tiresias's ability to obtain additional privileged knowledge. It is the transformation from male to female, from masculinity to femininity, which precipitates the renown Tiresias enjoys as a seer. Androgyny and prophecy are linked for Tiresias in a causal relationship; male possession of feminine knowledge generates prophecy. In the early Arthurian literature, as in the classical texts, mutability of gender plays an important role in the development of prophetic power. And in Arthurian literature, when we talk about prophecy, we cannot avoid thinking of that enigmatic old wizard, Merlin.

Merlin's representation in the English chronicles participates in the tradition of androgyny exemplified by Tiresias, whose echo continued to resound throughout medieval England (and well into the early modern period). One of the conditions of Merlin's prophetic power is his ability to participate in the most extreme of gendered behaviors at will, fluidly using the conventions of both masculinity and femininity to his advantage. In the chronicles, Merlin possesses a wondrous ability to adopt with equal facility behaviors conventionally associated with femininity and masculinity, strategically employing both poles of gendered binary systems such as active/passive, public/private, body/spirit, and presence/absence. This gender-blending contributes to the power and efficacy of Merlin's magic, which manifests occasionally as shape-shifting or engineering, but most frequently as prophecy. Merlin's characterization draws on a common trope for both the romance and chronicle traditions: the men who practice prophecy commonly possess gender mutability—so frequently, in fact, that the authors suggest an intricate connection between it and magical power, though Laȝamon's Merlin is the only figure who maintains an active control over his own androgyny. Prophetic power is, after all, transformative power, the power of breaking conventions, of crossing boundaries. Transforming the body and transforming the world are not so very different.

In Marie's "Yonec," the shape-shifting hawk-knight who fathers Yonec, Muldumarec, exhibits the power of prophecy after receiving his death-wound. From the beginning of the *lai*, Muldumarec has a great degree of control over his participation in gendered behaviors. He can transform from hawk to knight and back again, possessing powerful shape-shifting magic perfectly suited to gender mutability in its shifting appropriation of the forms of things. Though he could not appear to the unnamed lady until she had wished for him, thereafter the hawk-knight has the power to visit any time she is alone (131–34, 199–210). This arrangement juxtaposes masculine and feminine roles; it combines an active power—Muldumarec comes to her—with a reactive implementation of that power—he can only come once the lady calls for him.

Gender-Blending 39

Muldumarec's gender mutability becomes far more extreme than this subtle juxtaposition as the story progresses. As part of a plan to convince her of his Christianity, Muldumarec abandons the form of a "handsome and noble knight" and takes on the lady's form, transforming himself from an ideal male figure into an ideal female figure, from masculinity to femininity (115). He convinces her, and the two enjoy a clandestine relationship, the fruits of Muldumarec's magic, until the suspicious husband finally catches the lovers. When the husband gets involved, trapping and fatally wounding the hawk-knight, Muldumarec loses his transformative power, becoming permanently feminized, with a weakened body, leaking a trail of blood. The death-wound of this knight forces him into a permanently feminized role, an extreme example of passivity, silence, and feminine fluidity.

Before Marie's hawk-knight dies, while his body endures the suffering of his death wound but before his ability to self-construct has been snuffed out entirely, he displays a tremendous prophetic power. On his deathbed, the hawk-knight receives a visit from his lady, who travels to his otherworldly land by following his blood-trail, and he prophesies that their son, Yonec, will one day grow to be a great knight. At a feast, Muldumarec's son will discover his tomb, at which time the lady will tell Yonec his father's story and present him with his father's sword (342–436). The hawk-knight is a true prophet: when the fated feast finally happens, Yonec kills his stepfather, the murderous husband, fulfilling the prophecy and avenging his real father's death (465–544). Muldumarec's prophecy not only comes true, but secures his succession, as Yonec becomes lord of the land (544–550).

In this example, Muldumarec possesses powerful transformative magic—his prediction avenges his death and provides his child with wealth and power. But he accesses prophetic knowledge only after the destruction of his body and the consequent revocation of his transformative ability. Though Muldumarec's prophetic knowledge is accurate, Marie does not offer prophecy as an effective means for obtaining information for average people; in fact, she marks this prophet as unable to sustain life. The wages of prophecy are death, it seems. And yet, Merlin, the most popular Arthurian magician, whose mysterious life became fodder for both awe and mockery in the following centuries, is primarily a prophet. Unlike the abortive prophets of early Arthurian romance, the Merlin of the chronicles navigates the tricky waters of gender mutability with great skill and showmanship, landing himself eventually upon the fertile island of prophetic power.[35] Despite his success, even Merlin cannot fully escape the consequences of his prophetic power—it seems that while prevention of hyper-masculinity demands that men occasionally embrace their feminine side, too much yin in their yang proves just as fatal as too little. The French romances warn against the difficulty of using prophetic power without sacrificing one's life, and the chronicles reinforce that warning in the figure of Merlin.

In his extremely popular chronicle, Geoffrey represents Merlin's prophetic power as linked to his ability to appropriate masculine and feminine

40   *Crafting the Witch*

behaviors. The *Historia* presents Merlin as alternately masculine and feminine, a trend Laȝamon exaggerates in the *Brut* by emphasizing Merlin's careful and deliberate orchestration of his own gender construction.[36] Geoffrey commonly uses femininity to signal the prophetic moment, and Laȝamon builds on this, creating a Merlin who exploits gender mutability to achieve what he wants.

Geoffrey introduces us to Merlin very briefly. Advised by the local wisemen to find a fatherless boy to sacrifice, Vortigern sends his men on the search. They rest from their long search in the outskirts of Carmarthen, where some local children are playing in a field. Geoffrey writes, "A sudden quarrel broke out between two of the lads, whose names were Merlin and Dinabutius" (167). Geoffrey embroils Merlin in an argument as soon as we meet him, introducing him in the same way kings and knights are typically introduced—in the context of active, aggressive behavior, and Laȝamon's version of this scene also strongly marks Merlin as a bully. Laȝamon describes the scene as follows: "Vmben ane stunde heo bigunnen striuinge, / alse hit wes auer laȝe imong childrene plæȝe; / þe an þe operne smat and he þeos duntes abad" [After a while they began fighting, as it was ever among children at play; the one smote the other and he endured the dints] (7765–67). The one who smote turns out to be Merlin, accused by the unfortunate recipient of the blow, Dinabuz. Merlin thus begins his quick rise to fame by striking another child.

Geoffrey and Laȝamon both introduce Merlin by way of his aggression, a trait properly belonging to those ideal representatives of masculinity, the knights, but not necessarily to Merlin, a fatherless boy. Laȝamon's Dinabuz voices the argument against him: Merlin is inappropriately aggressive because Dinabuz is a "kinges sune" [king's son], whereas Merlin is "of noht icumen" [sprung from nothing] (7772). Dinabuz actually overstates the case: Merlin's maternal grandfather was a king, but his unknown paternity clearly convinces Dinabuz that Merlin is of no account. Though Merlin's gendered behavior transgresses what Dinabuz sees as a class boundary, potentially creating trouble for Merlin, it is precisely Merlin's appropriation of masculine gender conventions (regardless of their acceptability for his class or biological sex) that allows him to escape unharmed both the mildly dangerous situation with Dinabuz and the more deadly one to follow with Vortigern. Merlin's fight with Dinabuz reveals him to be the fatherless boy Vortigern's magicians claimed must be sacrificed to solve the problem of the king's unstable fortress foundation. This incident prompts his potentially deadly interaction with Vortigern, which in turn precipitates Merlin's fame, as it allows for the revelation of his prophetic power. Of the two, Laȝamon's is the more extreme representation, but both authors introduce this important figure as aggressively masculine. Though Merlin's aggressive behavior here causes him to be taken into custody, both writers characterize him as easily appropriating femininity and masculinity in order to reclaim authority over his body.

Merlin's inappropriate aggression places him at mercy of Vortigern and (temporarily) restricts him to a submissive, feminized role. In both chronicles, Merlin and his mother have no choice but to submit to the demands of the king: Vortigern's political and physical power force Merlin into a passive position, the recipient of threats and accusations. In the *Brut*, Vortigern's questions to Merlin's (unnamed) mother carry an implicit threat, as he repeats the phrase, "Gode læuedi, sæi me—sæl scal iwurðe" [Good lady, say to me—it would be good for you to do so] before asking about her family and Merlin's father (7819, and again at 7826). Telling her that it would be good for her to answer his questions is tantamount to threatening her should she refuse, and the subtlety is not lost on Merlin's mother, who submits reluctantly but politely, answering all Vortigern's questions, narrating her story humbly, and bowing her head demurely when she finishes (7805–55). Her obedient, submissive behavior marks her as conventionally feminine, and she remains properly within the boundaries dictated by conventions of class and gender.

Though he should be likewise constrained by his youth and class to submit to his monarch, Merlin does not wait for his questioners in either version, instead taking the initiative and interrogating Vortigern. Geoffrey includes a detail highlighting the presumptuous nature of Merlin's decision to question his sovereign. Vortigern's reaction to Merlin's demands in this scene reflects the strangeness of his behavior: "The King was amazed at what Merlin said" (168). Merlin uses masculine aggression—inappropriately questioning the monarch—to gain control of the situation, manipulating first the king and then the magicians. After challenging the king, Merlin frightens the magicians into silence, extreme passivity; his offense in this case is to challenge the magicians, asking them to explain what he knows they do not understand, and providing the answer when they are silent (168–9). His prophetic knowledge provides him with the crucial information that finally bests the magicians, and his calculated appropriation of aggression allows him to transgress the class boundaries that would otherwise prevent him from controlling the situation.

In the *Brut*, Merlin models his language after the king's questions to his mother, saying: "King, þine men me habbeoð inumen, and ich æm to þe icumen; / and ich iwiten wulle what beon þi wille, / and for wulche þinge ich æm ibroht to kinge" [King, your men have taken me, and I have come to you; and I will know your will, and for which reason I am brought to the king] (7884–6). Through his language here, Merlin assumes the masculine, questioning gaze of the king: just as Vortigern designates the social position of Merlin's mother by calling her "lady" at the beginning of his question, so Merlin specifies Vortigern's rank when he begins his interrogation, naming him as "king"; just as Vortigern provides motivation for Merlin's mother to answer him in his veiled threat, Merlin stresses the injustice of his unwarranted arrest before demanding to know why he is there; and just as Vortigern exposes Merlin's mother's private knowledge of Merlin's father to the

42 *Crafting the Witch*

whole court, Merlin publicly reveals Vortigern's sinister plans for him. This strategy reverses their roles, allowing Merlin to temporarily appropriate Vortigern's (masculine) power.

Both Geoffrey's and Laȝamon's narratives offer depictions of Merlin using aggression to help him overcome the powerlessness of his low-ranking position in society when taken into custody by Vortigern. In Laȝamon's version of this scene, Merlin uses the same aggressive questioning with Vortigern and his magicians as he did in the *Historia*, but couples it with a clever passive-aggressive strategy, arranging for someone else to perform the murder of Joram and his followers. In the *Brut*, Merlin's appropriation of masculine behavior—in this case, active pursuit of his potential enemies—begins as soon as his mother finishes her story about Merlin's spiritual father, as it does in the *Historia*. Challenging the king, dangerous behavior for a bastard of any age, would be particularly inappropriate for a child; that Merlin does it so aggressively speaks to the strategic extremity of his behavior—Laȝamon's Merlin is even more extreme.

In the *Brut*, when Merlin hears that Vortigern wants to kill him, he explodes into rage: "Nulle hit nauere God seolf, þe gumenene is lauerd, / þat þi castel stonde for mine heorte blode, / ne nauere þi stan wal stille ne ligge" [Never will God himself, who is lord of men, allow that the castle will stand for my heart-blood, nor will the stone wall ever lay still] (7906–8). Merlin identifies Joram as the false prophet whose prediction called for Merlin's blood, and he demands that the king give him the prophets' heads if he can prove them false (7909–22). These details do not appear in Geoffrey's text, and their inclusion here marks Merlin as extreme: he becomes extremely angry, presumes to speak for God, and then demands that Joram and his followers be executed if they cannot meet his challenge. The rest of the scene is similar to Geoffrey's, with Merlin questioning Joram and his followers, although Laȝamon draws it out, adding dialogue and new details to lengthen the scene and heighten the dramatic tension. Because Merlin has demanded Joram's death if he cannot answer correctly, however, this scene becomes more than Merlin's aggressive shaming of the older men; Merlin embraces a passive manipulation here, accomplishing an aggressive feat (murder—conventionally accomplished by men) by proxy, using a non-physical strategy to accomplish a bodily effect. Here Laȝamon's Merlin uses both active and passive strategies to accomplish not only the saving of his own skin (which he manages in the *Historia*), but revenge on his would-be executioners as well.

The chronicles' introduction of Merlin features his use of predominantly masculine behaviors to escape from danger, but the pendulum of behavior soon swings to the other side of the gender binary. The *Historia* characterizes Merlin as displaying exaggeratedly feminized behaviors just before and after his prophetic trances. Immediately after Merlin's aggressive confrontation with Vortigern, when asked to explain the meaning of the two fighting dragons discovered under the foundation of Vortigern's fortress, Merlin "burst into tears," entering a prophetic trance and narrating the *Prophetie Merlini* (171). Merlin moves from aggressive questioning to extremely feminized crying, and this shift marks his greatest prophetic utterance. Merlin cries before prophesying elsewhere in Geoffrey's narrative as well: when ordered by Uther to explain the ominous dragon-star that appears at Aurelius's death, Merlin "burst into tears, summoned up his familiar spirit, and prophesied aloud" (201). As Fiona Tolhurst Neuendorf argues, Merlin's tearful prophetic trances "evoke the prophetic powers of the Cumaean Sibyl and other prophetic figures in the *Aeneid*" (28). In addition to classical models, Geoffrey's descriptions of Merlin associate him with emotional sensitivity (his tears), affective spirituality (his tears, trances, and prophesy), and witchcraft (his familiar spirit), behaviors medieval authors often attribute to women.[37] Prophecy and femininity become intertwined here, as Merlin's prophetic knowledge appears during his bouts of feminized behavior. Geoffrey characterizes Merlin as feminine through behaviors like these and, in other scenes (like the one discussed below), hints at the self-conscious control of his own gender mutability that Laȝamon would develop more fully.

Geoffrey sets Merlin up in direct opposition to the masculine quality of strength during the trip to fetch Giant's Ring from Mount Killaraus. Merlin challenges Uther's troops: "Try your strength, young men . . . and see whether skill can do more than brute strength, or strength more than skill, when it comes to dismantling stones!" (197). Merlin designates "brute strength" as appropriate for "young men," implicating both gender and age in his construction of physical prowess, linking masculinity with youth (and conversely, by implication, femininity with age). When the young men fail to move the stones, Merlin derides strength, laughing at the men before dismantling the ring "more easily than you could ever believe" with his skill and his "gear" (198). By rejecting strength, Merlin aligns himself with femininity.[38] He does not use his body to move the stones, but his magical knowledge, accomplishing what he should not be able to do by embracing an otherness that convention suggests should not belong to him (he is, after all, a young man himself). Geoffrey explicitly condones Merlin's strategy in this scene: "Merlin . . . put the stones up in a circle round the sepulchre, in exactly the same way as they had been arranged on Mount Killaraus in Ireland, thus proving that his artistry was worth more than any brute strength" (198). In this scene, Merlin overcomes a physical obstacle while rejecting an important marker of medieval masculinity, strength, using a more feminine strategy involving magic to accomplish what strength could not. As he also employs masculine behavior to overcome a class barrier when he confronts Vortigern and his magicians, his success with both strategies seems to endorse his reliance on gender mutability to secure an advantage.

Merlin's brand of appropriated androgyny affords him great power, and Laȝamon's description of his ritual among the stones reflects the magical cachet he enjoys in the chronicles. Though Geoffrey's Merlin uses his skill

44 *Crafting the Witch*

and some equipment to move the stones, acting less like a wizard than an engineer (197), Laȝamon's Merlin performs a distinctly magical ritual in front of a politically important audience, an act that contributes to his carefully constructed (feminine) mystique. After Merlin clears the Giants' Ring, emptying his stage, he begins his show by riding around and examining the ring. Laȝamon describes the performance: "þrie he eode abuten, wiðinnen and wiðuten, / and sturede his tunge alse he bede sunge" [thrice he rode around, within and without, and moved his tongue as if he sang/chanted prayers] (8701–2). There is no special equipment, only the power of Merlin's magic, which Laȝamon tells us involves Merlin's body (moving throughout the stones) and his language (the chanting). Merlin's body and his language are critical for the efficacy of his magic—the men are able to move the stones when Merlin's ritual is complete (8708–9). Just as his magic works in this scene by relying on both his body and his speech, his appropriation of gender relies on the same two factors. Merlin absents his body from masculinity by *not* acting (and thus opposes strength, a physical manifestation of masculinity), yet he uses language aggressively to assert his authority over Uther and his men.

In the chronicles of both Geoffrey and Laȝamon, Merlin often appropriates the conventions of both masculinity and femininity. Though Laȝamon's Merlin is the only figure who practices gender ambiguity self-consciously, other Arthurian prophets also commonly display both masculine and feminine behaviors, often to such an extreme that their humanity is threatened. These extreme cases function as a warning which reinforces the normative gender conventions popularized by heroic figures; though magical manipulation of gender may be profitable, there is a catch. Even Merlin, adept at self-construction, sometimes spins wildly into the liminal spaces of humanity, where life and death are locked in infinite flirtation.

Shifting Subjectivities: The Prophet at the Border of Humanity

We have seen how the chronicles represent Merlin's magic as an ability to construct and reconstruct himself, especially through his calculated appropriation of gendered behaviors. His most important act of magic (the shapeshifting deception required to orchestrate Arthur's conception), however, moves from assumption of different gender roles to assumption of another subjectivity. Transformative prophetic power relies on gender mutability, but this is not the only kind of mutability available to the prophesying subject. Through their representations of Merlin, Geoffrey and Laȝamon work together to suggest that magical power relies not only on gender appropriation, but also on a more general kind of self-reconstruction. Successful magic happens when the practitioner can adopt alternate subjectivities and not lose the self. The two prophets examined here manage this task with greater or lesser success: Marie's Muldumarec excels at transforming his self, changing subjectivities with great facility until the husband's careful trap locks him into a permanently feminized form, but Merlin is far more successful.

Gender-Blending   45

In the *Historia*, Merlin arranges Arthur's conception by transforming Uther, Ulfin, and himself into Gorlois, Jordan, and Britaelis, respectively. The three must look, act, and speak as their likenesses for the disguises to work. Though Merlin's "new" and "unheard-of" drugs will make Uther "resemble [Gorlois] in every respect," Uther completes the ruse "by the lying things he said to [Ygerna], things which he planned with great skill" (206–7). Appearance is critical to identity, but a convincing imitation requires more than physical likeness—speech and behavior represent the subject as well. Construction of the self and construction of gender both demand a performance from mind and body: one looks and acts the part, whatever it may be.

Laȝamon's version of this scene expands the performative elements necessary for a convincing disguise. When Merlin offers to help Uther deceive Ygerne, he says: "ich con swulcne lechecraft þe leof þe scal iwurðen, / þat al scullen þine cheres iwurðen swulc þas eorles, / þi speche, þi dede imong þere duȝeðe, þine hors and þine iwede, and al swa þu scalt ride" [I know such magical craft as will be valuable to you, that your whole appearance shall become like the earl's, your speech, your behavior among the warriors, your horse and your clothes, and you shall ride like him] (9448–51). Laȝamon describes identity in terms of appearance and speech, as does Geoffrey, but also reminds readers that personal demeanor, clothes, equipment, and bodily movement must also reflect the person one wishes to imitate for a disguise to be effective: representing the subject thus involves an array of signifiers.

Laȝamon expands Geoffrey's construction of the self, but his characterization of Merlin's transformative power differs from that in the earlier chronicle. Geoffrey's Merlin uses drugs (reminiscent of the domestic potions crafted by Thessela) to transform Uther, Ulfin, and himself so that they can successfully imitate specific subjects. Laȝamon, however, creates an ambiguity that only intensifies Merlin's mysterious ability to shift his subjectivity—he simply doesn't mention how Merlin transformed his party. He offers an extended version of Merlin's explanation of identity, as I have discussed, but elides over the moment of magical transformation, saying only: "þas þinges forðrihte þus weoren idihte" [these things were done forthwith] (9472). Though he notes the difficulty of the magical operation in his lengthy list of elements required, Laȝamon doesn't explain how Merlin accomplishes the transformation—Merlin just does it. This strategy has a dual effect: 1) it emphasizes the impossibly difficult nature of the task, suggesting that only someone very powerful, like Merlin, could ever perform it, and 2) it implies that no one really understands how Merlin's magic works. Merlin is magic because he can transform one subject into another without recourse to drugs. Here, transformative magic is cerebral, not requiring the domestic props of feminine healing magic. Merlin has some other power, a power related to his ability to transform the future by predicting it. Merlin's secret knowledge gives him power: he fathoms the subject, and he is the only one who does. This is what makes him different from others, the foundation of his magical power.

46 *Crafting the Witch*

One of the effects of Merlin's unique representation in the *Brut* is that Laȝamon allows him to wrest his autonomy back from the kings who inevitably want to use his abilities for their own ends. Whereas the Merlin of the *Historia* is at each king's beck and call, the Merlin of the *Brut* commands the three kings with whom he interacts, only assisting when he chooses, and the kings must cajole and bribe him, sometimes with little success. The fact that the kings must search for Merlin in the *Brut*, instead of ordering him to come as they do in the *Historia*, reflects the increased stature Merlin enjoys in the later work. For example, when Aurelius's engineers are stymied by the problem of raising an ever-lasting monument to the fallen Britons, bishop Tremorien suggests that Aurelius seek Merlin's help. His advice stresses how careful they must be when entreating Merlin to come:

> ȝif æi mon hine mihte ifinden uppe þissere wælden
> and to þe ibringen þurh æies cunnes þinge,
> and þu his iwille driȝen woldest,
> he þe wolde runen selest ræden,
> hu þu mihtest þis weorc makien strong and sterk
> þet a mihte ilæsten þa while men leoueden. (8480–85)

> If any man might find him anywhere in the country, and bring him to you through any skillful means, and (if) you would do his will, he would provide you with the best counsel, how you might make this work strong and enduring so that it might last while men live.

Tremorian's long list of conditions for Merlin's participation emphasizes how much power Merlin has; *if* they can find him, *if* they can get him to come to the king, and *if* they acquiesce to his demands, *then* he will give them advice. When Aurelius's knights finally find Merlin, waiting for them by a spring, they are "afæred þat he fleon wolde" [afraid that he would flee], unsure that the king's authority will influence the mysterious "witeȝe" [prophet/magician] (8513). Merlin reminds them that he is not obligated to obey the king, telling them, "ȝif ich swa walde, ne mihte ȝe me finden" [if I so wished, you could never find me] (8517). Merlin's statement here reiterates his autonomy: no power but his own can possibly move him to answer the king's summons. Though the entire kingdom must obey the king, Merlin can do as he pleases, appropriating the masculine authority of the monarch.

Uther has more trouble than Aurelius in finding Merlin and obtaining his help. After Uther's coronation, Merlin disappears, and Laȝamon writes: "Merlin him ætwende, nuste he nauere whidere, / no nauere a worlde-riche to whan he bicome" [Merlin went away from him (Uther), he had no idea where, nor what in the world had become of him] (9070–1). Uther cannot locate Merlin at all, despite offering "gold and gersume" [gold and treasure] to anyone who can find him (9075). Merlin's protracted absence here fires

Gender-Blending 47

Uther's emotions: "þe king wes swiðe særi and sorhful an heorte / for ne les he næuere leouere mon seoððen he wes an liuen, / neouere nenne oðer, ne Aurilie his broðer" [The king was very sorrowful and sad at heart because he had never, in all his life, lost a man he valued more, not even his brother Aurelien] (9082–84). That Uther values Merlin over Aurelius reflects Merlin's elevated social position: he is more important than both monarch and brother. Though Geoffrey's Merlin is certainly a key figure in the *Historia*, Laȝamon's Merlin outshines every monarch he encounters.

In addition to Merlin's positioning as superior in power and influence to kings, Laȝamon presents Merlin as taking the initiative in matters Geoffrey assigns only to his monarchs. In the Giant's Ring episode, for example, whereas Geoffrey's Aurelius "ordered Merlin to erect round the burial-place the stones which he had brought from Ireland" (198), Laȝamon's Aurelius is not even there when Merlin reassembles the stones. When Aurelius, "i þan norð ende" [in the north end] of England, hears the news, he calls an assembly to celebrate Merlin's achievement (8718–25). Laȝamon praises Merlin's actions here: "Mærlin heom gon ræren alse heo stoden ærer, / swa næuer nan oðer mon þene craft ne cuðe don; / ne næuer ær þer biforen nes na mon swa wise iboren / þat cuðe þet weorc rihten and þa stanes dihten" [Merlin did erect them as they stood before, as no other man could ever do with magical arts, no never before was any man so wise born, who could perform that task and move the stones] (8714–7). Not only does Merlin act without consulting the king, but Laȝamon commends him as the only person capable of accomplishing this amazing feat. In the *Brut*, Merlin is more powerful than the king because he is unequalled in skill and wisdom, because he is unique. His power is a function of his singularity.

We have seen how Merlin occupies a unique position within Laȝamon's narrative as an androgynous magician. We have also seen how Laȝamon emphasizes Merlin's magical power, creating a figure of more mystery and influence than the Merlin of the *Historia*. In the *Brut*, Merlin's especially adept appropriation of both masculinity and femininity, and the consequent heightening of his magical prowess, distinguishes him from the other normative characters in the chronicles. In Laȝamon's chronicle, Merlin is more powerful, but his constant movement between genders and subjectivities becomes excessive, transgressive—prophetic power does not come without consequences. During his most powerful prophetic moments, Merlin faces the loss of his humanity.

Laȝamon's descriptions of Merlin's behavior during and after his prophetic trances emphasize Merlin's extreme difference, his liminal humanity. In *Powers of Horror*, Julia Kristeva describes the abject as liminal, as that which "disturbs identity, system, order. What does not respect borders, positions, rules. The in-between, the ambiguous, the composite" (4). In his ability to shift between different genders and subjectivities, Merlin occupies an abject, liminal space: as a prophet, he is "in-between" divinity

48   *Crafting the Witch*

and humanity; his gender frequently becomes "ambiguous," and his transformative power treats borders as malleable. Merlin is a figure of abjection,
but what kind of abjection? Kristeva distinguishes a pre-Christian abject
from a Christian notion of abjection, arguing that the pre-Christian sacred
is two-sided. One side, purity, privileges "the social bond" derived from the
father-murder fantasy described in Freudian psychoanalysis, and the other
"like a lining, more secret still and invisible, non-representable, oriented
toward those uncertain spaces of unstable identity" is the impure abject,
which must be expelled to reinforce social boundaries (57–8). For the
"Christic subjectivity," on the other hand, the abject "is no longer exterior.
It is permanent and comes from within," and it changes "the pure/impure
dichotomy into an outside/inside one" (113–4). Because Christian theology
suggests "nothing that enters a man from outside can make him unclean,"
a figure like Christ, whose inner purity is without question, can surround
himself with lepers, prostitutes, and other people of questionable cleanness.
Like Christ, whose abjection eventually leads to his martyrdom (further
proof of his purity), Merlin's outward signs of abjection—his beast-like
seizures, his deathly pallor—threaten his humanity.

In the *Historia*, as I discuss above, Merlin bursts into tears before prophesying. In the *Brut*, however, Merlin behaves ever more strangely. After his
first prophetic utterance, when he foretells the deaths of Vortigern, Aurelius, and Uther, Merlin falls into a lengthy silence (8007–41). This puzzling
silence is just the beginning: when Aurelius asks Merlin how the Giant's
Ring can be moved, he prompts a prophetic trance affecting Merlin so pro-
foundly that Aurelius offers him a private chamber in which to rest: "þus
seiden Mærlin, and seoððen he sæt stille, / alse þeh he wolde of worlden
iwiten. / þe king hine lette bringen into ane fære bure / and wunien þerinne
æfter his iwille" [Merlin said this, and after he sat very still, as if he would
depart this world. The king had him brought into a fair bower and let
him rest there as he pleased.] (8601–4). Aurelius fears Merlin will leave the
world, lose not only his humanity, but his life. Merlin's most ostentatious
display of oddity comes when Uther asks him to explain the dragon star
that appears at Aurelius's death:

> Mærlin sæt him stille longe ane stunde
> swulc he mid sweuene swunke ful swiðe.
> Heo seiden þe hit iseȝen mid heore aȝen æȝen.
> þat ofte he hine wende swulc hit a wurem weore.
> Late he gon awakien; þa gon he to quakien,
> and þas word seide Merlin þa witeȝe: . . . (8935–40)

> Merlin sat very still for a long time, as if he were dreaming busily and silently.
> They who saw it with their own eyes said that often he twisted as if he were
> a worm. Finally he began to awaken; then he began to quake and shake, and
> Merlin the prophet said these words. . . .

Gender-Blending 49

Here Laȝamon compares Merlin to a worm (or serpent) and gives him a seizure. Merlin is both bestial and close to death; his humanity hangs precariously in the balance between man and beast, life and death. Merlin, expert at crossing boundaries like male and female, scratches in these scenes at the thin gauze separating humans from the other animals, and almost transgresses the bounds that sustain life. The prophetic trance takes its toll on Merlin's body, and he becomes extremely tired after prophesying (8979). He must rest after his exertions; prophecy is demanding, dangerous work, and it threatens Merlin's life more seriously each time he uses his power. The more he prophesies, the more he becomes abject. The more abject he is, the more fame and goodwill he receives.

As Merlin's mysterious and strange behavior illustrates, transformative power propels prophets into the liminal spaces of humanity.[39] Merlin approaches the borders of humanity, but he never crosses them in the chronicles. Though he avoids the fatal results of liminality by avoiding death, Merlin's body vanishes nonetheless from the narrative immediately after he arranges for Uther and Ygerna to beget Arthur. His character disappears, but his prophetic power remains. Indeed, well after Merlin's disappearance from the narrative, his prophecies continue to appear, prompting Françoise H. M. Le Saux to make this observation: "Merlin's Arthurian prophecy is repeated at each of the turning-points in Arthur's life, to the extent that it may be considered a major artistic device in the episode" (139). Merlin's prophetic offspring continue to haunt the lines of the *Brut* long after his physical presence is gone, even appearing in the chronicle's concluding lines.[40]

In his representation of Merlin as the abject prophet, Laȝamon expresses an ambivalence towards the sacred reflected in the characterization by Kristeva discussed above. The prophet is both revered and estranged, divine and abstract. Ambivalence also pervades Laȝamon's treatment of prophetic knowledge. Laȝamon problematizes the power of prophecy through his characterization of Merlin, as we have seen, but also through his failure to include the *Prophetie Merlini* in his version of the British history. Laȝamon's primary source, Wace's *Roman de Brut*, omits the *Prophetie*, but Le Saux argues convincingly for Laȝamon's familiarity with both the *Historia* (which contained the *Prophetie* as its seventh book) and the *Vita Merlini* (94–117). That Laȝamon chose to omit the lengthy prophecies but lavish attention on their speaker reflects an ambivalence towards prophetic transformative power. He references the prophecies, but does not translate them; he cannot ignore them, but will not include them.[41]

The cultural reception of prophetic writing in the late twelfth and early thirteenth centuries likely influenced Laȝamon's attitude towards prophecy, intensely refined from Geoffrey's material, and his decision to omit the *Prophetie* from his chronicle. Jean Blacker argues that twelfth-century writers exhibited a "cautious" attitude towards political prophecy, as if an error in translation "might entail consequences" (37). Laȝamon may have been

50 *Crafting the Witch*

affected by a political climate which treated prophecy with ambivalence or worse, intolerance. While his chronicle explores a variety of liminal appropriations of gender and subjectivity afforded by transformative power, the textual ambivalence towards prophecy combats its threatening power by casting it as simultaneously generative and deadly. Laʒamon's prophet is like the phoenix: the fledgling prophecy is born only through the death of the fertile speaker, whose utterance is left to find a life of its own.

VI. NO LADIES EVER DID BETTER!

When Dorothy traveled the yellow-brick road, she feared "lions and tigers and bears," but it was wicked witches who posed the greatest threat to the success of her quest. We've negotiated a tricky narrative landscape without running into any wicked witches—a feat Dorothy was unable to replicate. Instead, we have met the giants, prophets, and healing ladies of four important early medieval authors in the Arthurian tradition. We have seen the threat posed by the hyper-masculinity of the giants and by the diminishing humanity of the prophets, and we've enjoyed the benefits of women who heal or who work together to diffuse the threat of male violence. These writers of Arthurian material helped to reinforce strict gender conventions through their representations of knights, heroines, and female magical characters. Representations of male magical characters took two main routes: 1) critiquing men who are unable to submit to hierarchy through the representation of giants, and 2) demonstrating the power of men who are able to transcend gender conventions via the male magical figures who wield transformative, prophetic power. Whereas options for female characters are limited primarily to the domestic sphere (with a few exceptions), options for male characters are wider, though not without their risks. What these writers tell us is that men must be strong enough to dominate, yet flexible enough to submit when necessary; they must walk a fine line between hyper-masculine excess and overly feminized and non-human estrangement. Under the feudal system, the most important relationships were those between men, as women had few legal rights, especially under Norman rule in England. Treatment of female characters and feminine magic reflects this one-sided view of women, as part of the system of economic exchange that accompanies feudal government. Though spaces did exist for women in the French romances and *lais* (the one thousand ladies, the good witch Thessela, the fairy mistress of "Lanval"), the chronicles neglect women in a substantive sense, using them as icing on the narrative cake.

The tensions present in early medieval English society do not exist for contemporary U.S. citizens, but the theme of female community working to eliminate a male threat still chimes pleasantly in our ears. For example, in the recent film, *Practical Magic* (based on the Alice Hoffman novel and directed by Griffin Dunne in 1998), the narrative features a family of (good) witches, ostracized by the community for generations, who finally gain acceptance when they ask their neighbors to join with them to destroy a male zombie-demon. One of two twin daughters, Gillian (played by Nicole Kidman), finds herself involved with an abusive beast of a boyfriend, Jimmy (Goran Visnjic), whom she has taken to drugging when she wants a few hours to herself. When her sister, Sally (Sandra Bullock), stumbles into the situation, the boyfriend ends up dead from an accidental overdose. A modern version of the monstrous giant of medieval romance, Jimmy's demonstration of overly aggressively masculine behavior precipitates the violent situation in which the necessary response turns out to be accidental execution.

The female community must intercede after the two sisters have failed in their various attempts to first reverse and then hide their crime. The film represents the magic as domestic, involving potions brewed in the rambling kitchen, herbs grown in a sunny breakfast nook, and women with brooms (and one mop)—and the exorcism ritual itself take place in the kitchen. These witches are like the twelfth- and thirteenth-century good witches, and their participation together allows them to destroy the masculine source of their problems, just as the thousand ladies saved Fenice from her victimization at the hands of the surgeons. The film, like Chrétien, suggests that when women come together to help curtail hyper-masculinized men, "no ladies ever did better!" Though we no longer suffer from the kind of rigidly oppressive laws our medieval sisters endured, and our situation compared to that of medieval women is so far improved as to hinder comparison, women (and men) in the U.S. still respond to narratives, such as that in *Practical Magic*, which provide strategies for defending against, avoiding, or otherwise mitigating the aggressive violence of men. That we still need such strategies points to the insidious pervasiveness of patriarchal tolerance (and thus promotion) of male violence, especially against women.

Medieval authors certainly did not forget the figures so common in these early texts, but they inevitably adapted them, as we do, to suit a changing set of social and ideological needs. Though the chronicle tradition continued in the fourteenth and fifteenth centuries, the authors did not change the tradition as radically as did the late Middle English verse romancers, who reinvented the game. No longer do the heroes find themselves presented with easy targets, and giants may turn out to be knights, or hags may turn into beautiful ladies. The world of romance becomes more insidious, more duplicitous, and we find a figure who held little interest for the authors considered in this chapter, the wicked witch. She's waiting for us.

3 From Rags To Riches, or The Step-Mother's Revenge
Transformative Power in Late Medieval Arthurian Romances

I. EXTREME MAKEOVER, MEDIEVAL STYLE

There's something deliciously enticing about watching someone get a make-over. You see the "before" shot, either as a photograph in its daytime television incarnation, or perhaps as a bedraggled, downtrodden figure whose mundane life occupies the screen behind the opening credits of a movie—and you see the "after" shot, too, when the beaming make-over recipient steps out to model her new look, or the bedraggled lady turns out to be drop-dead gorgeous after all. You always see the "after" shot—it's the pay-off—but its revelation is deferred. You don't get the climatic "after" until you've seen, in the most gloriously minute detail, the "during." What occupies most of the make-over narrative is describing the mechanisms which effect the make-over, the critical change from bad (or less preferred) to good. How does someone make change happen? What mysterious mechanism allows a prostitute to become a millionaire's wife, a "heartless guttersnipe" to turn into a lady, or a lowly farmer to transform into an inter-galactic Jedi knight? Judging by the prevalence of these narratives in popular U.S. media, we really want to know.

This is not a new narrative. The brothers Grimm dusted off an old version of this story when they collected the fairy tales of Europe. They called it "Aschenputtel," and the Cinderella story still resonates for twentieth- and twenty-first-century audiences, as evinced by the range of popular adaptations (both cinematic and televised), from Disney's *Cinderella* and the recent *Ever After* to looser adaptations such as *Annie, My Fair Lady*, or *Pretty Woman*. In all these stories, the Cinderella character gets what ABC would call an "Extreme Makeover." As in the television reality-show where recipients receive free plastic surgery and a new wardrobe in addition to help with hair and make-up (or an entirely remodeled house, in the "Home Edition" of the show), someone always provides Cinderella with what she needs to transform. Someone else transforms her. Cinderella can't help herself—she needs intervention. In all of the twentieth-century visual adaptations mentioned above, the intervening figure is either a fairy god-mother practicing magic or a rich, powerful man.[1] Magic and money occupy equivalent positions in modern versions of this tale, an equation I will discuss in the concluding section of this chapter, but this is not the case with late Middle English versions.

Two popular transformation—or "makeover"—narratives appear in a good number of Middle English Arthurian romances composed in the fourteenth and fifteenth centuries. These narratives focus on the makeover of a loathly lady and a churlish knight, the transformation of these carnivalesque, grotesque figures into idealized representatives of masculinity and femininity. The fact that there are two traditions, one focused on male-male relationships and one focused on male-female relationships, suggests that the romances in these sub-genres were explicitly concerned with structuring binary gender roles and identifying a normative set of gender conventions. Though there are many versions of these makeover romances, this chapter uses representative examples to explore and define the representations of gender privileged therein. My discussion of the churlish knight narrative focuses on late medieval romances featuring Arthur's nephew Gawain, including *Sir Gawain and the Green Knight* (henceforth abbreviated *SGGK*), *The Greene Knight* (*Greene*), *The Turke and Sir Gawain* (*Turke*), *Sir Gawain and the Carle of Carlisle* (*Carle*), and *The Carle of Carlisle* (*Carlisle*).[2] The loathly lady discussion utilizes four examples, including John Gower's "Tale of Florent" (henceforth abbreviated *Florent*) and Geoffrey Chaucer's "The Wife of Bath's Tale" (*Wife's Tale*) as well as the anonymous *The Wedding of Sir Gawain and Dame Ragnelle* (*Wedding*) and *The Marriage of Sir Gawain* (*Marriage*).[3] These Middle English romancers use the make-over narrative to revise radically the aggressive masculine *ethos* developed in the earlier French romances: England's is a kinder, gentler hero. At the same time, the Middle English authors reject an earlier French tolerance of aggressive behavior in love-stricken heroines, inscribing a static ideal femininity on the transformed body of the loathly lady. The English revision of gendered behaviors reflects a specifically economic anxiety: the low-brow figures are forced through an aristocratic filter.

It is economic anxiety that drives the other major revision of French models produced by the Middle English adaptations, the replacement of the giant with the witch. The fourteenth- and fifteenth-century romance writers rediscover the classical wicked witch, neglected by the previous Arthurian material, and they bring her across the channel to play the villainess. This mysterious mother-witch replaces the excessively masculine giants of earlier chronicle and romance traditions as the narrative threat. The rise of the wicked witch in the popular verse romances corresponds with an apparent increase in opportunity for women—especially young women— to wield economic and political power within fourteenth- and fifteenth-century England. Through their transformations of the two grotesques and their unique use of the witch-figure, the Middle English romancers give romance itself a most extreme makeover indeed.

Perhaps the most influential of all the French romancers is Chrétien de Troyes, whose five Arthurian romances forever marked the genre for which

54 *Crafting the Witch*

they were the prototype. In the Arthurian landscape imagined by Chrétien, shifting class boundaries are not what seems to be at stake; instead, knights quest, find royal princesses, fight evil giants, and return home to castles, ever secure in their nobility. Physical threats abound, but none of these threaten the social position of the hero, and in fact, when a hero does not at first appear noble (as in the "fair unknown" motif), the circumstances of the quest will usually reveal his inherent nobility. What Chrétien's narrative does highlight, as I discuss in Chapter 2, is the power of both love and magic to transform normative gender roles and allow for a temporary reversal of conventional masculine and feminine behaviors. In these narratives, the normative situation presents masculine aggressive action as the privileged behavior for male characters, whereas female characters must remain passive in the face of male desire, both that of suitors and enemies.[4] The force of love can reverse this gender binary, making heroes silent before their beloveds or heroines aggressive in pursuit of theirs. Whereas male characters suffer condemnation from this reversal, the reversal in female characters is not only tolerated, but admirable.[5] Through this dual positioning—men as laudable only when active, but women as able to become active through the force of love—Chrétien's romances create a masculine *ethos* of aggression that endorses extreme violence for men and active agency for love-stricken women.

The Middle English romancers don't brook this representation. Through their use of the transformation motif, the Middle English authors gentrify the central figures (the grotesques), employing a system of strict chivalric courtesy to transmute the inappropriate aggression of the male and female grotesques into aristocratic submission. In both versions of the make-over tale, the strategy is similar: the authors first identify the inappropriate figure with visual and behavioral cues, then provide a positive example whose exaggerated courtesy releases the grotesque from the magically-induced cocoon of iniquity, allowing the noble butterfly within the freedom to fly up, up, and away. And fly up they do—one of the most important changes the transformation effects is the restoration of class privilege to the seemingly lower-class grotesques. This imbrication of class and inappropriate behavior offers insight into the cultural work being performed by the medieval makeover narrative, suggesting that these tales (and their representations of ideal gender roles) exist in service of an aristocratic ideology.

It has often been argued that the medieval romance genre deals with issues of class, or what medieval scholars call the "estates," though the analyses of what stance the romances take towards the estates varies considerably. Susan Crane sees insular romance as promoting an ideology of upward class mobility, for example, whereas Stephen Knight reads the romances as ultimately endorsing a static feudal estate system. Harriet E. Hudson, on the other hand, sees romance as mitigating class tension, allowing the medieval hero to travel a tricky line between two opposing viewpoints:

From Rags To Riches, or The Step-Mother's Revenge   55

class mobility as possible through accumulation of capital vs. class mobility as impossible because of its inextricable connection to lineage. Debates such as these are exacerbated by the nature of romance itself—romances offer complicated, multi-layered representations of characters and situations, and their thematic valences shift as each layer peels away.

Before we can analyze the operation of class dynamics in these romances, we must first decide what it is we mean when we talk about "class" in the medieval period. This decision requires a more specific date range than the description "medieval" offers, as the three traditional medieval estates began to look more like a modern class system as the centuries progressed. Though the earliest extant copies of these transformation stories date from the fourteenth century, the tales of the churlish knight and loathly lady are much older than that. A version of the loathly lady story was performed for Edward I in 1299, and the circumstances of its performance suggest that the audience must have already been at least somewhat familiar with the story.[6] There is also evidence that the beheading game featured in the churlish knight romances has origins in early Irish literature. The central episodes in these romances were probably in circulation before the thirteenth century, but it was in the fourteenth century that authors composed the most well-known and highly-regarded literary versions, *Sir Gawain and the Green Knight* and Chaucer's "Wife of Bath's Tale." With the exception of Gower's version, the rest of the romances considered here are what I call "popular"—that is, verse romances written down between 1460 and 1650 and likely performed orally with music for a diverse audience. My discussion of class will focus primarily on the economic situation in fourteenth- and fifteenth-century England, as those are the centuries in which production of manuscripts including churlish knight and loathly lady stories begins and proliferates, respectively.

Writers in England from Aelfric (c. 1000) to Langland (c. 1370) conceptualized society within the framework of the "estate" system—consisting of 1) those who rule (or fight), 2) those who pray, and 3) those who farm.[7] Despite the usefulness of this classification for both medieval writers and modern scholars, it was never that simple. Each estate contained within it different kinds of people: degrees of nobility developed (nobles—those with inherited landholdings vs. gentry—those who purchased or married into land), as well as specialized groups of farming folk (serfs—those legally bound to their land vs. peasants—those with small, rented holdings vs. farmers—those with large, rented holdings). As time wore on, and certainly by the late fourteenth century, the three-tiered system was less apt in its description of actual social and economic relations. During the fourteenth and fifteenth centuries in England, the economic system can best be described as "in flux," in that the predominantly agricultural economy of earlier centuries began to allow for increased trade in the face of a growing European mercantilism.[8] The resultant capital created by this shift only accelerated the development of groups of people who did not fit easily into

56   *Crafting the Witch*

the traditional estates—merchants and tradespeople, a *nouveau-riche* gentry, and farmers with more land and resources than the usual peasantry.[9] This reorganization of the traditional estates was bound to cause tension, upsetting the smooth operation of a divinely-ordained social hierarchy, and it is precisely this tension which is mitigated by the transformations of the loathly lady and the churlish knight.

II. RAGS TO RICHES?: THE MYTH OF CLASS MOBILITY

You sit down to eat, grateful for the bountiful feast spread before you. You chat with your friends about the latest tournament, about your fashionable outfit, about the roast fowl. You lift your glass to take a drink of wine, and you notice, out of the corner of your eye, the biggest man you've ever seen. You turn to get a better look, and your gaze lingers on his muscular body and expensive clothes until you suddenly, joltingly realize—he's bright green. What do you do? What do you think? A trick? Make-up? Some strange play of the light? When the characters in *Sir Gawain and the Green Knight* are confronted by the huge, "enker-grene" [bright green] knight who shows up on his horse in the dining hall, the people at King Arthur's court wonder what it could mean, eventually deciding that the apparition must be the result of "fantoum and fayryȝe" [illusion and 'fairy'-magic] (240).[10] The Green Knight is so remarkably different, so incredibly other, that his physical presence creates a logical problem for those attending Arthur's holiday feast. Something's fishy. Is it magic?

After introducing the Green Knight, the mysterious author of *Sir Gawain and the Green Knight* indulges our curiosity, using nearly 100 lines to describe the "aghlich mayster" [terrible master]. The poet does not tell us first, as we might expect, that the Knight was colored "in grene" (151), but that his body is extraordinarily large. He appears to be "most in þe molde, on mesure hyghe," a "half-etayn" [the biggest man in the world, tall in measure, a half-giant] (137). The poet focuses his initial description on the Green Knight's body: his broad "bak" and "brest," his "worþily smale" waist-line, his "lyndes" and "lymes so long and so grete" [back, breast, worthily thin, loins, and limbs so long and so great] (143–144, 139). The Green Knight's physical perfection is exaggerated—he is a super-knight, a super-man, excessively masculine. Other details contribute to this hyper-gendering, such as the Green Knight's bushy beard, which "ouer his brest henges" [over his breast hangs] (182), and his behavior, which is unruly and aggressive. The Green Knight's masculinity is so excessive, in fact, that his humanity is simultaneously threatened and expanded—he's a half-giant, beyond the bounds of the merely human. He is an ambivalent figure whose appearance silences the entire court, which waits for Arthur to address his transgressive behavior.

Though the poet meticulously describes the great mass of the Green Knight before mentioning that he was "all ouer enker-grene" [all over

From Rags To Riches, or The Step-Mother's Revenge 57

bright green], he uses the word "grene" eight times in the next forty lines, emphasizing the non-human color of the creature. As men or women were about as likely to have bright-green skin in medieval England as they are in the twenty-first-century U.S. (the Incredible Hulk notwithstanding), this detail marks vividly the Green Knight's incongruity—he is a supernatural marvel, and his presence creates a carnivalesque rupture.

In medieval literary tradition, outward form often reflects inward character—if it looks bad, you better believe it's bad! In particular, medieval romancers make use of carnivalesque imagery, described by Mikhail Bakhtin in his influential book, *Rabelais and his World*. One of the most common figures associated with carnival and the carnivalesque in literature is the grotesque—the exaggerated and degraded human body. Grotesque realism, a defining characteristic of carnivalesque representation, is described by Bakhtin as relying heavily on a stylized "bodily element" (19). The body, in grotesque realism, is not necessarily that of "the biological individual," but of "the people," and it is therefore "grandiose, exaggerated, immeasurable" (19). The body is universal—everyone has one—and in festive imagery the body is most commonly exaggerated, represented as the hyper-body, the extra-large, extra-old, extra-young, extra-masculine, extra-feminine, extra-disgusting, extra-human body. "Exaggeration, hyperbolism, excessiveness are generally considered fundamental attributes of the grotesque style," Bakhtin writes (303). Bakhtin also emphasizes the "nonofficial, extraeccelsiastical and extrapolitical aspect" of carnival and its iconography (6). Carnivalesque figures are not members of the aristocracy, not court officials or clergy. The world of carnival is the world of the third estate—the world of the working classes, from peasant to merchant.

Twenty-first century western audiences are familiar with carnivalesque exaggeration, as it is employed frequently in western film and television. For instance, we have no trouble determining that the step-sisters of Disney's *Cinderella* are ugly. We know this because the filmmakers use carnivalesque imagery to show us the difference between the ugly girl and the pretty girl. Cinderella, the heroine from whose perspective the story is told, is petite with dainty features, but the step-sisters are tall and gangly, with exaggeratedly large noses, brows, hands, and feet. Their clothes are brightly colored and highly decorated, festive compared to the muted tones of Cinderella's work clothes or her white, fairy ball-gown. Exaggeration is one of the key elements of carnivalesque imagery, and its use here signals to the audience the humorous awkwardness of Cinderella's step-sisters. The director reinforces their deviance from the conventions of feminine beauty by showing us a scene of the sisters trying to make music: one sister stumbles along a melody with her flute as the other sister stretches her voice almost up to the notes. From this scene we travel to another room in the house where Cinderella's soft, delicate voice picks up the melody, and she seems to be a natural soprano. See the difference, the film asks us? See how feminine Cinderella is?

58   *Crafting the Witch*

Carnivalesque exaggeration functions via its immediacy—we recognize the visual cues, and they signal otherness, deviance. Like the gangly stepsisters, the grotesques of popular romance are immediately recognizable negative examples: beware the loathly lady and the churlish knight! I've already provided some examples of the way the knight's description in *SGGK* marks him as carnivalesque, and this imagery pervades the other versions as well. In each of the versions of the churlish knight story, the knight is characterized by his carnivalesque appearance, a descriptive trope not used in the earlier Arthurian material. Sir Bredbeddle, the knight in *Grene*, for example, evokes the carnivalesque by dressing festively in "full gay" clothes and armor, "a jolly sight to seene, / When horsse and armour was all greene" [very festive; a jolly sight to see, when horse and armor were all green] (74, 79–80). In *Carle*, the churlish fellow is "two tayllors yardus" wide and "nine taylloris yerdus" high [two tailor's yards; nine tailor's yards] (256, 258). Not only is he a giant, but his features are also grotesque, overly exaggerated:

He semyd a dredfull man:	He seemed a dreadful man:
Wytt chekus longe and vesage brade;	with cheeks long and visage broad;
Cambur nose and all full made;	turned-up nose and all foully made;
Betwyne his browus a large spane;	between his brows a large span;
Hys mogth moche, his berd graye;	his mouth large, his beard grey;
Over his brest his lockus lay	over his breast his locks lay
As brod as anny fane.	as broad as any basket.

(*Carle* 248–54)

The language of this passage constructs the figure as radically other—the poet first tells us that the knight is "dredfull," and then narrates each of the details causing the condition of dreadfulness. The poet goes on to note that his "fyngeris" are as large "as anny lege that we ber" [fingers; as any leg that we bear] (266–7), prompting the audience and the narrator to join together as the "we" who bear the normal legs against the "he" whose fingers stand out so clearly. The *Carlisle* poet reins in the exaggeration slightly, describing the churlish knight's hands as the size of "breads that wives may bake," but adds demonic lights to his eyes: "With two great eyen brening as fyer, / Lord, hee was a lodlye syer" [with two great eyes burning as a fire, Lord, he was a loathly sire] (186, 181–2). The *Turke* poet eschews excess description, relying instead on widespread knowledge of exotic stereotypes to fill in the details, saying merely, "He was not hye, but he was broad, / And like a Turke he was made / Both legg and thye" [He was not tall, but he was broad, and like a Turk he was created, in both leg and thigh] (13–15).

The loathly lady's grotesqueness is even more exaggerated. Two of the romances, Gower's *Florent* and the anonymous *Wedding*, relish the initial description of the loathly lady, spending more than a few lines detailing her grotesque appearance. The descriptions appear below (with facing translations):

From Rags To Riches, or The Step-Mother's Revenge   59

Florent his wofull heved uplefte
And syh this vecke wher sche sat,
Which was the loathlieste what
That evere man caste on his yhe:
Hire Nase bass, hire browes hyhe,
Hire yhen smale and depe set,
Hire chekes ben with teres wet,
And rivelen as an emty skyn
Hangende doun unto the chin,
Hire Lippes schrunken ben for age,
Ther was no grace in the visage,
Hir front was nargh, hir lockes hore,
Sche loketh forth as doth a More,
Hire Necke is schort, hir schuldres
  courbe,
That myhte a mannes lust destroube,

Hire body gret and nothing smal,
And schortly to describe hire al,
Sche hath no lith withoute a lake;
Bot lich unto the wollesak
Sche proferth hire unto this knyht,
And bad him, as he hath behyht,
So as sche hath ben his warant,
That he hire holde covenant,
And be the bridel sche him seseth.

Florent his woeful head uplifted
and saw this creature where she sat,
which was the ugliest person
that ever man cast his eye on:
her nose low, her brows high,
her eyes small and deep set,
her cheeks wet with tears,
and wrinkled as if empty skin
hung down unto the chin,
her lips shriveled with age,
there was no grace in the visage,
her front was narrow, her locks hoary,
she looks as does a Moor,
her neck is short, her shoulders
  curved,
(so much) that (it) might disturb a
  man's lust,
her body great and nothing small,
and shortly to describe her all,
she has no limb without a fault;
but like a woolsack,
she proffers herself to this knight,
and bade him, as he promised,
as she had been his warrant,
then he should hold to their covenant,
and be the bride-groom, she says to him.
        (*Florent* 1674–97)

Her face was red, her nose snotyd
  withalle,
Her mowithe wyde, her tethe yalowe
  overe alle,
With bleryd eyen gretter then a
  balle.
Her mowithe was nott to lak:
Her tethe hyng overe her lyppes,
Her chekys syde as wemes hippes.
A lute she bare upon her bak;
Her nek long and therto greatt;
Her here cloteryd on an hepe;
In the sholders she was a yard brode.
Hangygng pappys to be an hors lode,

And lyke a barelle she was made.
And to reherse the fowlnesse of that
  Lady,

Her face was red, her nose completely
  snotty,
her mouth wide, her teeth yellow
  all over,
with bleary eyes even greater than a
  ball.
Her mouth was not too small:
her teeth hung over her lips,
her cheeks as wide as women's hips.
A lute she bore upon her back;
her neck long and very wide;
her hair clotted in a heap;
in the shoulders she was a yard broad.
Hanging paps (large enough) for a
  horse,
and like a barrel she was made.
And to rehearse the foulness of that
  Lady,

60 *Crafting the Witch*

There is no tung may tele, securly;	there is no tongue that may tell, surely;
Of lothynesse inowghe she had. . . .	of ugliness enough she had. . . .
She had two tethe on every side	She had two teeth on each side,
As borys tuskes, I wolle nott hyde,	like boars' tusks, I will not hide,
Of lengthe a large handfulle.	of length a wide hands-breadth.
The one tusk went up and the other doun.	The one tusk went up and the other down.
A mowthe fulle wyde and fowlle igrown,	A mouth full wide and foully made,
With grey herys many on.	with many gray hairs thereon.
Her lyppes laye lumpryd on her chyn;	Her lips lay lumped on her chin,
Nek forsothe on her was none iseen—	neck therefore was not seen—
She was a lothly on!	She was a loathly one!
	(*Wedding* 231–45, 548–556)

Both descriptions follow the conventions of romance, focusing first on the lady's facial features and then discussing her body, highlighting the lady's grotesqueness. Instead of conventional gray eyes that shine with an inner light, the loathly lady has orbs of the bulbous, "bleary" variety. Her nose is large and "snotty," she has "shriveled" lips and "yellow" teeth, and her neck is not fair and white, but "wrinkled," "very wide," and brown. Her body is always large; exaggerated size is common to both the churlish knight and the loathly lady. The author of *Marriage* is far briefer, but this loathly lady is the most deformed figure of the four romances:

Then there as shold have stood her mouth,	Then there where her mouth should have stood,
Then there was sett her eye;	then there was set her eye;
The other was in her forhead fast,	the other was securely in her forehead,
The way that she might see.	so that she might see.
Her nose was crooked and turnd outward,	Her nose was crooked and turned outward,
Her mouth stood foule awry;	her mouth stood foully awry;
A worse formed lady than shee was,	a worse formed lady than she was,
Never man saw with his eye.	never man saw with his eye.
	(*Marriage* 57–64)

This description, which positions the lady's eyes in her mouth and forehead and turns the nose inside-out, pushes the loathly lady from carnivalesque to deformed; this woman exists only through the help of magical life support. Only Chaucer eschews the chance to linger over a lurid description, saying simply, "A fouler wight ther may no man devyse" (999). Whether described at length or invoked by a few telling details, the iconography of carnival would have been immediately recognizable to a medieval audience; thus the carnivalesque marking of characters like the churlish knight and the loathly lady helps signal to the audience not only that something is "up"

From Rags To Riches, or The Step-Mother's Revenge   61

(that things are not as they seem, that perhaps magic is involved), but also that these figures belong to the lower classes, the "folk."

If their appearances construct the two grotesques as radically other, their behaviors work to emphasize their inappropriateness by positioning them as decidedly third estate. In particular, the behavior of *Wedding*'s loathly lady at her wedding reception reveals her disregard for the aristocratic system of etiquette that includes such niceties as appropriate table manners or moderate food intake. The loathly lady is "nott curteys," according to those at the wedding, eating "as moche as six that there wore" [not courteous; as much as six who were there] (602–3). The implication is obvious; the other guests eat only one-sixth of what she eats, so she stands out as voracious, excessive, another carnivalesque trope at work. In fact, she eats everything set before her, continuing to consume until the servants "drewe clothes and had wasshen" [drew (off) the table-clothes and washed up], physically preventing any more consumption (620).

The romances also position the loathly lady as a member of the third estate through her aggressive sexuality. For example, *Wedding*'s loathly lady is far more active in obtaining her marriage than even the most aggressive of Chrétien's love-driven heroines. She asks Arthur for Gawain's hand as the reward for saving her king's life, the reverse of the more traditional scene wherein a groom asks the father of the bride for permission to wed his daughter. Not only does the loathly lady pursue marriage, but she also initiates sexual activity. In the three loathly lady tales featuring a wedding-night bedroom scene, the bride pursues the husband.[11] In *Florent*, the loathly lady takes action when her husband turns himself away from her in bed: "In armes sche beclipte hire lord, / And preide, as he was torned fro, / He wolde him torne ayeinward tho; / 'For now,' sche seith, 'we ben bothe on" [In arms she clasped her lord, and prayed, as he was turned away, that he would turn again towards (her); "For now," she said, "we are both one."] (1790–3). Her pleading is effective, as Florent turns around shortly thereafter. In *Wedding*, Ragnelle makes the connection between Gawain's sexual prowess and his reputation as a knight (his courtesy) when discussing his martial obligation: "A, Sir Gawen, syn I have you wed, / Shewe me your cortesy in bed; / With ryghte itt may nott be denyed [Sir Gawain, since I wed you, you must show me your courtesy in bed; by rights it may not be denied.] (629–31). Ragnelle goes on to say that Gawain should at least kiss her "for Arthours sake" [for Arthur's sake] (635). This ploy works too; Gawain says that he'll "do more / Then for to kysse" [do more than merely kiss] (638–9). Chaucer's loathly lady also asks the rapist knight about his less-than-amorous behavior in bed, smiling while she asks him, "Fareth every knyght thus with his wyf as ye? / Is this the lawe of kyng Arthures hous? / Is every knyght so dangerous?" [Does every knight behave with his wife as you do? Is this the law of King Arthur's house? Is every knight so disdainful?] (1088–90). As in *Wedding*, Chaucer's lady explicitly connects the husband's behavior in the bedroom to his reputation as a knight

62   *Crafting the Witch*

of Arthur's house. In each of these examples, the loathly lady turns the gendered sexual hierarchy upside down, taking over the role of sexual aggressor. In her manipulation of Arthur and Gawain, the loathly lady most resembles Chrétien's servant-girl, Lunete, who actively orchestrates the marriage between her mistress and Yvain. Aggressive femininity thus aligns with servants, representatives of the working estate, in this interpretation of the legend.

Likewise, it is the churlish knight's behavior towards Gawain that most clearly demonstrates the class-based nature of his threat to the aristocratic investment in chivalry. In the churlish knight romances, the churl's association with the third estate is demonstrated by his disdain for aristocratic hospitality, both as a host (in the two "Carle" romances) and as a guest (in *SGGK*, *Grene*, and *Turke*). In *Carle* and *Carlisle*, the churlish knight brazenly flouts the romance convention that demands of hosts a most generous hospitality; instead, the churlish knight provides a surly porter who hems and haws before granting the hunting party lodging for the night, he scares his guests with his wild animals and grim greeting, and he goes so far as to strike a man of the cloth, Bishop Bodwin. Each of these behaviors flouts the dictates of aristocratic etiquette—like the loathly lady, the churl's refusal to behave properly marks him as low-brow, as "churlish." The churlish knight's behavior reflects his designation as the "carle" of Carlisle; the Middle English word, *carle*, was used as a pejorative term for men of low estate. In fact, the word often referred to serfs and slaves as well as free farm workers.[12] The carle is a churl indeed.

If the churlish knight of the "Carle" romances is a bad host, the churl in *SGGK*, *Greene*, and *Turke* is a bad guest. His initial visit in each episode, for example, is a two-part demonstration of bad behavior: a) it challenges Arthur's reputation for courtesy by testing his tolerance for insubordinate behavior and b) it probes the Round Table's reputation for unparalleled courage by challenging the knights' bravery when confronted with a clearly-marked, exaggerated threat. Instead of asking for hospitality, as knights in romances usually do when they approach a new castle, the churlish knight of these narratives demands a boon.[13] In *SGGK*, the churlish knight's behavior is particularly rude: from his initial appearance, when he rides his horse into Arthur's hall, the Green Knight challenges the conventions of romance, and by implication, the dictates of chivalry. The green churl flouts the established hierarchy, pretending not to recognize the King, and rudely impugns the knights' masculinity, calling them "beardless children." Despite his provocative challenge, the churl asks not for a fight, but to play a "Christmas game" (283). The behavior of the churl in *Grene* is less pronounced, but similar to that of his 14th-century cousin. Likewise, though the churl in *Turke* simply demands a blow-exchange upon entering Arthur's hall, this behavior is strange enough to cause Gawain to wonder whether "that man want of his witt" [that man lack his sanity] (31).

From Rags To Riches, or The Step-Mother's Revenge 63

The bad behavior of the grotesques reinforces their carnivalesque physical appearance, and the combination of these characteristics functions as a harsh indictment of the third estate. Economic lack equals ugliness, in these tales, reinforcing medieval hierarchy through the conventional conflation of outward sign with inward truth. But there's a trick—in this case, outward appearance only seems to reflect reality, as we learn when the spell is finally broken. What does it take to break the spell, to reveal that what seems to be the innate grotesqueness of deprivation and poverty is actually a façade? Let's see.

III. NIPPING THE BUD: TAMING THE GROTESQUES

Towards the end of the story, the titular character of *Turke* asks Gawain to "strike of [his] head" (276). Gawain answer is nothing if not courteous: "'That I forefend!' said Sir Gawaine, / 'For I wold not have thee slaine / For all the gold soe red'" ['That I forbid!' said Sir Gawain, 'for I would not have you slain, for all the gold so red.'] (277–9). He declines politely, asserting the importance of the Turk's life, thus mitigating his otherwise impolite refusal. Likewise, in *Carle*, Gawain says that he "had rather be dead" [would rather be dead] than do what the churl asks (386). When the churl presses him, Gawain finally submits, saying, "Sir, your bidding shall be done" (396). Gawain's courtesy first demands that he protect the churlish knight's life, but the same courtesy then dictates that he must comply. This choice is a happy one for both Gawain and the churl, as it turns the churl into a noble knight who then rewards Gawain handsomely.

In both the churlish knight and loathly lady versions of the makeover romances, it is Gawain who finally transforms the grotesque figures into beautiful, noble ideals. Aristocratic courtesy is Gawain's transformative tool, the mechanism by which he effects the makeover. His chivalric demeanor emphasizes the changing construction of masculinity in the romances, and differs from the masculine ideal endorsed by earlier French romances in that his submissive obedience, rather than his aggressive violence, wins him accolades. This chivalric code is exemplified by the trials of the churlish knight narratives, wherein the churl challenges Gawain in a series of tests measuring his ability to negotiate male-male relationships by adhering to chivalric virtues such as keeping one's word (*trowthe*), showing respect to other men regardless of their station (*cortaysye*), remaining pure and chaste (*clannes*), and being brave and strong in the face of fearsome challenges (*corage*).

Just as the lack of hospitality was an indicator of the churlish knight's working-class position, hospitality is an important aspect of Gawain's ideal courtesy, including demonstrating respect for the rules and possessions of his host. A perfect example is a scene in both *Carle* and *Carlisle*, where

64   *Crafting the Witch*

Gawain wins his host's respect with his kind treatment of the churl's foal, stabled with the war-horses belonging to Gawain and his companions. Kay and Bishop Bodwin treat the foal poorly, throwing him out into the rain, and they each earn themselves a hard blow from the churl for their pains. But Gawain brings the foal in from the rain, covering the rain-sodden creature with his own mantle, and the churl thanks him graciously for the favor. Immediately following this scene, dinner ends, but whereas Kay and Bodwin go to one chamber, Gawain goes to the lady's bed; the sequence of events here suggests causality—it is because Gawain passes the test of courtesy (represented by the foal episode) that he continues on to the test of his chastity (represented by the episode in the lady's bed), and it is because Gawain passes the test of chastity that he eventually goes on to the beheading sequence, discussed below.

Part of the chivalric code demands that a guest respect the host and his household, including his wife and children (*trowthe*); another aspect suggests that a knight should be chaste (*clannes*). Both Gawain's *trowthe* and his *clannes* are tested in a bedroom scene common to four of the five romances, where the churlish knight's wife offers herself to Gawain, who may kiss but must go no further. In the Carle romances, the churl asks Gawain to undress, climb into bed, and kiss his wife in front of him. In both versions, Gawain goes overboard: the narrator of *Carle* tells us, "When Gawen wolde have doun the prevey far, / Then seyd the Carle, 'Whoo ther! / That game I the forbede'" [When Gawain would have done the private act, then said the Carl, "Whoa there! That game I forbid you."] (466–8); and in *Carlisle*, though Gawain is warned to "doe no other villanye" while in bed, his "flesh began to warme" and he "had thought to have made infare" [do no other villainy; flesh began to warm; had thought to have intercourse] (338, 342–3). In each case, the churl stops Gawain from proceeding, but praises him for obeying orders. Apparently, though Gawain wanted to have sex with the churl's wife, the fact that he stops when told redeems him. Compared to Gawain's response to the wife in the two Green Knight romances, though, Gawain's behavior here seems motivated more by the churl's presence (the test of *trowthe*) than a desire to remain chaste before the Lord (the test of *clannes*).

Though *SGGK*'s Gawain is also driven by respect for his host and loyalty to his oath, Gawain's dedication to chastity is connected explicitly to his Christianity in the most famous of the churlish knight romances, *SGGK*.[14] Not only does the poet spend roughly fifty lines expounding upon Gawain's pentangle and its connection to Christian chivalry (619–669), but the titular hero also enjoys a special relationship with the Virgin Mary. A picture of Mary appears on Gawain's shield, and Gawain prays to Mary when lost in the wilderness on his way to the Grene Chapel. In fact, Castle Hautdesert materializes as if in answer to Gawain's prayer: "Nade he sayned hymself, segge, bot þrye / Er he watȝ war in þe wod of a won in a mote" [He had not blessed himself, the man, but thrice before he was aware in the woods of a dwelling within a moat] (763–4). The poet invokes Mary on the third morning of the bedroom sequence, reminding us that "gret perile" stood between the Lady and Gawain "nif Mare of hir knyȝt mynne" [great peril; if Mary did not think of her knight] (1768, 1769), and the virgin indeed keeps him safe from sexual dalliance, in the end.

Gawain's motivation for maintaining chastity in *Greene*, an adaptation of *SGGK*, is more ambiguous than in the earlier version. When Sir Bredbeddle's wife comes to Gawain's bedchamber to kiss him and tempt him sexually, he tells her: "Your husband is a gentle knight, / By Him that bought mee deare! / To me itt were a great shame / If I shold doe him any grame, / That hath beene kind to mee" [Your husband is a gentle knight, by Him who bought me (at a) dear (cost)! For me it would be a great shame if I were to do him any harm, who has been kind to me.] (383–6). His chastity is not motivated by Christian idealism; rather, he doesn't want to offend his gracious host. He is obligated to respect his host, and he does so even though the churlish knight is not present. Gawain's desire to obey the chivalric obligation to his host is in fact his greatest strength, as most of the challenges Gawain faces in these tales require him to mitigate his aggressive brutality with deference before men and women with more economic, social, or political power. The aggressive masculinity of the twelfth- and thirteenth-century romances and chronicles has been refined, preserving a chivalric, courtly morality even as the economic situation in England moves further away from the feudal model.

Despite the importance of submissive obedience, Gawain must still prove that he can fight when necessary, and tests of *corage* (courage and strength) appear in all five romances. In *SGGK*, *Greene*, and *Turke*, they come at the beginning, when the churlish knight offers the blow exchange. By accepting the challenge, Gawain demonstrates both strength (in chopping the knight's head off) and courage (in defeating a monstrous foe). By showing up for the return blow, Gawain shows that he has courage in the face of certain death. In *Carle*, *Carlisle*, and *Turke*, Gawain also performs feats of strength, beating a group of giants at giant-tennis in *Turke* and lifting huge wine goblets in *Carle* and *Carlisle*. In the latter two romances, the churlish knight asks Gawain to throw a spear at his head, and Gawain complies, chucking the spear with such force that it shatters upon hitting the wall above the churl's head. He clearly passes with flying colors. Of course, the most fascinating of the tests of strength performed by Gawain is the notorious beheading exchange.

The beheading sequences of the churlish knight tales are critical moments in the male makeover narratives, in part because of their relationship to the beheadings presented in the French romance tradition. Chrétien's many giants exhibit an excessively aggressive masculine essence, one which ultimately compels their execution, often via beheading. When a giant is killed, he is dead. There is no coming back. Not so in the later Middle English versions. Though the Middle English poets echo Chrétien in beheading the

66   Crafting the Witch

"giant-esque" churl (symbolically castrating him), they don't kill him out-right. Instead, the beheading releases their "true" essence—the churls are transformed into perfect models of aristocratic chivalry. Gawain, as ideal representative of chivalric knighthood, performs the makeover ceremony, and it is easy to read this moment as one of castration, as Gawain removes the churl's hyper-masculinity by removing his head. The result is an emas-culated churl, a man who submits to the feminizing demands of courtesy. As the challenges have proven, Gawain's victory comes because he is the best example of aristocratic knighthood. Gawain's courtesy, inextricably linked to his class status, is what gives him the transformative power to break the grotesque spell—his conformity to upper-class conventions is transferred to the churl through the act of removing the lower-class façade. Beneath the mask lies a noble man after all.

The situation is similar in the female version of the makeover narrative. The loathly lady, like the churlish knight, may represent all that medieval authors encouraged women not to be, but this loathly veneer also hides a most lovely core. Unlike the churlish knight, the lady does not require a beheading. Instead, to tame her a chivalrous knight must marry her and be willing to consummate the marriage. Marriage replaces (symbolic) castra-tion in this story, and the replacement is significant: though adherence to a submissive chivalric ideal is what allows men to move into the ranks of the privileged classes, women's entrance to the world of nobility is a form of "class by association." That is, women are exchanged in a traditional format, through marital bonds, which have always been a means for female upward mobility.[15] The submissive chivalric ideal is still important to this exchange, as it is not merely the marriage which catalyzes the loathly lady's transforma-tion, but the reversal of sexual roles created by the lady's aggressive behavior and the knight-hero's corresponding submission in the bedroom.

In fact, it is at the precise moment when the marital roles have been completely reversed, when Gawain (the husband, the traditional sexual aggressor) is turned into a passive (i.e., feminine) recipient of sexual desire, that the loathly lady makes the first step of her transformation into the beautiful maiden. This step demands a decision, as the loathly lady of all four versions offers Gawain a critical choice about her physical appear-ance. In three of the loathly lady romances (Chaucer deviates from the formula), *after* transforming, the lady offers the knight the following choice: would he rather see her beautiful during the day and grotesque at night, or the opposite? We learn, as he does, that he has not yet won, as the loathly lady will still be loathly for half of each 24-hour period. It is only when he grants her license to make the decision herself, validating her authority over her own body, that the spell is broken and the loathly lady becomes permanently beautiful. In this transformation story, then, the knight's courtesy relies on his complicity in relinquishing the conven-tionally masculine role: he must not be the sexual aggressor, he must not make decisions, and he must submit to the lady as if she were a lord.

From Rags To Riches, or The Step-Mother's Revenge 67

Gawain's submissive courtesy in these romances is parallel to the churlish knight stories: he obeys the will of his lady as he would obey the will of his host, lord, or king. Granting the loathly lady her own will is the chivalric response—and, indeed, chivalry breaks the magical spell, providing the all-important upward mobility: we see that only through a close connection with richness can one become rich.

These tales thus seem to promote a particular kind of social mobility; the participants are freed from the yoke of poverty (and its attendant grotesqueness) through an association with an ideology that demands proper respect for one's betters. Moving up, the tales suggest, requires the help of one well-versed in a chivalric ideal—the grotesques do not and cannot transform themselves. Gawain saves them. Significantly, his connection to aristocracy is tied to his willingness to maintain a submissive position within a strict class hierarchy, and he teaches that submission to the decidedly aggressive grotesques. Class conformity releases the third estate upstarts from their inappropriate behavior, their grotesque appropriation of class privilege.

But are these grotesques really lower-class, despite the visual and behavioral cues I have just described? To answer this, we must peel away a layer from the complicated soap-opera offered by these romances. Indeed, in all five of the churlish knight romances, after the transformation occurs we learn that the churlish knight was never really a churl at all: in *SGGK*, he is Sir Bertilak, master of a chivalric homestead rivaling Camelot; in *Grene*, he is Sir Bredbeddle, "a man of mickele might" in "the west countrye" (41, 39); in *Carle*, he is a landed knight who chose to abandon his nobility when confronted by the lack of chivalry apparent in the members of his own estate (517–28); in *Carlisle*, he is also a landed knight, whose appearance as a churl was a result of malicious magic (401–15); and in *Turke*, he is really Sir Gromer, who is crowned "King of Man" (329–30). Likewise, three of the four loathly lady stories feature transformations revealing the lady's aristocratic origins: in *Wedding*, Ragnelle's family was originally landed, but was dispossessed by the king, as we learn in the initial episode that launches the adventure (54–72); in *Marriage*, though the loathly lady's father is a knight, she has been bewitched (175–82); and in *Florent*, the loathly lady is the daughter of the king of Cizile (1832–38). In both *Wedding* and *Marriage*, Gawain restores the social position of the loathly lady's family, righting the wrong that led to the (grotesque) downward social movement, and Florent plays the same role in Gower's version of the tale.[16]

With the underlying nobility thus exposed, what are the implications? On the one hand, these medieval makeovers revise the threatening behavior of third estate figures. On the other hand, the figures were (always?) already land-owning members of the first estate. In light of this contradictory doubling, questions spring to mind: To whom are these stories directed? Whom do these figures represent? What kind of "folk" are the carnivalesque grotesques? What kind of nobility are the landed families behind the grotesque knight and lady? Exactly which people require transformation?

68 Crafting the Witch

In the mid-fourteenth century, famine spread across England, followed by plague, war, and social unrest.[17] The results of this series of crises were widespread, eventually allowing for shifts in power between the workers of the third estate and the aristocracy. Population declined dramatically, offering farm laborers a chance to increase their incomes and forcing land-owners to relinquish some of their control over agricultural production.[18] With fewer people to work it, land value decreased, encouraging many land-owners to move from managing their own demesnes to renting parcels of land to peasants and farmers.[19] The resulting economic surpluses allowed agricultural production to support the growing populations of merchants, craftspeople, and traders in towns and cities.[20] Christopher Dyer notes that the lowered land-values also allowed "lawyers, merchants and wealthy peasants" to acquire "a sufficient quantity of land" (339–40), and Hudson suggests that the gentry amassed large estates rivaling those of the knightly families (81). The loss of power for the aristocracy effected by the shift in land ownership created a tension manifested in historical and literary texts. A. J. Pollard suggests that it was in the late fourteenth and fifteenth centuries that the distinction between "gentility and lack of gentility" became "articulated" (186–7). In other words, it became increasingly important during this period to distinguish between "old money" and "new money." This distinction flavors the details of the makeover narratives considered here.

In particular, the loathly lady romances reflect anxiety about land ownership. *Wedding*'s Sir Gromer Somer Joure is a lesser noble whose hold on his land is not hereditary, as the king is able to grant possession to Gawain. He is like the gentry, who have purchased their way into the first estate, and the grotesque appearance and behavior of his sister (the loathly Dame Ragnelle) both mark her as a peasant and reflect the tenuousness of her family's social position. Once she marries Gawain, this validates her family's position, as evinced by the fact that Arthur promises to be a "good lord to Sir Gromer" thereafter (812). Marriage is clearly a more acceptable route for upward mobility than business in *Wedding*. The same is true in both *Florent* and *Marriage*, which feature dispossessed daughters who restore their family's social standing through marital advancement (*Florent* 1832–60; *Marriage* 188–9). If the loathly lady stories warn against social advancement without the familial privilege afforded by marital bonds, the churlish knight stories address the problem of how to behave once successful upward mobility has been accomplished.

In the churlish knight narratives, land is not the immediate problem. The churlish knights are just that—knights, or landed nobility (whether lesser or greater), who do not adhere to the idealized chivalric code associated with the aristocracy throughout the romance oeuvre.[21] The anxiety expressed here is directed at the ability of capital to simulate what land had always represented for the first estate—power. Sheila Delaney analyzes the representation of money as possessing what seems almost like "magic power": "The creative power of money is that it compensates for

From Rags To Riches, or The Step-Mother's Revenge   69

the deficiencies of nature: The ugly person can buy a beautiful mate; the stupid person can buy intelligent employees; the bad person is honored for his or her social position" (87–8). Here, the peasant can buy nobility. If anyone can purchase and thus own land, the stories ask, what can we use to distinguish "us" from "them?" If land no longer provides a clear boundary, what does? The answer given in the churlish knight romances is clearly "ideology."

It seems the makeover narratives reflect two sides of a social "coin": on one side, the threat of increasing economic power for lesser nobility and third estate workers is soothed by the loathly lady's dependence on marriage for social mobility; on the other, the crisis precipitated by a changing economic system allowing merchants, lawyers, and gentry to achieve wealth rivaling that of the landholding aristocracy is mitigated in the makeover narrative by the behavioral transformation of the offensive churlish grotesque. For both sides of the coin, the message is similar: it is not economic power, but adherence to aristocratic ideology, which determines one's true class association.

Most of the make-over narratives discussed here clearly valorize the knight-hero's submission to feudal hierarchy, but one of these tales, written by an unknown author far removed from the courtly world of Chaucer and Gower, problematizes the effects of this ideological position on traditional masculinity. *SGGK* is, in many ways, a typical churlish knight tale, involving the transformation of a gigantic, grotesque churl into a perfectly chivalrous knight through the extraordinary courtesy of Gawain, as we have seen. But that narrative doesn't fully describe what happens in this unique adaptation. What that description leaves out is that fact that, in *SGGK*, it is Gawain himself who undergoes the most radical metamorphosis.

In both *SGGK* and its later adaptation, *Grene*, when the churlish knight tests Gawain's mettle, our hero fails one of the tests! This is big, huge, momentous—not because the knight has a flaw (Chrétien's knights are notorious for mistreating their lovers, as do Erec and Yvain, among other misdeeds), but because of the nature of the flaw. It's not that Gawain is a coward. As I document in Chapter Two, knights often use magic rings to prevent harm in exactly the same fashion as Gawain intends to use the girdle. It's that Gawain breaks his word. The word of a knight is sacrosanct; it is only because knights keep their word that the whole system of sending hostages back to the king can operate as it does in medieval romance. Specifically, Gawain breaks his word by keeping the girdle when he should have given it to Bertilak. At the moment he does this, Gawain's transformation is complete—his hiding the girdle is the culmination of a transformative process that begins the moment Gawain arrives at Castle Hautdesert. When he first leaves Arthur's court, Gawain occupies a powerful masculine position: he has chopped the head off his enemy, armed himself in the dual protective glory of Christianity and chivalry, and set off on a quest to honor his word as a knight. Once he enters the world of the churlish knight, a

70 *Crafting the Witch*

world of carnivalesque inversion, Gawain slowly metamorphosizes from masculine aggressor into feminine object.

When Gawain arrives at Castle Hautdesert, it is not unlike Arthur's court: the denizens feast for the holidays, play games, exchange kisses, and foster a festive atmosphere where even the losers laugh (60–71). Bertilak engages Gawain in the exchange game, laying the groundwork for what will become the primary inversion of the poem. Bertilak's game prohibits Gawain from hunting with the men for the duration of his time at Castle Hautdesert, requiring him to keep the company of the Lady Bertilak. Romance convention dictates that Gawain should be an honored guest at the hunt, but Bertilak restricts Gawain to the domestic world of the castle, physically imposing a spatial inversion, as it were. Gawain soon internalizes this externally imposed inversion, becoming more and more feminized as the poem goes on.

The bedroom scenes, offered in tandem with the hunting episodes, highlight Gawain's incremental journey towards internalizing a feminine subject-position. Henry Savage noted the way this parallel structure situates Gawain as the Lady's prey and shows Gawain's behavior to be similar to that of the beasts hunted each day by Bertilak, and critics have made arguments in the same vein ever since.[22] Gawain becomes the passive love-object, and the Lady becomes the active pursuer, the temptress who both possesses and seeks to be the object of the phallic gaze.[23] The Lady reveals more of her body each day, tempting Gawain more aggressively each time, until she enters his bedchamber on the third and final day with barely any clothes on at all: "Her þryuen face and hir þrote þrowen al naked, / Hir brest bare birfore, and bihine eke" [Her lovely face and her throat were laid all naked, / Her breast bare in front, and her back also bare.] (1740–41).

The first conversation between Gawain and the Lady centers on her control of his body. The Lady says Gawain has been "tan as-tyt" and threatens to "bynde" him to his "bedde" [quickly trapped; bind, bed] (1210, 1211). Gawain yields to the Lady, but begs her to release him. She refuses, saying that even though they are sitting on a bed, they should merely "karp" [talk] (1225). Though the Lady invokes sexuality through her near nakedness and her intrusion into Gawain's boudoir, she immediately revokes any chance for Gawain to act, channeling his bodily tension into discourse, and positioning him as the passive recipient of her action. The poet is careful to note that, in every instance, the Lady kisses Gawain—she is the kisser, and Gawain the kissee. Her deliberate inversion of conventional gender roles forces Gawain's involuntary inversion, his adoption of a sexually passive behavior pattern. Though the Lady forces Gawain's initial inversion, he participates more actively in his own feminization as the story develops.

If Gawain spends his days being seduced by Lady Bertilak, he spends his nights seducing her husband. Gawain must kiss his host, and the poet delicately gestures towards both the homoeroticism of the act and its feminizing

From Rags To Riches, or The Step-Mother's Revenge   71

elements. The description of Gawain's kiss on the first knight illustrates the awkwardness of his situation: Gawain "hasppeȝ his fayre hals his armeȝ wythinne, / And kysses hym as comlyly as ho couþe awyse" [clasps the lord's neck within his arms, and kisses him as courteously as he could devise] (1388–9). He must adhere to his bargain with the Lord, and yet remain within the bounds of heterosexual masculinity. On the second day, Gawain adopts the same stance as before, holding his host around the neck and kissing him "hendey" [nobly] (1639), ritualizing the interaction. By the last day, however, Gawain's attitude has changed; his kisses are offered "as sauerly and sadly as he hem sett couþe" [as enthusiastically and soundly as he could place them] (1947). Gawain has moved from reluctant sharing to assertive, passionate kissing. His repeated kissing of the lord juxtaposes the lord/vassal relationship with the heterosexual relationship; this parallel positioning marks Gawain as vassal or beloved—servant or wife.

In the final stage of his feminine inversion, Gawain chooses to use the green girdle rather than face his opponent with no defense. The girdle, like the carnivalesque Green Knight with whom it shares its color, is a harbinger of feminine inversion, given to him by a woman, and allegedly imbued with powerful defensive magic. At Arthur's court, bastion of idealized chivalric masculinity, Gawain was the aggressor, using his strength for offensive maneuvers. At Castle Hautdesert, Gawain is on defense, helpless against the threat of decapitation but for the girdle. Though his feminine talisman can protect him from death, it cannot protect him from his symbolic castration—Gawain's grand finale.

Though the churlish knight's beheading sequence results in his return to glory in *Carlisle* and *Turk*, for *SGGK*'s Gawain the process of his symbolic castration is humiliating: the Green Knight knicks him, causing a permanent scar, a signifier of Gawain's flawed knighthood. Gawain's change from perfect knight to dishonorable man is as complete a transformation as the churlish knight's; Gawain has lost perfection, Edenic innocence. When the Green Knight tells Gawain that he only "lakked a lyttel," Gawain cries, his face turning red, and he shrinks "for shome" [lacked a little; for shame] (2366, 2370–2). Gawain's confrontation with his own lack (i.e. his castration), marker of feminine difference, results in an explosive diatribe against women of no less than fifteen lines (2414–28).

Though he blames women, the poem emphasizes that it is Gawain's strict adherence to the masculine chivalric ideal that in fact fosters his inversion and his eventual transgression against that ideal. Gawain originally volunteers for the Green Knight's challenge to free Arthur from the obligation; his commitment to knightly courtesy then embroils him in the exchange game with Lord Bertilak; finally, his dual loyalties to chivalry and Christianity demand that he deflect the Lady's advances with tact and grace, preserving her feelings and his own chastity. Adhering to the masculine ideal causes Gawain's feminine inversion—being a man turns Gawain into a woman. Within masculinity lies femininity.

72 *Crafting the Witch*

The *SGGK*-poet's construction of gender is by no means conventional. This version of the churlish knight story exists in a single manuscript, written in the north of England for a literate, rather than a popular (i.e., illiterate), audience. While the short verse romances use Gawain's figure to reinforce the Christian-infused ideology of chivalry, *SGGK*'s representation of Gawain invokes a carnivalesque inversion of gender roles. This is a reversal of the crisis of masculinity reflected in the excessively masculine giants of medieval chronicles. Instead of behaving too aggressively, *SGGK*'s Gawain is overly passive, a feminized version of what used to be the premier masculine icon, the knight. Rather than promote chivalric masculinity, this poem mourns it—participating in the trend toward submissive courtesy, the games of court, can only lead to losing all maleness and becoming a woman. Though the theme of this poem is certainly different from those of the popular romances, all the romances considered here respond to a similar problem: the difficulty of constructing and maintaining strict gender roles in the face of economic change.

If the popular romances promoted an ideology critiqued by the Gawain-poet, did those messages reach audiences for whom they would be relevant? Were the newly-wealthy merchants and gentry likely to hear these romances? To answer this question, we might begin by taking a brief look at the probable audience of the romances. This is a tricky task, however, as the evidence is difficult to interpret: the general consensus is that the romances reached a diverse range of people, from the nobility and gentry to merchants and farmers, to both women and men.[24] Hudson has made the case that romances were probably most commonly consumed by the gentry classes, in particular, and if that is true, then the answer to my question is "yes." The precise way in which this set of narratives affected the perhaps extremely diverse groups of people who encountered them is of course impossible to determine, but the ideology offered by the stories must have been fairly satisfying, judging by the prevalence of extant versions. That the romances seemed to have a broad appeal to a wide cross-section of people from different estates or classes is not surprising in light of the range of themes and motifs offered within the genre. The complexity of tensions expressed by the manifestation of transformative power in these makeover stories—the textual layers—likewise kept them circulating for generations.

The makeover narrative—the Cinderella story—still resonates for twentieth- and twenty-first-century audiences, as evinced by the range of popular adaptations (both cinematic and televised), from Disney's *Cinderella* and the recent *Ever After* to ABC's musical *Cinderella* and looser adaptations such as *Annie*, *My Fair Lady*, or *Pretty Woman*. However, rather than reacting to the threat of economic power with an assurance that only upper-class ideology can create upper-class people, modern makeover narratives privilege the role of capital itself. As in "Extreme Makeover," it is

From Rags To Riches, or The Step-Mother's Revenge 73

the intervention of money (and all it brings) which provides the transformative power. In twentieth-century visual adaptations, Gawain's magical courtesy becomes the magical power of a rich man, an equation especially evident in the terribly popular film *Pretty Woman*. That money occupies the space previously held by chivalry reflects the mystification of wealth that inevitably pervades a society predicated, as ours is, on a capitalist economy. It seems there is one truth after all, one these romancers feared but we celebrate with gusto: money changes everything.

IV. IN BED WITH PATRIARCHY: THE PRICE OF FEMALE DESIRE

The churlish knight and loathly lady stories provide "his" and "her" versions of what is still an extremely popular narrative trope, the make-over. Both versions of this story circulated in England for generations; their repeated retelling and their structural similarities demand their comparison—these are gendered stories. Specifically, the gendering of this narrative suggests that medieval authors saw the need to distinguish an appropriate male (or masculine) response to economic changes from an appropriate female (or feminine) one. Though both the male and the female versions of the transformation tale focus on appropriate ownership of land, exposing the threat to aristocracy posed by a shifting economic system, analysis of the structural differences in these tales offers a unique glimpse at medieval gender construction in operation. It is no surprise, considering the western literary tradition, to find that the aristocratic ideology privileged in these popular romances is securely aligned with patriarchy. The parallel tales work together to privilege a binary system which equates maleness with the normative world and femaleness with the domestic world, wrapping the patriarchal convention neatly in a pretty make-over story and presenting it proudly as a gift for future audiences.

I will begin by providing a brief summary of the generic structure of the "male" and "female" versions of the make-over tale. Though the details of each version differ slightly, both sets of tales share critical plot movements. The churlish knight stories proceed as follows: a) Arthur and court are engaged in a communal, aristocratic activity (i.e. feasting or hunting) when the initial conflict develops; b) the conflict centers around the figure of the churlish knight, who either shows up at court to challenge Arthur[25] or is encountered by chance as a few knights seek lodging for the night[26]; c) Gawain accepts the challenge and visits the churlish knight's castle; d) at the castle, Gawain undergoes a series of tests or challenges, during which he usually performs very well; e) the challenges culminate in a final beheading sequence, which releases the churlish knight from the enchantment that made him churlish to begin with; f) Gawain is (joyfully) reunited with Arthur's court.

74 *Crafting the Witch*

Likewise, all four loathly lady romances follow a similar plot line: a) the main knight acts to place himself in a dire situation (either by making foolish choices or by attempting to save Arthur from the consequences of his actions); b) to prevent his execution, the knight must learn the answer to the question "What do women desire?" within a specified time period; c) the knight searches, but cannot find the answer; d) he comes across the loathly lady, who offers to provide the answer if he will grant her a boon; e) he agrees to this exchange, and uses her answer to save himself when the time comes; f) the lady claims her boon, the knight's hand in marriage, and he is obligated to comply; e) they marry, and the lady encourages the knight to consummate the marriage, which the reluctant husband finally agrees to do; f) upon demonstrating his willingness to perform the marital duty, the knight sees the loathly lady transform into a beautiful maiden and is given a choice related to her physical appearance; g) rather than choosing, the knight grants the choice to the lady, who is then truly released from her spell and will remain beautiful ever after.

Structurally, the loathly lady and churlish knight versions of the transformation narratives share many important features: the conventional opening, which sets up the entrance of the carnivalesque character; the unconventional behavior of the grotesque, which presents a challenge to the knight-hero's chivalry; the knight-hero's unparalleled courtesy, which breaks the enchantment; and the final scene, which reasserts the importance of the normative royal court. The differences in structure occur in those places where the female sex of the carnivalesque figure necessitates alternate strategies to ensure a binary gender system where male equals "person" and gender equals "female." To use a modern analogy, the differences between the "male" and "female" versions of the story have the effect of rendering the loathly lady story "chick lit" while pitching the male version as a best-seller for everyone. The loathly lady story is clearly about class-appropriate femininity, and the writers brandish that fact like a mace, swinging it around so that we notice it; the churlish knight story is clearly about class-appropriate masculinity, but the issue of gender never arises overtly within the narrative. Both the loathly lady and the churlish knight narratives explore gender through the transformation of the inappropriate figure into the perfect specimen, but the version dealing with femininity is marked as overtly concerned with the question of gender difference. The fact that the female version of the narrative is the one that signifies difference both reflects the medieval scientific view of woman as the "second sex" and anticipates the situation in U.S. academia, where the mention of "gender" may still be understood to mean a discussion of women (rather than of both men and women). While there are certainly many writers and teachers engaged in the project of making women's interests so integral to the operation of normative society that we no longer desperately need a field like Women's Studies, maleness and masculinity still remain in many spaces as the unquestioned and untheorized norm.[27] When we allow "gender" to constitute "female," we inherit the patriarchal tradition of the west, the tradition embodied by the make-over romances of the fourteenth and fifteenth centuries.

The first difference between the two tales I want to explore involves the challenges faced by the knight-hero. Both versions of the tale ultimately test the knight-hero's *trowthe*, his ability to keep his pledge unfailingly, even in the face of great danger or humiliation, but the particular demands made by the grotesques demonstrate the gendering of their interests. A comparison between the two traditions exposes the binary positioning of desire: male interests and desires appear to be polyvalent and wide-ranging, but female desire is singular and simple. The trials of courage, chastity, and courtesy comprising the central episodes of the churlish knight tales involve a range of activities reflecting a variety of interests: for example, the overt displays of physical strength reveal the churlish knight's interest in the knight-hero's ability to serve in battle, whereas the bedroom sequence allows the churlish knight both to demonstrate his sovereignty over his wife and the knight-hero and to confirm the knight-hero's virility. The tests of *trowthe* demonstrate that the churlish knight is interested in the knight-hero's abilities in a number of different male arenas—his physical prowess, his sexuality, his social position as knight and guest, his animal husbandry skills, and so on. Despite the fact that martial skills, feudal obligations, and virility appear in western literary tradition almost exclusively as male/masculine motifs, the narrators never mention that fact or represent the exchange as related specifically to maleness or masculinity. For the narrators, the interests of the churlish knight are generic, not connected to gender.

This is not the case with the loathly lady tales. The narrators of these stories announce themselves immediately as interested in women and the nature of women's desire—topic today, women! This story revolves around an exchange of information; in exchange for marriage to the knight-hero, the loathly lady provides the answer to variations of the question "What do women most desire?"[28] The narrative of the loathly lady is thus overtly concerned with female desire. The addition of the question about female desire marks the story as not the usual fare—this isn't about people, it's about women. The wording of the question eerily foreshadows Freud's language (Was will das Weib?) and makes explicit the way in which this tradition is linked to what modern feminists have described as the masculine questioning gaze, which seeks to uncover the mystified woman. The poets take great fun in answering the unanswerable question—sometimes at length. Women are so different! So unknowable!

Upon first glance, the interests attributed to women by the various male figures of the loathly lady romances seem polyvalent and far-reaching. In *Wedding*, Gawain's search provides him with "many an answer," as reflected in the following list:

76 Crafting the Witch

Somme sayd they lovyd to be welle arayd,	Some said they loved to be well-arrayed,
Somme sayd they lovyd to be fayre prayed,	Some said they loved to be beautifully beseeched,
Somme sayd they lovyd a lusty man	Some said they loved a lusty man
That in theyr armys can clypp them kysse them than.	Who in his arms can hug them and kiss them then.
Somme sayd one, somme sayd other;	Some said one thing, some said another,
And so had Gawen getyn many an answere.	And so had Gawain gotten many an answer.

(199–204)

This list, by no means unique, features what are still predominant stereotypes about women: we like clothes, we like flattery, and we like sex. Later, when Dame Ragnelle presents her answer to Arthur, she reiterates the list of claims, but is careful to specify that these are the things men say:

Summe *men sayn* we desyre to be fayre;	Some *men say* we desire to be beautfiul;
Also we desyre to have reparyre	Also we desire to have relations
Of diverse straunge men;	With diverse strange men;
Also we love to have lust in bed;	Also we love to have pleasure in bed;
And often we desyre to wed.	And often we desire to wed.
Thus *ye men nott ken*	This *you men do not understand,*
Yett we desyre anoder maner thyng:	Yet we desire another manner of thing:
To be holden nott old, butt fresshe and yong,	To be held not old, but fresh and young,
With flatryng and glosyng and quaynte gyn—	With flattery and cajolery and quaint arts—
So ye men may us wemen evere wyn	*So you men make us women ever joy*
Of whate ye wolle crave.	*In whatever you would crave.*

(408–18, italics mine)

In answering the question about female desire, Dame Ragnelle elucidates male desire, a fact she notes in the last two lines of this passage: what men want is for women to want the things men think they want. For Ragnelle and the other loathly ladies, men want women to be sexy, appearance-driven flattery-whores, obsessed with their bodies. Sounds like the same women described by cosmetics ads and weight-loss fads, the ones who occupy the covers of magazines (and their centerfolds) and decorate the arms of Hollywood action heroes.

Though *Marriage*'s incomplete manuscript does not include the list of what women want, both Gower's and Chaucer's versions do. Chaucer presents a list of female stereotypes similar to *Wedding*'s, but Chaucer's

From Rags To Riches, or The Step-Mother's Revenge 77

is longer and more thorough: he highlights women's interest in "riche array" and "lust abedde," as well as women's desire "oftetyme to wydwe and wedde" [rich array, sexual pleasure in bed, often to be widowed and to wed] (927–8); he includes "flaterye," but adds that the flattery should include comments about how "wise" and "clene of synne" the women are [wise, absent of sin] (932, 944). *Florent*'s men are so completely baffled that they can't come up with anything at all, finally concluding that "Such o thing [as women's desire] conne thei noght finde" [Such a thing could they not find] (1507). Though the lengthy lists (which reach more than twenty lines in *Wife's Tale*) imply a wide range of female interests, a closer look reveals that they all circulate around physical appearance and sexuality. What women want, these lists suggest, is to be perfect sex objects, to look beautiful and love sex. Men's desire is thus revealed through the speculation about female desire.

Establishing what men think women want (sometimes acknowledging the irony of the list), sets the stage for the all-important revelation central to the loathly lady stories, the revelation of what women *really* desire. The false list thus authenticates the "real" answer: if women don't want to be what men want them to be, then what they really want must be next. All four authors (two of whom we know to be male) agree here: women want sovereignty over men. As Chaucer puts it, "Wommen desiren to have sovereynetee / As wel over hir housbond as hir love, / And for to been in maistrie hym above" [Women desire to have sovereignty, over her husband as well as her lover, And to be in mastery above him] (1038–39). *Wedding* takes it a step further, noting that women "desyren of men above alle maner thyng / To have the sovereynte, without lesyng, / Of alle, bothe hyge and lowe" [desire of men, above all manner of things, to have the soveriegnty, without lying, of all (men), both high and low] (422–4). And Gower simply says, "all wommen lievest wolde / Be soverein of mannes love" [all women desire most to be sovereign over men's love] (1613–4). From the many possibilities, one truth emerges. This shift is both sly and insidious, essentializing female desire while pointing to the underlying patriarchal truth: women want sovereignty over men because men have sovereignty over women. If women don't desire what men want them to desire, they must want to decide for themselves what they desire. Obtaining sovereignty over her husband allows a woman to maintain sovereignty over herself. The logic here is impeccable, and I can personally attest to the importance of self-sovereignty. But though the women in the stories say they want sovereignty over men, an analysis of their maneuvering reveals yet another desire, one which seems to undermine the desire for sovereignty: the desire to be married.

In these make-over tales, the knight-hero's test begins when he has to face the loathly lady's demand, which is specific and singular—she wants the knight to marry her. Just as the loathly lady's access to the aristocratic world must be confirmed through marriage ("class by association"), her access to

78 Crafting the Witch

the masculine world (and her ability to obtain agency within that world) is dictated by the same institution. In patriarchal cultures, a man's wife is a reflection of him (a fact which is just as true in a capitalist system as it is in a feudal one): in most of Chrétien's romances, for example, the heroine's beauty matches the hero's good looks so perfectly that everyone knows she must surely be meant for him. To marry a loathly hag is to risk tainting yourself with her physical grotesqueness (and for the medieval world, the implied spiritual grotesqueness that must accompany the outward sign). Marriage to the loathly lady is therefore a test of the knight's willingness to keep his word despite humiliation in a public venue, but the test doesn't end there. The medieval marriage contract demanded consummation—payment of the marital debt—a requirement the loathly lady invokes when her husband is reluctant to perform his duty. Again, the challenge is that the knight-hero must keep his word, despite his obvious disgust, and the venue is the bedroom. The loathly lady ultimately desires marriage, and her tests circulate within a domestic sphere. The range of the churlish knight's interests contrasts vividly against the loathly lady's one-track mind, circumscribing female desire firmly within the bounds of domesticity.

For the loathly lady, marriage fulfills the same narrative function as the beheading sequence in the churlish knight tale. The churlish knight's beheading isn't a real beheading, however, as the knight not only survives it, but is healed by it. The beheading thus figures as a kind of castration, reigning in the overly aggressive, masculine behavior of the churl and replacing it with preferable submissive courtesy. The loathly lady's situation is different here precisely because she is female; gender difference is an *a priori* assumption of the romance writers. Even if she behaves aggressively, displaying masculine behavior, castration won't fix her, because she's already castrated. In this version of the tale, marriage replaces castration (and the replacement speaks for itself). If emasculation ensures class hierarchy within the patriarchal system represented here, marriage ensures female submission. Without a husband to restrain her, the (loathly) lady is free to behave as a man herself. Just as the churlish knight wants the knight-hero to behead him, the loathly lady wants the knight-hero to marry her, and it is the knight's acquiescence to these external desires that fuels the grotesques' transformation. Once the knight has married the loathly lady, positioning her securely within the realm of patriarchal heteronormativity, the lady (no longer loathly) immediately acknowledges his powerful position as husband, offering him a choice about her appearance. This is the key point— the question she offers reveals the power he already possesses over his wife's person. He grants her sovereignty over her appearance because he has it to grant. Once he does, he wins: the lady becomes the perfect (heterosexual) wife, beautiful and obedient. Women may say they want sovereignty, and men can pretend to grant it, but what women really want, in these stories, is to be married. Marriage tames the savage female by simultaneously ensuring her lack of and precipitating her desire for sovereignty.

From Rags To Riches, or The Step-Mother's Revenge   79

Despite the ever-present undermining of female agency within the loathly lady make-over narratives, these stories offer active female characters who manage to get exactly what they want, women who pursue their own marriages in an era when arranged marriages were still common (though not necessarily prevalent outside of aristocratic and wealthy merchant groups). And when the story is placed in the mouth of the Wife of Bath, as it is in Chaucer's *Wife's Tale*, the power of the loathly lady looms in sharp relief. In a number of ways, Chaucer's version is unlike the others, not least because his version adapts a popular folk motif for a courtly, literate audience.

Unlike the three other versions of the tale considered here, the action in *Wife's Tale* does not work to display the knight-hero's innate ability to act chivalrously, instead focusing on the transformation of an unrepentant criminal into a proper knight: just as *SGGK* folds the loathly lady story into its churlish knight structure (a fact I will discuss in the next section), *Wife's Tale* includes an element of the churlish knight tale. A comparison of *Wife's Tale* with the other loathly lady stories provides insight about Chaucer's appropriation of traditional material to suit the richly developed characters who populate *The Canterbury Tales*. Chaucer's attribution of this tale to the Wife of Bath facilitates the change of focus that so completely transforms the tale's meaning, creating a narrative about the transformation, effected by women, of an unruly knight into a submissive husband, rather than on the returning of an inappropriately "loathly" monster to the form of a docile, beautiful woman. Although there are many differences between the versions of the loathly lady romances, an examination of the following key points makes the shift in focus clear: the premise for the quest, the appearance of the loathly lady, the circumstances of the marriage arrangements, and the circumstances of the final choice. It is in these areas that the crucial distinctions can be made.

From the beginning of the tales, it is clear that the quests to determine what women really want are predicated on significantly disparate circumstances. In *Wife's Tale*, the knight has "rafte" the "maydenhed" from an innocent "mayde walkynge hym bifron" [ripped; maidenhead; maid walking before him] (886–88). When the knight is brought to Arthur's court for justice, the Queen and her ladies beg for his life and present him with a challenge: his life for the answer to the question, "What thyng is it that wommen moost desiren?" (905). On the other hand, in *Wedding* and *Marraige*, Arthur and Gawain do not quest to discover "whate wemen love best in feld and town" as a punishment for rape (91); rather, Arthur must answer the question to satisfy the challenge of a figure who echoes the churlish knight (*Wedding*'s Sir Gromer Somer Joure and *Marriage*'s Baron). *Florent*'s knight slays a man who attacks him, and his kinship to the emperor is the only reason the man's relatives offer him the question quest rather than killing him outright in revenge. Though the crimes committed by Arthur and Florent show their abuse of power (by being a careless lord and by killing another man, respectively), the rapist commits a crime related directly to the issue of women's sovereignty.

80   *Crafting the Witch*

In Chaucer's rendition of the tale, the question asked is germane to the crime the knight committed; the knight rapes a woman (taking away her sovereignty) and then must spend a year thinking about what women want. This makes the question paramount—it is, in fact, what the knight needs to learn to prevent future occurrences of rape. In the other versions, however, the question of what women desire is completely unrelated to both the circumstances that bring Arthur (or Florent) to the woods and the crime Arthur (or Florent) allegedly commits. One effect of this is to trivialize the question being asked; it is less important that the knight think about what women want and more important that he exhibit noble character by keeping his word during the ensuing adventure. Another consequence of these differences is that in *Wife's Tale*, it is difficult to like the rapist knight, whereas the knights of the other versions suffer manipulation at the hands of strangers, making their characters far more sympathetic.

The circumstances under which the knight-hero first encounters the loathly lady further distinguish the narratives. The Wife of Bath tells us that the knight, after searching for the answer until "the day was come that homward moste he tourne" [the day had come that he must turn homeward], meets the loathly lady in a glade he passes on his way home (988). Chaucer is careful to point out that the knight heads home only "Whan that he saugh he myghte nat come therby . . . what wommen love moost" [When he saw that he might not come thereby . . . what women love most] (984–5); in other words, the knight has given up—he has admitted that he does not know what women want, can not name it and thus assert control over it—when he "chances" upon the true answer. *Wedding*'s Arthur, on the other hand, returns from his search with "a monethe" left, and decides to "seke a lytelle more / In Yngleswod Forest" when he meets Dame Ragnelle [a month; seek a little more in Inglewood Forest] (216–7). Arthur receives his answer while in pursuit of it, whereas Chaucer's knight is rescued by circumstance (much like his earlier rescue by the Queen and her ladies), or more specifically, by the chance intervention of a woman. The popular romance casts its hero as an active participant in his own salvation; had Arthur not decided to search further, he may not have been saved. *Wife's Tale*, on the other hand, presents a relatively passive knight saved purely by the intervention of female characters.

Once the wedding has been negotiated, the answer given, and his life saved, the knight-hero in the three versions of the loathly lady romance not penned by Chaucer does not have much else to do. Whereas Chaucer's knight must listen to a lecture of over one hundred lines from his new wife and make a difficult decision before any change happens, Gawain and Florent simply agree to consummate their marriages and are immediately rewarded by seeing their wives transformed into beautiful maidens. In *Wedding*, Dame Ragnelle requests that Gawain "kysse [her] att the leste," and Gawain replies by assuring her that he "wolle do more / Then

From Rags To Riches, or The Step-Mother's Revenge   81

for to kysse" [kiss her at least; will do more than kiss] (639). Immediately, Dame Ragnelle becomes "the fayrest creature / That evere he sawe, withoute measure" [the fairest creature that ever he saw, without measure] (641–2). Gawain, already rewarded with a beautiful wife, is then offered the choice between having a wife who is "fayre on nyghtes" and "foulle on days" or just the opposite [fair at night; foul during the day]. Similarly, in *Florent* the knight turns away from his bride when he sees her naked body, but after some pleading, she convinces him to turn back towards her. When he sees her, she has already transformed into a beautiful maiden of eighteen.

In *Wife's Tale*, the above sequence of events is altered. Before he agrees to anything—before he even speaks in response to the long lecture, the lady presents Chaucer's rapist-knight with the question of whether he would prefer an ugly, but "trewe, humble wyf" or a "yong and fair" bride likely to have extra-marital urges [true, humble wife; young and fair] (1221, 1223). His inability to make a choice between these two undesirable options, as indicated by his "sore" sighs, is presumably one of the things that prompts him to offer the choice to his wife (1228). Importantly, though, the knight in Chaucer's tale chooses to grant his wife sovereignty before being rewarded with his wife's announcement that she will be "bothe fair and good" (1241). Chaucer's knight does not get to make his decision while looking at a lovely damsel, nor is he assured of a beautiful wife at least half the time, regardless of his decision, as are Gawain and Florent. In the version of the tale offered by *Wedding*, *Florent*, and *Marriage*, the knight's decision to let the bride decide her own fate seems perfunctory when compared to the decision Chaucer's knight grants his lady. The genre more commonly features the transformation of the loathly lady (and thus the knight's decision can be superficial), but Chaucer's focus on the transformation of the knight necessitates a more substantial choice.

Whether Chaucer's focus on the female characters and women's desire for sovereignty is the result of his appropriation of a lost text, the manifestation of his "reading" of the tale, or a variation deliberately altered to suit the Wife of Bath's character is less important than the effect of his decision to present the familiar loathly lady tale in the manner he did. Chaucer's tale is clearly about the rehabilitation of an errant knight, whereas the focus of the later popular romances is parallel to that of the churlish knight, transformation through interaction with the most chivalrous knight. *Wife's Tale* is unique among surviving versions of the loathly lady legend in its representation of women as central figures of authority and controllers of the action. Chaucer's adaptation of the legend allows the Wife of Bath to transform a phallocentric interrogation of women into a literary world where women can effect positive changes in the men around them, where "sovereignty" is not merely a dream, but a powerful truth.

82   *Crafting the Witch*

Part of what gives Chaucer's loathly lady such power is the fact that she seems to have enchanted herself. We do not know what originally caused her transformation into loathly lady, and the omission of that important information has the effect of suggesting that the loathly lady is herself in control of transformative power. This is another point at which Chaucer's version of the make-over narrative differs from the rest; usually, there is some additional agent of transformation, some person who causes the grotesque to be grotesque in the first place, thus setting the entire chain of events into motion. Someone created the wrong that the knight-hero must right, and that someone is the final piece of our puzzle. Who's the villain? The answer is easy: the wicked witch.

V. STEPMOTHERS ARE WICKED: THE WITCH AS EVIL MOTHER

If it is the knight-hero (usually Gawain) acting as the ideal representative of aristocratic knighthood who breaks the spell enchanting the grotesques, who is it that bewitches them in the first place? What force turns a noble knight into a grotesque churl, or a beautiful maiden into a loathly hag? These romances offer only two alternatives: 1) they did it themselves, or 2) a witch transformed them. We have already seen how Chaucer's loathly lady seems to have enchanted herself. Likewise, in *Carle*, the churl is responsible for his own initial transformation: twenty years ago, the churl "maked a vowe" to God, saying "Ther schulde never man logge in my wonys / But he scholde be slayne, iwys, / But he did as I hym bad" [made a vow; there should never any man lodge in my dwelling, but he should be slain, in truth, unless he did as I bade him] (518, 520–3). Just as Merlin controlled the way others perceived him in the chronicles, this knight can summon divine power to achieve his metamorphosis into a churl. His oath is effective, as his reputation attests, and Gawain is the only one to whom God grants the victory. This form of transformative power, which relies on the divinity for its efficacy, links chivalric courtesy with Christian morality: God rewards the perfect knight. But *Carle* and *Wife's Tale* are in the minority: most of the tales assign responsibility for transformation to a specific villain. The villainous wielder of transformative power in these romances is that nefarious figure, my obsession in this study, the wicked witch.

Let's start with a witch we've seen before, a familiar face from both the romance and chronicle traditions, Morgan le Fay. *SGGK* relies on Morgan le Fay's reputation within both the romance and chronicle traditions, positioning her as a famous magic-worker with the power to heal a knight whose head has been chopped off. The Morgan of *SGGK* is a far more ambivalent figure than the royal half-sister with whom twelfth-century Arthurian audiences were so familiar. Unlike the chronicle tradition, in which Morgan is a beautiful lady, her physical appearance in *SGGK* is

From Rags To Riches, or The Step-Mother's Revenge 83

grotesque, and the poet explains precisely what's wrong with her by comparing her hideousness to the beauty of Lady Bertilak:

Bot, vnlyke on to loke þo ladyes were,
For if þe ȝonge watȝ ȝep, ȝolȝe watȝ þat oþer.
Riche red on þat on rayled ayquere;
Rugh, ronkled chekeȝ þat oþer rolled.
Kerchofes of þat on, wyth mony cler perleȝ,
Hir brest and hir bryȝt þrote bare displayed,
Schon schyrerþen snawe þat schedeȝ on hilleȝ.
þat oþer wyth a gorger watȝ gere ouer þe swyre,
Chymbled ouer hir blake chyn wyth mylk-quyte vayles;
Hir frount folden in sylk, enfoubled ayquere,
Toret and treleted wyth tryfleȝ aboute,
þat noȝt watȝ bare of þat burde bot þe blake broȝes,
þe tweyne yȝen and þe nase, þe naked lyppeȝ,
And þose were soure to se, and sellyly blered.

But unlike to look upon those ladies were,
for if the young was vibrant, withered was the other.
Rich red adorned the one's face everywhere;
rough, wrinkled cheeks rolled down on the other.
Kerchiefs on the one, with many clear pearls,
her breast and her bright throat displayed bare,
shining more brightly than snow shed on hills.
That other with a gorget was clothed over the neck,
bound over her black chin with milk-white veils;
her front wrapped in silk, veiled every where,
with embroidered edges and meshed with details about,
so that nothing was bare on that bird but the black brows,
the two eyes, and the nose, the naked lips,
and those were sour to see, and extremely bleared.

(950–63)

Preceding and following this description, which is remarkably similar to descriptions of the loathly lady, the narrator asserts that Morgan is "hegly honowred wyth haþeleȝ aboute" and "a mensk lady on molde" [highly honored with nobles all around; an honored lady on the earth] (949, 964). By juxtaposing claims to the ancient lady's honor with a long statement of how ugly she is, the poet creates an ambivalent picture—she is noble and important but ugly and old. Her duality is another side of the carnivalesque inversion represented by the grotesques; because she is noble, her grotesque physical appearance subverts the usual privileging of beauty as nobility, turning conventions of ideal femininity upside-down. Through this description in particular, the *SGGK* poet explicitly invokes the figure of the loathly

84 Crafting the Witch

lady. The loathly lady, like the churlish knight, presents a grotesque exterior which hides a "good" interior—for the loathly lady, it is a conventionally feminine interior. But Morgan is not a loathly lady, exactly, as her appearance does not change; instead, she's the one who transforms others.

In the case of Morgan le Fay, the golden nugget her loathly exterior disguises is her transformative power. The poet takes great pains to obfuscate Morgan's identity early in the poem; he describes her at length, but gives her no name, and hides her true function in this churlish knight story by appropriating the conventions of the corollary tale of the loathly lady. The narrator preserves the mystery until the shocking revelation of her true identity in the last section of the poem. Gawain asks the churlish Green Knight to say his name, and he replies:

Bercilak de Hautdesert, I hat in þis londe	Bercilak of Hautdesert, I am called in this land
þurȝ myȝt of Morgne la Faye, þat in my hous lenges,	through might of Morgan le Fay, who in my house lives,
And koyntyse of clergye bi craftes wel lerned,	and knowledge of lore through crafts well learned,
þe maystrés of Merlyn mony ho taken,	the mysteries of Merlin many has she acquired,
For ho hatȝ dalt drwry ful dere sumtyme	for she had dallied in delight once
With þat conable klerk; þat knowes alle your knyȝteȝ	with that competent master; all your knights know that
at hame.	at home.
Morgne þe goddes	Morgan the goddess
þerfore, hit is hir name;	therefore, it is her name;
Weldeg non so hyȝe hawtesses	none wield so much pride
þat ho ne con make ful tame.	whom she cannot make fully tame.

(2445–55)

Bertilak's explanation names Morgan as the force behind his political power, through her magical craft. He calls her a "goddes" [goddess] (rather than a witch), but there are enough goddess-witch figures traipsing around classical literature to provide a model for this kind of witch (Medea and Circe are two examples that immediately come to mind). In addition to authenticating Bertilak's lordship, Morgan devises the plan to send him to Arthur's court, "For to assay þe surquidre, ȝif hit soth were / þat rennes of þe grete renoun of þe Rounde Table" [In order to test the pride, whether it was true, that which has spread, (rumor) of the great renoun of the Round Table] (2457–8). Assessing the pride of the Round Table knights is certainly a worthy reason to send a knight to court, in the world of romance—such a test allows the knights to show their courage and flaunt their courtesy. This makes Morgan seem like an ally of the court, helping the nobles to realize their flaws and therefore correct them. But Bertilak's explanation includes a strange detail:

Ho wayued me þis wonder your wytteȝ to reue,	She cast this enchantment on me to remove your wits,
For to haf greued Gaynour and gart hir to dyȝe	for to have grieved Gwenevere and caused her to die
Wyth gopnyng of þat ilke gomen þat gostlych speked	with the sight of that same man who spoke frighteningly
With his hede in his honde birfore hyȝe table.	with his head in his hand before the the high table.

(2459–62)

Apparently, in addition to testing the court, Morgan wanted to scare Gwenevere to death. The inclusion of this detail casts doubt over the entire enterprise; if the whole thing was just a way for one woman to hurt another woman, then what does it mean? Is it really a test of the Round Table?

SGGK's Morgan le Fay, the witch-goddess lurking behind the carnivalesque churl who invades Arthur's hall and threatens Gawain's life, is a problematic figure. Is she good or bad? Does she want to hurt the queen or help the court? Is she loathly or honorable? Is she a powerful magical force or merely Merlin's lackey? Is she marginal or foundational to the story (or both)? It's difficult to say exactly how Morgan functions within this complex narrative, as evinced by the still-raging critical debates about her character. Part of that difficulty can be attributed to the deliberately ambiguous and ambivalent representation of her figure in the poem, but part of the trouble comes from the poem's overarching narrative arc, which critiques the feminizing influence of courtly behavior on the violent masculinity of knights. Though it would be difficult to characterize her representation in this poem as entirely positive, it would also be difficult to argue that she is simply villainized. The villainization of the witch-figure in the make-over narrative is readily apparent, however, in the rest of the romances considered here.

Grene, for example, the late-fifteenth-century adaptation of *SGGK*, turns Morgan into Agostes, a decidedly wicked witch (and the Grene Knight's mother-in-law to boot!). The *Greene* poet does not merely name the witch, but provides a detailed description of her powers:

Itt was witchcraft and noe other That shee dealt with all	It was witchcraft and no other that she dealt with.
Shee cold transpose knights and swaine	She could transform knights and servants
Like as in battaile they were slaine,	(to look) as though they had been slain in battle,
Wounded in lim and lightt.	wounded in arm and leg.
Shee taught her sonne the knight alsoe	She taught her son the knight also,
In transposed likenesse he shold goe	(so that) he could go in transformed disguise,
Both by fell and frythe.	both by moor and by the woods.

(50–7)

86 *Crafting the Witch*

The text explicitly designates "witchcraft" as transformative, transferable power—witches like Agostes can make things appear different than they are, and they can pass their magical knowledge on to others. This magical heritage is assured, definitive, unlike the problematic inheritance of land (which may or may not bring money in post-plague England) or nobility (which can be simulated by wealthy upstarts).

The *Greene* author provides a less ambiguous explanation of the churl's interest in Arthur's court (and Gawain in particular) than does the *SGGK* poet. Agostes's daughter, married to Bredbeddle, is in love with Sir Gawain because of his prowess in battle. Agostes sends Bredbeddle to court with the hope of luring Gawain to their castle so her daughter can meet him. Bredbeddle's reasons for taking the trip echo those of *SGGK*'s Bertilak:

To Arthurs court will I mee hye	To Arthur's court will I go
For to praise thee right,	to give you [the court] your due,
And to prove Gawaines points three—	and to test Gawain in three areas,
And that be true that men tell me,	whether that which men tell me is true,
By Mary most of might.	by Mary, most mighty.

(68–72)

The transformation sequence in *Greene* is a deliberate test of a specific knight in the court, as in *SGGK*, but the motives of the witch are not ambiguous at all. Agostes tries to help her daughter commit adultery, a sin that not only undermines the foundation of Christian marriage, but, should Gawain comply, also threatens his reputation as a noble knight. Agostes's tactic is trickery and illusion, and it is only because Bredbeddle already knew about his wife's interest in Gawain that the happy ending is possible. Here, masculine chivalric behavior contains and subverts the attempts of women to enact (inappropriate) female desire. Agostes attempts to provide her daughter access to a famous knight, in effect side-stepping the aristocratic reliance on patriarchal marriage, in which female desire is unimportant. Just as the transformation of the grotesques eases anxiety about the changing economy, the foiling of Agostes provides reassurance that even witchcraft can't successfully challenge convention as long as men loyally support one another. Female agency is no match for male chivalry!

The ability of hierarchical chivalric behavior to combat subversive female agency grounds the representation of the witchy villain in *Carlisle* as well. The author of *Carlisle* doesn't name or describe the witch directly, preferring to leave her in the shadows, and provides only the following explanation:

The Carle sayd, "Gawaine, God blese thee!	The Carl said, "Gawain, God bless you!
For thou hast delivered mee	For you have delivered me
From all false witchcrafft—	from all false witchcraft—

From Rags To Riches, or The Step-Mother's Revenge 87

I am delivered att the last.	I am delivered at last.
By nigromancé thus was I shapen,	By necromancy thus was I shaped,
Till a knight of the Round Table	until a knight of the Round Table
Had with a sword smitten of my head,	had with a sword smitten off my head,
If he had grace to doe that deede."	if he had the grace to do the deed."

(401–08)

The churl does not say it was a witch who transformed him, but the term "witchcrafft" implies the unnamed witch. The poet neglects establishing clear motivation for the witch's transformation of the churl—unlike the descriptions of Morgan and Agostes, here we have no sense of what the witch might gain from transforming a knight into a churl. All we know is that her witchcraft is "false" and that she uses "nigromancy," a medieval variation of the classical form of magic known as necromancy (raising the dead). The shift in spelling is significant: this is "nigro" or "black" magic. The association of witchcraft with deception and evil magic leaves no ambiguity—this is no healer-lady, no helpful magic-user or goddess. This is a wicked witch.

Unlike the witches of the churlish knight story—a goddess, a mother-in-law, and an unknown, generic witch—the wicked witches of the loathly lady romances are far more uniform: in all three of the loathly lady romances featuring witches, the perpetrator is the loathly lady's evil step-mother. In *Wedding*, for example, Ragnelle tells Gawain that she was "shapen by nygramancy" and "by enchauntement" at the hands of her "stepdame" [created by necromancy; by enchantment; step-mother] (691–3). She was doomed to appear loathly, as she says:

Evyn tylle the best of Englond	Until the best (knight) in England
Had wedyd me verament,	had wedded me truly,
And also he shold geve me the sovereynte	and also should give me sovereignty
Of alle his body and goodes, sycurly.	over his whole body and all his goods, surely.
Thus was I disformyd.	In this manner was I deformed.

(695–9)

The step-mother enchants Ragnelle, forcing her to live in the woods, without a home or family, until she finds herself a husband who will grant her property and wealth. The enchantment effectively rids the step-mother of an irksome heir, a child who might challenge the step-mother's access to her husband's possessions; the condition of unenchantment, marriage to a worthy and wealthy knight, ensures that the daughter's potential threat as heir will be forever neutralized. Once a medieval daughter marries, she is no longer her father's (or her step-mother's) problem—marriage makes her the legal responsibility of her husband.

The situation is similar in Gower's version of the tale. Florent finds himself married to the daughter of the King of Cizile, who tells him:

88   *Crafting the Witch*

My Stepmoder for an hate,	My stepmother, because of the hate
Which toward me sche hath begonne,	She had developed towards me,
Forschop me, til I hadde wonne	Transformed me until I had won
The love and sovereinete	The love and sovereignty
Of what knyht that in his degree	Of whichever knight of his station
Alle othre passeth of good name.	Exceeds all other knights of good name.

(1844–49)

Here, as in *Wedding,* the step-mother's witchcraft ensures that the daughter will remain loathly (and thus unrecognizable as her father's daughter) until she obtains a new, wealthy warder. In this version, the hate of the step-mother for her step-daughter takes a privileged position: it's the first detail we learn. This is the only loathly lady story to provide an overtly-stated reason for the step-mother's witchy behavior, but the logic is circular at best: the step-mother bewitched her step-daughter because she hated her.

In *Marriage,* the confession scene is likewise familiar, though interrupted by a missing page in the manuscript. The loathly lady tells the story of her father, "an old knight" who married "a younge lady":

Shee witched me, being a faire young lady,	She bewitched me, being a fair young lady,
To the green forrest to dwell,	(Banishing me) to the green forest to dwell,
And there I must walke in womans likenesse,	And there I must walk in this woman's likeness,
Most like a feeind of hell.	Most like a fiend of hell.
She witched my brother to a carlish B—	She bewitched my brother into a churlish B—

(179–83)

The writing stops here, with what may have been the word "baron," implying that the wicked step-mother bewitched both children born to her husband's first wife. Though we are not privy to the conditions of the enchantment because of the manuscript damage, the tale's resolution is the same as the other versions, implying that this daughter, too, must marry to escape the wrath of her step-mother. Must step-mothers hate their daughters? These medieval authors do not spend time explaining the step-mother's antagonism, treating it as a self-evident fact. Who is this evil mother who lurks behind transformative power, using it to punish her step-children?

Of the nine loathly lady and churlish knight romances considered here, six feature witches as the villainous wielders of transformative power. Of those six witches, four are mothers—three step-mothers and one mother-in-law. What's up with all these evil mothers? Psychoanalytical theory has an answer for mother-hate, and one that I believe makes sense when applied to individual psychology.[29] What psychoanalytical theory does not explain,

From Rags To Riches, or The Step-Mother's Revenge 89

however, is why the fourteenth and fifteenth centuries saw the rise of villainized mother-figures (cast as witches) in its popular literature. Earlier Arthurian tales do not utilize the witch as a villain; the villains of Chrétien and Geoffrey are giants whose threat is physical rather than economic. Anxiety about land ownership comes to its climax with the new maternal breed of villains who populate these make-over stories. The wicked witches are the ones who try to dispossess the grotesques, who initiate the action, and on whom blame securely falls. The replacement of evil giants with evil mothers is the crux of the connection between the rise of witches in the Arthurian tradition and the tension created by the shift from a feudal to a capitalist economy.

As we have seen, the rise of the wicked step-mother begins in the fourteenth century, after the decline of Norman feudalism saw a nascent mercantile economy grow in its vacancy. During and after the crises of the fourteenth century, witches begin to appear frequently in a genre where they had not appeared before, and their representation is intimately connected to an ideological crisis precipitated by the decreasing value of land and increasing value of capital, as demonstrated by the make-overs of the third-estate grotesques. Economic factors may have created class-based tension, but this does not explain why wicked witches should suddenly become prevalent in a literary genre where they had previously been rare, why step-mothers who possess magical power should be evil. Germane to this study is the following question: if economic changes created class tension, did that class tension increase for women and, more specifically, for step-mothers? This is no easy question to answer, especially since people disagree when delineating the ramifications of nascent capitalism on women's lives in the late medieval and Renaissance periods. The dominant version of the story goes like this: because the emergent mercantile economy and the labor crisis precipitated by the plague blurred the boundaries of the previously rigid class system, making it more fluid, women enjoyed increased economic power and a temporary reprieve from some of the most oppressive aspects of feudal life.[30] Specifically, there are two changes that have special relevance for the mothers of the make-over narratives: an increase in female property-ownership due to changing inheritance laws and an increase in the number of women involved in the workforce.

In feudal England, women stood to inherit very little, especially if they had brothers. They could be reasonably sure they would receive their dower portion if widowed, but children (especially sons) often challenged their ownership or usufruct of dowered land.[31] By the fourteenth century, noblewomen were becoming more successful at holding their dower against the claims of children, and widows increasingly served as guardians of their underage children (rather than being considered the "ward" of their male children) and administrators of family lands.[32] Kim Phillips argues that female landholding rose during the fourteenth century, demonstrating that on the Havering manor in Essex, in 1251, 11.5% of the tenants were female,

90 Crafting the Witch

but by 1352–3, the number of female tenants had risen to 17% (123–6). On another manor, Englefield, in Berkshire, 32% of the landholders were women in 1349 (126–7). Frances and Joseph Gies pinpoint the development of jointure, a new type of marital contract providing for "joint tenancy of land by husband and wife during their lifetime," as contributing to the rise in female administration and ownership of land (190). Upon the death of her husband, "A jointured widow might acquire most or even all of her husband's estates instead of merely the dower third" (190). In the wake of labor shortages precipitated by the plague, land became more available to both men and women, and female landholders were responsible for the same kinds of rent and service obligations as male tenants.

If the landholding, rural communities more frequently saw women playing roles as estate "lords" and heads of household, the urban communities watched women perform larger roles within the trade economy. P. J. P. Goldberg has found evidence that women's involvement in trade in towns increased throughout the fourteenth century, reaching its height in the early fifteenth century.[33] In particular, women were active in the many guilds, and female membership in guilds was not prohibited until the mid-fifteenth century. Women could conduct business in most towns as a *femme sole*, which allowed them to trade without a male representative and released their husbands from any debt they might incur. Helen Jewell pinpoints the most common trades engaged in by women, including victualling and many aspects of the textile industry (such as seamstresses, silkweavers, and spinners); women participated with lesser frequency in leatherworking and metalworking (92–3). Goldberg's work also provides evidence for another area in which urban women were often employed, domestic service. In urban areas, twenty to thirty percent of the population were employed as domestic servants (as opposed to ten percent in rural areas); in towns, most of the servants employed were women, whereas in the more agricultural rural areas, servants were more commonly men.[34] Frances and Joseph Gies argue that even in rural areas, after the Black Death, "a considerable number of the laborers were unattached women" (239). In part because of the changing economic system and in part because of the labor shortage after the plague, then, women apparently played an expanded role in the developing mercantile economy of the fourteenth and early fifteenth centuries.

So who did enjoy the benefits of the changing economy? Which women were most affected by economic opportunity, and which women went about their daily lives unaware that later scholars would pinpoint them as beneficiaries of a historical windfall? The extent to which economic changes affected women's lives depended almost entirely upon their relationship to men, whether they were singlewomen, wives, or widows. While married, wives could expect their husbands to represent them in the public world in many circumstances and on most occasions: in court, in property-ownership, in legal documents, in business (with some urban exceptions), in almost every arena except the domestic sphere. Legal power is not the

From Rags To Riches, or The Step-Mother's Revenge   91

only kind of power, as we know, and the simple fact of a husband's presence does not preclude his wife's participation in decisions; we need only to glance briefly at the Paston letters to see evidence of wives acting as powerful partners in their husbands' businesses and households, acting with a great degree of autonomy in the patriarchs' absence.

The basic economic unit in both rural and urban economies seems to have been the family—a husband and wife team working with children and (sometimes) parents or other relatives to secure the household's survival. Married women participating in urban trade most commonly worked with or for their husbands (with the exception of women who acted as *femme sole*), assisting the family trade, sometimes while also baking, brewing, or sewing to supplement the family income. Dyer, for example, argues that especially in the early stages of the shift to a mercantile economy, working-class wives were increasingly expected to contribute to the family's income, and this change increased women's economic power within the family while adding yet another marital obligation (159). Rural wives performed similar functions in their family's agricultural or pastoral endeavors; while the husband worked the field or tended animals, the wives ran the house, cooking, cleaning, caring for children, brewing, raising vegetables and herbs, tending pigs or chickens, making, mending, and laundering clothes, and pitching in with the farming, especially at harvest time, while also sometimes attempting a small business (such as selling ale or textile products). What this means is that wives did play an expanded role in the economy, and while sometimes that role became a public one, more often than not it was a role within a family unit. Wives benefited within the family, so an individual wife's access to personal and public power ultimately depended upon the socio-economic and idiosyncratic circumstances of her family— something which was just as true in the feudal period as in the changing fourteenth and fifteenth centuries.

If the effect of the changing economy on wives was dependent upon individual familial situations, the impact on widows was less ambiguous. Widows, especially of landholding and wealthy merchant families, enjoyed a marked increase in legal and economic autonomy in the fourteenth and early fifteenth centuries. Claudia Opitz identifies three areas in which widows gained legal independence after the thirteenth century: 1) the right to distribute and dispose of property, 2) the right to serve as guardian of underage children (rather than as a ward of their male children), and 3) the right to inherit and assume control of a guild business (308–11). Though widows still needed a male representative when bringing suit in court or completing official documents, the above changes afforded many widows the opportunity to govern their own lives, sometimes for the first time in their lives. Widows had a great deal of autonomy in choosing both whether to remarry (though they sometimes experienced great pressure to do so) and whom they would marry.[35] When they chose not to remarry, they usually headed their own households or ran their own estates; in fact, Jewell

92   Crafting the Witch

suggests that some noble and gentry widows controlled their dower and jointure lands to the detriment of male heirs (147). Though widows certainly did not enjoy the kind of legal and economic autonomy available to men within their class, they were, as a group, the medieval women with the most economic agency.

The last group impacted significantly by the economic changes of late medieval England with relevance for this study is young, unmarried women. Overwhelmingly, singlewomen in urban areas worked in domestic service. They often migrated from the countryside and worked in the households of merchant and victuallers, sometimes compensated only with room and board, sometimes with wages (earning roughly one-half the wages of their male counterparts).[36] Outside of service, the most common occupation for unmarried women was spinster, and because women employed as spinsters were poorly compensated, they often lived communally and relied on charity to make ends meet (Jewell 109–110). The other occupation frequently engaged in by unmarried women was prostitution, but it is extremely difficult to determine to what extent singlewomen were engaged in prostitution as a viable economic option.[37] By the beginning of the fourteenth century, argues Judith Bennett, young unmarried women had a temporary, but significant, access to power: gifts often placed them in control of large amounts of land and they received the benefits of participation in the legal system in their own right ("Public Power" 22–23). Marriage, of course, ended this temporary access to power. Singlewomen married later in the fourteenth and fifteenth centuries than they had in feudal England (in their twenties rather than late teens), which offered them the chance to play a larger role in choosing their husbands. As Judith Bennett and Amy Froide note, while singlewomen and widows generally had fewer resources than married women, they usually had more freedom in administering those resources (*Singlewomen* 14).

The expansion of women's economic power provides a compelling explanation for the kind of economic scapegoating apparent in the late medieval make-over narratives. We must consider the impact of economic shifts carefully, however, as it is difficult to determine the extent to which these changes affected the day-to-day existence of most women. How can we determine the real effects of economic changes on women's lives when those women are long dead and the extant texts that have been published frequently leave women out of the picture or on the sidelines (and those which haven't been published are, of course, readable only by those trained in both medieval languages and paleography)? Judith Bennett notes that while late medieval women did contribute more fully to the economy than in previous centuries, those contributions were almost exclusively situated in the domestic realm, even when those women were single ("Medieval Women" 51–3). Women were employed most frequently in "domestic service, but also laundering, making clothes, and victualing," areas which have traditionally been devalued in every capitalist economy, including that

From Rags To Riches, or The Step-Mother's Revenge 93

of twenty-first-century America. Though women's domestic work perhaps had the potential to earn more money than in previous centuries, Bennett argues that "women were firmly subordinated to men in the productive functions of the medieval family economy" (52). While women clearly had a larger role in production as the economy shifted, this does not necessarily mean that all women enjoyed equally large gains in relative power. The two groups of women whose gains were most significant, and who were therefore most able to step outside traditional gender roles as the economy developed, were widows and young, unmarried women. Bennett describes the situation as follows: "As long as adolescent daughters had to prepare for independent marriage and widows had to take over the households left by their husbands, power wielded by women, no matter how anomalous, had to be tolerated" ("Public Power" 24).

Not only did widows and young, unmarried women wield more power than previously, demographic shifts meant that these two groups comprised a greater percentage of the population than ever before. According to Maryanne Kowaleski, in England in 1377, women who had not ever been married comprised about one-third of the adult female population over fourteen, twice the number of singlewomen in Italy around the same time ("The Demographic Perspective" 46). Elsewhere, Kowaleski examines the number of widows in pre-plague London, citing that "about 61 percent of male testators left surviving widows" ("The History of Urban Families" 55). This percentage rises to 82 in urban areas by the end of the century (55). Lisa Bitel makes the case that women outnumbered men in England after the plague, a disparity which increased the numbers of widows and singlewomen and facilitated the temporary relaxation of the strictly gendered division of labor characteristic of the feudal economy (232–6).

If the economic changes impacted widows and singlewomen most drastically, what does that have to do with lurking and plotting wicked witches, those dispossessing meddlers of the late medieval make-over tales? The wicked witches of the make-over narratives are mothers, but not birth mothers: they are step-mothers and mothers-in-law. While mothers-in-law might be married, they might also be widows. Indeed, Agostes, the mother-in-law in *Greene*, operates as a *witch sole*, working her magic without the nuisance of a husband; as she has a daughter, the implication is that she's a widow. As women cannot legally remarry while currently married, it is clearly young, unmarried women and widows who are available to be step-mothers. In fact, the narrator of *Marriage* tells us explicitly that the witch is a "faire young lady" (i.e., a singlewoman) who married an old widower knight (175). According to the Gieses, young widows often remarried, a situation fraught with potential perils: "the remarrying young widow (or the girl marrying a widower) frequently found herself confronted with another problem: stepchildren" (284). Because of the changing inheritance laws, "Stepchildren sometimes sued stepparents over rights to property" (285). The conflict over economic power in the make-over narratives points the finger squarely at

94 *Crafting the Witch*

usurping widows and young women. Step-mothers are threatening in part because they can potentially disinherit children, and this threat finds its metaphor in the transformation of the attractive, upper-class child into the grotesque, lower-class loathly lady or churlish knight by the step-mother. Doing the chivalric thing, following the rules, these romances tell us, will restore the children to their rightful state (as landowners).[38]

If on the one hand, step-mothers pose a threat to their stepchildren because of their increased power to hold land, the other hand finds them in a unique position in relation to maternity. In the medieval world, the primary role designated for women is a domestic one, focused on bearing and raising children and maintaining the household in which those children are raised. The presence of large numbers of unmarried women with the potential to support themselves (albeit often barely) threatens an essentialist view of females as mothers. What will happen to the maternal bond when women can achieve power and value without bearing children? The daughter-hating step-mother manifests a cultural anxiety about the possibilities open to women who usurp the position of birth-mother. Though the material existence of all medieval English women may not have been drastically altered by the economic and legal shifts described above, we must be careful not to underestimate the potential threat of even small ideological and economic shifts. The make-over romances considered here respond to the newly-developed possibilities for female economic and legal agency; they mitigate an anxiety about the effect of increased economic power on the traditional familial position of women as mothers, representing the potentially disastrous ramifications of motherhood gone awry in the figure of the wicked witch. In early modern England, when the population was faced with a living example of strong, capable, and (perhaps most importantly) non-maternal female power, as embodied by the unmarried and childless Queen Elizabeth I, the anxiety was surely even more intense, a fact that has received no small amount of attention in early modern studies.

In fact, the connection between maternity (or its lack) and witches occupies an important place in Renaissance scholarship. Diane Purkiss argues that in early modern England, "some women's stories of witchcraft constituted a powerful fantasy which enabled women to negotiate the fears and anxieties of housekeeping and motherhood" (93). Purkiss also examines the way in which the body of the witch in Renaissance texts is a "fantasy-image of the huge, controlling, scattered, polluted, leaky fantasy of the maternal body" (119). Deborah Willis argues also that "the figure of the witch was closely intertwined with that of the mother" (17). In an analysis of witchcraft conflicts at the village level in England, Willis notes that "early modern women and men were most likely to fear a specifically magical danger when they got angry at someone who resembled their mother or nurse" (29). Both Purkiss and Willis situate the conflation of witchcraft and motherhood as an early modern phenomenon. Based on the examples considered here, it may be that the association of motherhood and witchcraft has its roots in medieval soil.

From Rags To Riches, or The Step-Mother's Revenge 95

We are still keenly aware of the delicate economic situation of non-traditional families, and our literature and film reveals our continued anxiety over the role of mothers and step-mothers within the family. The director of *Ever After* (1998), a recent cinematic adaptation of *Cinderella*—perhaps the most well-known make-over story in western literature—represents the conflict between the daughter and the step-mother as rooted in common interest in ownership and management of the land once belonging to the deceased father/husband. In this film, Drew Barrymore's Cinderella (Danielle de Barbarac) becomes a servant in her father's home after he dies suddenly, under the rule of the petty, self-centered step-mother, Baroness Rodmilla de Ghent (played with delightful wickedness by Angelica Huston). Danielle expresses her interest in her father's manor when she tells a friend that she would be glad if her step-sister married the prince, because the step-family would then move to the castle and she would be free to "turn things around" on her struggling farm. Certainly one thing to keep in mind as we consider any version of Cinderella is that, at its core, this is a story about a bad mother—a mother who abuses her power to help or hurt the children in her care.

Though there are likely to be as many factors involved in the late medieval rise of the romance wicked witch as there are surviving manuscripts, what is clear is that her popular literary debut was a resounding success. She appeared with more frequency as the fifteenth century wore on, and by the sixteenth century, she was everywhere. The wicked witch retains her maternity as she travels into the Renaissance, and in many ways the maternal connection grows more intense and more complicated. In the late medieval romances, the step-mother is certainly wicked, but like the modern make-over fairy-tale, her power can easily be thwarted if folks just follow the (aristocratic) rules. The wicked witches of the Renaissance are more slippery, less easy to tame or outdo, more sinister and more exaggerated as well. The early modern maternal witch is not merely bad, but downright evil, and magic itself becomes suspect and frightening. Something wicked this way comes.

4 The Lady is a Hag
Three Writers and the Transformation of Magic in Sixteenth-Century England

I. WHO IS THE FAIREST ONE OF ALL?

The first thing we hear from the lips of the Wicked Queen in Disney's *Snow White* isn't the line for which she is famous, the line repeated by generations of American children, "Magic mirror on the wall, who is the fairest one of all?" Instead, her first words summon the spirit within the magic mirror, commanding her "slave" from the "furthest spaces" to attend her. Her spirit possesses secret knowledge, knowledge that allows the queen to make important personal decisions, like whether or not to kill her step-daughter because of her unparalleled beauty. The evil Queen is known for being vain and self-serving, but we seldom remember that she's a conjurer of mysterious, knowledgeable spirits. First and foremost, in fact, the Queen is a conjurer, what medieval and Renaissance audiences might have called a necromancer or a demonologist.

Her interest in beauty is undeniable—she does seem to care very deeply about her success on the local fashion scene. Isn't it true that beauty is power, after all? Especially for women, the (beauty) myth goes.[1] The Queen is quite shrewd, actually, to watch the competition closely, but her Machiavellian tactics in her dealings with Snow White make her unsympathetic. Some mother, right? Her apparently vain interest in outward appearance only seems vain when read in the context of the late twentieth-century U.S., where it has become unfashionable to value beauty overtly (even as our mass media joyously engages in worshipful adoration of outward beauty and youth). In medieval texts, as we have seen, outward physical appearance reflects inward moral character: when we meet a grotesque hag in the forest or a club-wielding giant on the road, it is a clear signal that Something is Up. But the evil step-mother of Disney's *Snow White* is not a grotesque hag, nor does she have the exaggerated features of the "ugly" sisters in *Cinderella*, Drizella and Anastasia, though her story is also an adaptation of a fairy tale collected by the Grimms (called "Schneewittchen"). Quite the contrary, in fact—she's beautiful, with sumptuous clothing and a delicate red mouth under dark, mysterious eyes. The action of the tale requires the Queen to be vain about her beauty.

I think the Wicked Queen is quite lovely. But as far back as I can remember, whenever I watched the film, she scared the bejesus out of me. When

The Lady is a Hag 97

her pale face first appears, reflected in the smoky magic mirror, it still sends shivers skating across the back of my neck. She's beautiful, but she's ee-vil! She's the opposite of the loathly lady, whose grotesque shell hides a pearl of goodness: the queen's beautiful veneer covers a core of pure hatred and ill will. Her transformation into the old hag with the tempting apple reconstructs her figure in a way that aligns it more closely with medieval typology—it is as if her moral character has been moved from the inside to the outside, the mask removed. Again, this feels like the loathly lady story in reverse, except that the transformation is supposed to make the lady less threatening. But what's less threatening about the classic witch-hag figure, the old lady stooping and hunching her way up to a little cottage, eyes glittering maniacally over a warty nose and cragged features?

What's less threatening is that in her hag guise, the Wicked Queen is recognizable as wicked (at least by the audience, as Snow White seems to have no sense about these things). She fits the profile. In the U.S., a number of horror and thriller movies which did very well at the box office feature villains who are not what they seem to be or who do not fit the cinematic stereotype of the "crazed killer": from the hugely influential *Psycho* to films such as *Kiss the Girls*, *From Hell*, or *Scream*. These villains are frightening because they seem so harmless, they seem to be the good guys.[2] The same principle is at work in *Snow White*, whose Wicked Queen is first revealed to be evil and then destroyed. In these kinds of stories, it's especially horrifying when you can't tell who the bad guys are, when evil appears good.

For the authors considered in this chapter, one of the most pressing problems about magic is that it disguises and deludes, allowing wickedness to mask itself. There's no way to tell whom to fight, because the magician may appear to be a pious hermit, the witch may seem a beautiful queen. The villains can hide because of their magical illusions and tricks, and magic itself becomes implicated through constant association with malicious and manipulative deception. As magic becomes more and more debased, dependent upon demons and deceptive illusion, it becomes more and more a practice of wicked old witches: in England, the Renaissance is the time for witches. In Malory's *Morte Darthur*, Spenser's *Faerie Queene*, and Shakespeare's plays, witches lurk everywhere, cackling and brewing potions, trapping men and making mischief in an abundance unmatched by the earlier medieval Arthurian romances.[3] And as the Wicked Queen in *Snow White* shows us with the very first words she speaks, witches rely on evil spirits to help them do their work, on those nefarious nasties we know as demons.

The connection of witches with demons in the fifteenth and sixteenth centuries marks one of the most important paradigm shifts for knowledge-production about witches in England. The first section of this chapter traces the development of demonology: demonic magic relies on the coercion of spirits who provide magical power based on illusion and deception, the primary tools of the devil. Widespread belief in demonology, beginning in

98   *Crafting the Witch*

the late fifteenth century and flourishing in the sixteenth, coupled with a backlash against women after crisis and economic change in fourteenth- and fifteenth-century England, contributed to the development of specific cultural constructions of maternity *vis a vis* witches. When these forces collided, the result was the Renaissance witch, whose presence marks all magic as potentially evil. The wicked witch of the early modern period exhibits a specific kind of maternity, in the tradition of the medieval witches, but the writers of the later texts construct a maternal "Catch 22" by stigmatizing pre- and post-maternal women while simultaneously rejecting the maternal body. Renaissance witches push women into a particular kind of maternity, at the same time that the literature punishes women for choosing maternity by providing no cultural space for the mother. This witch has proven deeply satisfying to both nascent and full-fledged capitalist audiences, so much so that she is still with us. It is the Renaissance wicked witch we meet when we turn on our televisions or slip into darkened movie theaters with popcorn; it is this wicked old witch whose cackle still strikes that tiny flame of horror. I'll get you, my pretty!

II. BREWING TROUBLE: DEMONIZING MAGIC

By the sixteenth century, two traditions of magic, which can be roughly equated with the categories "natural" and "divine," had merged into one.[4] The "natural" tradition, as described by Michael Bailey, featured "a widespread and diffuse system of common spells, charms, blessings, potions, powders, and talismans employed by many people at all levels of medieval society" (965). The "divine" tradition posited that "through very complex and detailed invocations of demons," a magician with "the prerequisite ritual training and Latin literacy" could coerce demonic spirits and thus make use of the spirits' magical power (966). "Natural" magic includes, for example, the practice of healing magic and the love-potions brewed by Chretien's good witch Thessela. "Divine" magic, on the other hand, lurks behind the prophetic knowledge of Merlin, whose father is a fiend, and motivates the witches' sabbath, a celebration of the devil. During the fifteenth century, these two traditions combine to leave the sixteenth century the cursed legacy of full-blown demonic magic.

It is well documented that religious, scientific, and (to a certain extent) popular thinking about magic coalesced during the late fifteenth and early sixteenth centuries into a firm belief that all magic—and witchcraft in particular—derived from demonic pacts.[5] When natural and divine magic can no longer be distinguished, when good and bad magic are the same, every instance of magic use might involve supplication to the supernatural and reliance on demonic power. Traffic with demons was heretical, and the punishments could be severe, even fatal.[6] The impact of this heightened belief in the Satanic connection to magic on the magic-users of Arthurian legend is clear: Malory, Spenser, and Shakespeare structure magical power so that the control of demonic spirits becomes solely responsible for its efficacy.[7] In these works, the appearance of "feends," "spirits/sprites," and "demons" is so frequent that demons become inseparable from the magic with which they are associated. Beginning at least as far back as the representations in the Bible, the devil (and thus his demon pals) has been associated with temptation via the power of illusion and deceit. As Brian Levack summarizes, "One of the most important powers that the Devil had was the power to create illusions" (33).[8] In some romances, a knight who meets a foul hag may end up marrying a beautiful maiden. But in others, a knight who meets a lovely maiden may actually be in league with the devil himself. "Things are not always what they seem," a modern fantasy film warns, a refrain picked up from the lingering voices of the likes of Malory, Spenser, and Shakespeare.[9] For these authors, whose works circulated during the sixteenth and early seventeenth centuries, magic is deceptive, false, and tricky—it is illusion. Disguises, deceptions and lies, fake or false people and objects: there is no end to the medley of wriggling and twisting forms of magic swimming in the early modern sea of illusion. All the magical figures in the Arthurian stories were affected by the rise of demonic magic, but while the representation of male magical figures (namely, wizards) maintains the traditions inherited from the twelfth and thirteenth centuries, the construction of female magical figures changes radically, participating in a cultural backlash against the changing roles occupied by women in a rapidly shifting economy.

Merlin's Ilk: Male Magical Figures

Malory, Spenser, and Shakespeare connect male magical figures more closely with demonic magic and Satan than previously in the Arthurian tradition; while more demonic, Renaissance wizards are nevertheless situated firmly within Arthurian magical conventions. Male magicians of the twelfth-century possess transformative power over the body, which both feeds their magical prowess and threatens their humanity, situating them with a framework of ambiguity and ambivalence. For twelfth-century chroniclers, Merlin, in particular, embodies ambiguity: son of a nun and a mysterious spirit, Merlin possesses great transformative power, manipulating gender and occupying a liminal position between humanity and divinity. The writers of the late fifteenth and early sixteenth centuries utilize the same tradition of ambiguous transformative power to revitalize the centuries-old message that male manipulation of power is both extremely beneficial and extremely dangerous.

Malory's Merlin illustrates well the limited effect of demonic magic on the construction of masculinity in late medieval and early modern Arthurian narratives. In the earliest Arthurian chronicles, Merlin plays an important role—his mysterious power enables the story of Arthur's conception.

100 *Crafting the Witch*

In Malory's romance, he plays an even larger role in Arthur's life, sticking around after pandering for Uther to teach the lad Arthur a few things, but still disappearing from the text very early (on page 81 of Vinaver's 726-page edition). Generally, he serves as Arthur's advisor, giving him military advice, as he does in both Geoffrey's and Laȝamon's texts, but also providing marital advice.[10] With a few notable mistakes (namely, murdering baby boys and letting Arthur marry Gwenevere), Merlin's advice is usually helpful, and in some cases, absolutely necessary to Arthur's success. Malory's Merlin follows the chronicle tradition in making Merlin an important, beneficial part of Arthur's early reign. Merlin's primary function in the *Morte* mimics that in the chronicles—he's the possessor of special knowledge and the resident prophet—but Malory emphasizes that he is also a deceptive and wily master of disguise, a fiend.

Merlin has an arsenal of deceptive transformative magic at his disposal: he turns himself and Arthur invisible to avoid re-fighting Pellinore, he disguises himself as a beggar, a fourteen-year-old child, an old man, and Jordan, and he makes others fall asleep.[11] One of his favorite tricks, designed to showcase his knowledge and teach his pupil through experience, is to show up disguised and administer a set of questions, a test of sorts. When the examinee fails, Merlin lectures the chastened student, often Arthur. This kind of deception benefits Arthur's reign and demonstrates Merlin's importance, and his fondness for this kind of trick is characteristic of his association with deceit and illusion in the *Morte Darthur*.

Merlin is obviously a trusted advisor for Arthur, but he is not an unambiguously "good" person by any means: he is both a hero-magician and a mysterious and potentially dangerous sorcerer. His paternity remains in question, but Malory highlights the possibility that Merlin's spiritual father is a demonic, rather than a benevolent, spirit. Uwayne tells Morgan, for instance, that "men seyde that Merlyon was begotyn of a fende" [men say that Merlin was begotten by a fiend] (90). Merlin is the son of a demonic spirit, and his fiendish nature must have come to mind when audiences heard Malory's retelling of one of Merlin's more insidious deceptions, the transformation of Uther into Gorlois for the purpose of getting Igerne into bed. This scene reads as a rape, and indeed comes off that way in the chronicles, where Igerne responds positively to his sexual advances only because she thinks Uther is Gorlois. Malory takes steps to mitigate the deception in his version: a) by the time Uther reaches Tintagel, Gorlois has been dead "more than thre houres" [more than three hours], a fact that erases the sin of adultery, and b) the narrative elides over the actual moment when Uther deceives (and therefore rapes) Igerne, spending more time on the after-effects of Arthur's conception (5). Igerne nonetheless finds out about the deception almost immediately, and though "she merveilled who that myghte be that laye with her in lykenes of her lord," she takes no public action: "she mourned pryvely and held hir pees" [she wondered who that might be who lay with her in the likeness of her lord;

she mourned privately and held her peace] (5). Igerne's private mourning speaks to her feelings about the situation: she feels there is something to be mourned, a loss about which she would like to speak, but must hold her tongue instead. Details like this tarnish Merlin's reputation, a fact Malory emphasizes when his characters call Merlin a "wytche" after learning the truth about his role in Arthur's conception (12). Merlin's moral ambiguity leaves him open to accusations of witchcraft, a practice that marks him as allied with the devil.

If Merlin's transformative magic seems dangerous and "witchy" to the rebel kings allied against Arthur, how sinister must Merlin seem when he advises Arthur to "sende for all the children that were borne in May-day," and put them "in a shyppe to the se" [send for all the children who were born during May; in a ship (headed) out to sea] (37). The ship founders, and all the "lordis sonnys" and "knyghtes sonnes" [lords' sons; knights' sons] are killed except, of course, Mordred (against whom the murderous episode was directed, in a desperate attempt to prevent a prophecy foretelling Mordred's murder of Arthur). Merlin takes the rap for the dirty deed, as "many putte the wyght on Merlion more than on Arthure" [put the blame on Merlin more than on Arthur] (37). Just as Igerne is silenced by Merlin's deceptive ploy, the parents whose children were callously murdered remain silent as well: "So what for drede and for love, they helde their peece" [So whether for dread or for love, they held their peace] (37). Like Igerne, these people felt (either out of fear or out of love) that they must remain silent in the face of Merlin's fiendish cruelty. His magic makes him morally ambiguous, but provides him with great power to control the behavior of others. Ultimately, Merlin works for the "powers that be," assisting Arthur to rule his kingdom effectively, participating in the normative social world and perpetuating patriarchal hierarchy.

Demonic magic heightens both Merlin's power and his risk—the consequences for Merlin's connection to magic in the *Morte* are dire indeed. It is clearly Merlin's demonic connection that prompts Nineve to imprison him, as Malory tells us that "she was aferde of hym for cause he was a devyls son" [she was afraid of him because he was a devil's son] (77). Her solution avoids the executions that awaited both literary and accused witches of the Renaissance, but prevents the disease of demonic magic from spreading to other men.

Though Merlin's prophetic moments far outnumber his seedier exploits, when it comes to the figure of Merlin the prophet, his story sometimes horrifies rather than impresses. Malory's Merlin, though substantively similar in behavior and role to Geoffrey's and Laȝamon's, has lost some of his earlier grandeur, tainted by his association with the devil, magical deception and manipulation, lechery, and the murder of innocent children. Malory heightens the moral ambiguity of male magical use, but retains the basic principle: male magic is a positive (though sometimes dangerous) force for maintenance of social control. Merlin works for the good of the patriarchal

102   *Crafting the Witch*

kingdom—for the good of Arthur—and is therefore situated firmly within the conventional Arthurian literary tradition.

In addition to linking the most magical male character in the *Morte Darthur* with demons, Malory's dialogue makes frequent use of an idiomatic curse using the word "devil." For example, Sir Borce uses the expression during a pre-battle pep-talk to criticize cowardly behavior: "And he that faynes hym to fyght, *the devyl have his bonys!*" [And he who fears (refl. himself) to fight, *the devil have his bones!*] (italics mine, 128).[12] This idiom is particularly useful for this discussion because of the way it constructs the speaker's relationship to the devil. In this kind of expression, a person speaks aloud a desire for the devil to perform a specific service. If the short-hand of this idiom were to be written out long-hand, it might be something like the following statement: I wish the devil would perform revenge on someone I can't/won't perform revenge on myself. Even when intended in a metaphorical sense, such a statement creates a parallel power structure to that of demonic magic, where the person controls the demon by means of a performative utterance. Specifically, this idiom suggests that people can turn to demons for assistance, a practice clearly frowned upon by orthodox Christians. Though Malory makes greater use of demonic figures and language than both the writers of the French romances and the short Middle English verse romances, his text merely scratches the surface of a bottomless pit of demonological rhetoric. Spenser and Shakespeare, on the other hand, have fallen in.

Demonic spirits and deceptive illusion pervade representations of magic in *Macbeth*, *A Midsummer Night's Dream*, and *The Tempest*, three of Shakespeare's most magical plays. In these plays, almost every instance of magic involves spirits or demons. Two of the three feature masculine magical pairs in which an older male magician commands a male spirit (Oberon/Puck and Prospero/Ariel).[13] These pairs are morally ambiguous, sometimes acting for the good of others, but often using illusion to support selfish or malicious agendas. In both plays, the male magical figure uses power over demonic spirits and secret knowledge to gain the advantage over his adversary: Oberon has both the knowledge of the magical love-flower and the power to command Puck to fetch it, giving him an edge in his quarrel with Titania; and Prospero has both the knowledge that his enemies travel by ship off the coast of his island and the ability to force Ariel into creating a tempest, giving him the opportunity to strand his foes. Both men use their knowledge and their control of spirits to torment and torture their foes, using magic in the service of deceit and manipulation. Despite this, both avoid serious negative consequences for their behavior— in fact, they are ultimately rewarded for their efforts in happy endings that restore normative patriarchies.

In *A Midsummer Night's Dream*, Oberon's magical knowledge is tinged with a deceptive hue. After deciding to torture his wife in response to their custody battle, Oberon confesses to Puck, his spirit, that he knows of a magical love-charm because he happened to observe as Cupid's stray arrow fell into "a little western flower" (II.i.66). Oberon's sneaky spying provides him with magical power, and he uses that power in an ever-widening sphere of influence. His ability to become invisible—another deception—allows Oberon a perfect opportunity to delude the lovers into believing they are alone, thus providing him with an opportunity to meddle. Oberon's prank on his wife and the lovers makes magic into the play-toy of revenge, the power to create an illusion of love as a tool for punishing women (and men?).

Though not overtly connected to the Arthurian tradition (and the infamous, witchy Merlin), Oberon's characterization fits securely into the centuries-long tradition of wizards wielding transformative power. Oberon's power is nothing if not transformative, but whereas the twelfth-century Merlin often targeted himself with his transformative power, Oberon favors transforming others: he changes Demetrius's scorn into love and Lysander's love into hate (and this change in turn catalyzes the shifting of Hermia from demure to shrewish and Helena from foolish to divine); he transforms an indifferent Titania into a love-struck maiden (thus transforming her rebellion into subservience); and his minion, Puck, turns Bottom into precisely what his name suggests. Oberon turns things on their heads, inverts things, and this process causes its female victims, in particular, serious psychological harm. Hermia endures the loss of both her beloved and her best friend's favor; Helena thinks her beloved and best friend conspire to humiliate her; and Titania not only falls in love with a donkey-headed human, much to her own dismay, but loses the little Indian boy she vowed to care for. When things are topsy-turvy, there is danger, Shakespeare tells us, a fact that Helena explains early in the play as she chases Demetrius:

> Apollo flies, and Daphne holds the chase;
> The dove pursues the griffin; the mild hind
> Makes speed to catch the tiger—bootless speed,
> When cowardice pursues and valor flies. (II.i.231–4)

Helena presents an inverted world, where fierce predators like tiger and griffin are chased by the notoriously mild-mannered deer and dove, a vision more prescient than she knows, as the fairy world she is about to enter will prove more topsy-turvy still.

Evidence of the fairy world's inversion presents itself as soon as we enter it, when we learn of the fight between Oberon and Titania over the little Indian boy. Unlike the opening of the play, where Theseus has dominated Hippolyta in true masculine style, Titania will not submit to Oberon; thus the fairy forest initially presents a space for challenging normative conventions. Despite the potential for subversion presented by the forest, Oberon's magic ultimately restores a perfectly hegemonic state of affairs. At the end of the play, male magical power has restored the heterosexual love couples; each person—Demetrius/Helena, Lysander/Hermia, Theseus/Hippolyta,

104 *Crafting the Witch*

Oberon/Titania, Pyramus/Thisbe?—is paired off happily and, in the women's case, submissively. The world order has been restored, and while gender may have been more flexible in the fairy world, it in the real world it is oppressively rigid. All trace of the rebellious Hermia who defied her father to sneak away with a lover in Act 1 is gone; by Act 5 she is reduced to complete silence, uttering not one word during the entire act. Helena is likewise strangely quiet. Silent and obedient, indeed. Both Lysander and Demetrius, on the other hand, speak more than ten times each. Like Merlin, in the end it seems Oberon works for The Man.

Though Oberon clearly impacts the human world (changing Demetrius permanently and blessing the couples' marriages, for example), he is not ever truly part of it. Like Merlin, Oberon and the fairies are liminal figures—they exist outside the human world, but they interact with it, creating a borderland between the fairy forest and the human city. Oberon in particular lurks around the edges of the human world, playing with his human dolls, interfering if and when he chooses, but never quite revealing himself to anyone human (unlike his unlucky wife, tricked into consorting with a human male). The fairies are in a perpetual state of in-between, affecting things in the human world but not joining it, at the border of humanity, but not quite human. Their liminality is constitutive of their magic, and their magic of their liminality. Oberon is magic because he is a fairy because he is magic. He joins Merlin in a long line of wizards on the borders of humanity.

The Tempest's resident wizard, Prospero, also borrows from the Arthurian tradition as he works to control the residents of a small island. Like Merlin, Prospero works in service of a kingdom (his own!), with a personal interest in getting Milan back for himself and Miranda. Prospero is more sinister than both Merlin and Oberon, as he exerts his power with people not nearly as threatening as Merlin's foes: Stephano and Trinculo are harmless buffoons who simply like to drink and boast, and neither Ferdinand nor Alonso has done anything to deserve the cruel deception that makes each of them think the other is dead. Though Prospero is vindicated in the end when he regains his dukedom and finds a royal husband for his daughter, he flirts with moral ambiguity, behaving sympathetically one minute but becoming mean-spirited and tyrannical the next (especially with Ariel and Caliban, his beleaguered slaves).

Prospero's relationship with Ariel, his spirit, demonstrates the deceptive nature of Prospero's *modus operandi*. Prospero exerts influence over Ariel in part because, as he often reminds the spirit, he released Ariel from the tree in which Sycorax imprisoned him—he uses guilt to control the spirit, despite Ariel's pleas for freedom.[14] Prospero uses the illusory promise of freedom to manipulate Ariel into performing complicated tasks, a practice he continues until the very last lines of the play.[15] Prospero's last statement to the spirit still does not grant him freedom, but provides yet another condition of release. Prospero promises to provide "calm seas" and "auspicious gales" for the return voyage to Naples, and then tells Ariel to arrange it all: "My

The Lady is a Hag 105

Ariel, chick, / That is thy charge. *Then* to the elements / Be free, and fare thou well!" (V.i.317–9, italics mine). In one last "if" clause, Shakespeare emphasizes that Prospero's control over Ariel is based on the duplicitous manipulation of the spirit's sense of gratitude and the terms of his indentureship. It is the (demonic?) spirit who provides most of the magic Prospero utilizes in the play, as we only hear rumors about, but never witness, what Prospero can do with his magic book. All the magical power in the play comes directly from the manipulation and deceit of a spirit.

In addition to holding the carrot of freedom in front of Ariel's nose, Prospero also deludes and abuses Caliban. Though Caliban did "seek to violate the honor of [his] child" (I.ii.346–8), a heinous offense, Prospero's abuse of the wretched monster has no limit: Prospero calls Caliban a "poisonous slave," and accuses him of being begotten "by the devil himself" (I.ii.319–20). Caliban returns the abuse without hesitation, but his story reveals the underlying power dynamic of their relationship:

> This island's mine by Sycorax my mother,
> Which thou tak'st from me. When thou cam'st first,
> Thou strok'st me and made much of me, wouldst give me
> Water with berries in't, and teach me how
> To name the bigger light, and how the less,
> That burn by day and night; and then I lov'd thee
> And show'd thee all the qualities o' th' isle,
> The fresh springs, brine-pits, barren place and fertile.
> Curs'd be that I did so! All the charms
> Of Sycorax, toads, beetles, bats, light on you!
> For I am all the subjects that you have,
> Which first was mine own king; and here you sty me
> In this hard rock, while you do keep from me
> The rest o' th' island. (I.ii.331–44)

Though Caliban is heir to the island through his mother, he nonetheless willingly becomes Prospero's subject, and Prospero ultimately rewards his help by enslaving him.[16] With Sycorax gone, Prospero becomes a surrogate mother for Caliban, caressing, feeding, and instructing him as a mother might. Prospero's skillful appropriation of maternal roles here echoes Merlin's manipulative feminine crying fits, and his strategy works, as Caliban volunteers important information about "all the qualities of the isle." Prospero takes advantage of this information, and by the time the play starts, Prospero and Caliban are deeply embroiled in a master/slave relationship wherein Prospero rules Caliban by tormenting him with magic.

Prospero's magical power can be cruel, as with Ariel and Caliban, but in the end, it restores the patriarchal line of rulers and provides an aristocratic marriage to continue the line. Like Oberon and Merlin, Prospero's magic is deployed in service of a normative ideology which still grounds modern

106 *Crafting the Witch*

representations of gender. Prospero represents male-dominance, from his participation with Ferdinand in the exchange of his daughter through marriage to his literally replacing a maternal power with a masculine one on the island. Shakespeare's most "mature" romance offers the same message as one of his earliest comedies: men can and should have power, especially over women. Magic is just another tool in the arsenal.

The impact of demonic magic is plain in these texts, as these magical men use a fundamentally deceptive and manipulative form of magic. Though Merlin, Oberon, and Prospero are ambiguous figures—sometimes cruel and sometimes benevolent—they are not imbued with evil through and through, as are the witches. They are dubious sorcerers, dabblers in the demonic arts, whose motivations cannot be trusted, and whose magic tends towards illusion, but they are also members of a semi-divine elite, celebrated within their own worlds and connected with the ruling hierarchy.

Malory and Shakespeare both link magic with illusion and demonic spirits, but it is Spenser's *Faerie Queene* that demonstrates most strongly the representation of magic as demonic illusion and the potential negative consequences of association with Satanic power. His epic is filled with tricky magicians and false ladies who turn out to be witches or demonic spirits, impressive men or women who turn out to be monstrous creatures, and manipulative villains. The best example of a Spenserian specialist in deception is the master of disguise himself, Archimago. Whether or not he is a demon or even Satan, Archimago's association with hellish fiends and demonic spirits is the most extreme example of the association of magic and those who use it with demons.

From the moment he appears, disguised as a pious hermit, Archimago operates by means of deception and illusion. After convincing Redcrosse and Una to lodge with him because he's disguised as a holy palmer, Archimago uses his "Magick bookes and artes" to deceive Redcrosse and split up the couple (I.i.36.8). He conjures two demonic spirits, one who visits Morpheus to beg a "fit false dream, that can delude the sleepers," and one who becomes a false Una (I.i.38–43, 45–6). He combines the lusty dream (illusion) with the presence of the false Una (deception) to tempt Redcrosse into wavering in his knightly commitment to chastity or, even better, abandoning it entirely. When Plan A doesn't work, Archimago moves on to Plan B, setting up a scene where the false Una and another spirit provide a peep-show for Redcrosse. Archimago's tenacity pays off, as Redcrosse does abandon Una. Archimago's magic here is pure illusion, and he deceives the pair for no other reason than that he loathed Una "as the hissing snake, / And in her many troubles did most pleasure take" (I.ii.9.8–9). His hatred appears unmotivated, hatred for hatred's sake, and we later see Archimago opportunistically abuse nearly everyone he meets.

The name "Archimago" points to the allegorical meaning behind the duplicitous magician's malignance: glossed variously as "the great master of the false image," the "architect of images," or simply "archmagician," the two parts of the name suggest 1) that the figure is exceptionally good at what he does, which 2) has something to do with illusion.[17] The great master of the false image is the devil himself, and Archimago's hatred is thus allegorically motivated: falseness battles the truth in the clash between Archimago and Una. Though his later encounters do not fall as easily into perfect allegory as this first episode, Archimago needs no external motivation to deceive: he simply is deception.

Spenser's representation of Archimago relies on the Arthurian magical tradition—Archimago, like Merlin, possesses transformative power, as we learn in this passage where the wily wizard considers his options for luring the unprotected Una to his side:

> He then deuisde himselfe how to disguise;
> For by his mightie science he could take
> As many formes and shapes in seeming wise,
> As euer Proteus to himselfe could make:
> Sometime a fowle, sometime a fish in lake,
> Now like a foxe, now like a dragon fell,
> That of himselfe he oft for feare would quake,
> And oft would flie away. O who can tell
> The hidden power of herbes, and might of Magicke spell? (I.ii.10)

Archimago can transform himself into anything he wants, as Satan's disguises are limitless. Archimago uses magical illusion throughout the poem until his disappearance in Book III, but his manipulative ploys do not always require as large an expenditure of magical energy as does Redcrosse. Sometimes Archimago just lies.

Spenser associates Archimago with deception in both magical and non-magical arenas; in addition to the transformative magic mentioned above, Archimago often manipulates his victims by spinning a convincing yarn, by garden-variety lying rather than magical illusion. When Archimago meets Guyon in Book II, for example, our evil enchanter is on Redcrosse's trail, but as Redcrosse has proven difficult to re-ensnare, the enchanter "chaungd his minde from one to other ill: / For to all good he enimy was still" (II.i.5.4–5). Archimago is the enemy of all good knights and ladies, too opportunistic to be devoted singly to one foe. As soon as he sees Guyon, he begins "to weaue a web of wicked guile" (II.i.8.4). His deception is a masterful performance, as he must first adopt "a faire countenance and flattring smile," then switch to "feigning then in euery limbe to quake," and finally become "pale and faint" when he discusses his main subject, the rape of a "virgin cleene" by Redcrosse knight (II.i.8.5, 9.3, 9.4, and 10.4). Though his story is detailed enough to incite Guyon's "fierce ire," it does not require magical power—it requires good acting. Archimago consistently engages in deception, using any means available to manipulate his victims.[18] His use of magic subordinates magical power to deceit, casting it as a tool for deception, part of the trappings of illusion. Lying and magical illusion are two sides of the same coin in this story, a coin stamped with Archimago's face.

108   *Crafting the Witch*

The male magic-users I have discussed in this section do not, as a group, personify evil (although Archimago may do exactly that), but they certainly all practice a tainted magic, a magic thick with the guilt of its marriage to those nefarious minions of evil, the bane of Christianity, the demons. These figures suffer limited pejorative changes as they become connected with evil, but they still share a great deal with their Arthurian grandfathers. The Renaissance wizards did not turn into unambiguously evil creatures, as did their witchy sisters—they suffered no widespread villainization, no transformation into wicked beasts. Why not? What accounts for the continuity of the figures in the midst of a changing world? The answer—the gendered division of labor. While women's roles changed (albeit in a limited and brief way) as a result of the economic shifts of the late medieval period, men's roles did not. Men still worked outside the home, provided for themselves and their families, and operated in the public sphere. When women encroached on the public sphere, working both outside the home and within fields previously dominated by men, they appropriated, rather than challenged, male roles. Since men's roles did not change dramatically, male figures did not need to function as a warning. Female roles changed, so female figures changed with them. And what the change produced was the wicked witch.

III. "THAT SAME WICKED WITCH": (STILL) VILLIFYING FEMININE MAGIC

Here is a story. Once upon a time, there was a woman who lived on the edge of a village. She lived alone, in her own house surrounded by her garden, in which she grew all manner of herbs and other healing plants. Though she was alone, she was never lonely; she had her garden and her animals for company, she took lovers when she wished, and she was always busy. The woman was a healer and midwife; she had practical knowledge taught her by her mother, and mystical knowledge derived from her closeness to nature, or from a half-submerged pagan religion. She helped women give birth, and she had healing hands; she used her knowledge of herbs and her common sense to help the sick. However, her peaceful existence was disrupted. Even though this woman was harmless, she posed a threat to the fearful. Her medical knowledge threatened the doctor. Her simple, true spiritual values threatened the superstitious nonsense of the Catholic church, as did her affirmation of the sensuous body. Her independence and freedom threatened men. So the Inquisition descended on her, and cruelly tortured her into confessing to lies about the devil. She was burned alive by men who hated women, along with millions of other just like her.

(description of the "Burning Times" myth,
from Diane Purkiss's *The Witch in History* 7)

The Lady is a Hag   109

In the above description, Purkiss has captured a number of elements characteristic of a popular understanding of the Renaissance witch—but as Purkiss compellingly argues, this attractive description is deeply flawed, for many reasons. In short, women who were accused of witchcraft in Renaissance England were not usually single women living on the outskirts—they were typically wives and mothers, women who were involved (sometimes heavily) in local social networks (7–29). But there is something within this familiar description that resonates with literary and legal descriptions of witches in the late 15th and 16th centuries. The modern stereotype of the lonely hag on the outskirts of the city writes the witch as economically stable on her own—without relying on a male to provide the primary income for the family. In fact, it is on this point that the stereotype hinges—for there to be a hag who lives without a man in town, there must be female access to capital. Economic stability is the key for female empowerment both in this modern fantasy and in the literary representations of witches I consider here.

As I documented in Chapter 3, female participation in the economy grew in the wake of the crises of the fourteenth century. Though access to capital was still limited, two groups of women achieved some economic independence: young, unmarried women and widows. Judith Bennett and Amy Froide document that numbers of singlewomen began increasing in the mid-fourteenth century, with a dramatic increase in the sixteenth century (4–5), and P. J. P. Goldberg provides evidence that female involvement in trade and selling in at least one town reached its height during the early fifteenth century.[19] These small gains resulted, as is often the case when dispossessed groups make progress, in a social and economic backlash. During the mid-fifteenth century, many of the achievements of women were reversed. Goldberg describes the shift as follows: "men sought to preserve their own position in a period of recession by excluding competition from female labour. Women were thus forced back into positions of dependency within marriage" (7). Women's small movement toward economic independence not only stopped short, but stepped backward in the face of reasserted male dominance.

Economic backlash can also be seen in the declining numbers of female-headed household renters. Kim Phillips demonstrates that while female renters made up 17% of the tenants on the Havering manor in Essex and 32% on the Englefield manor in Berkshire during the mid-fourteenth century, these numbers decreased dramatically during the fifteenth century (123–7). By 1405–6, only 1.5% of the Havering tenants were women, and by 1445–6, no women held land at Havering; likewise, female tenants at Englefield comprised only 4% of the total in 1402, 8% in 1441, and none in 1474 and 1496. This data reveals that in the late fifteenth century, female landholding had been almost entirely eliminated. It was not only in the area of landholding that the backlash operated: economic recession in the mid-fifteenth century contributed to the exclusion of women from trade guilds,

110   *Crafting the Witch*

falling wages for female laborers, and decreased job opportunities.[20] By the sixteenth century, the situation for women was so dire as to prompt Joan Kelly's famous question, "Did Women Have a Renaissance?" The answer to her question seems to be a resounding "no."

If the evidence for economic backlash can be found in the records and documents analyzed by the scholars cited above, evidence for social backlash screams from the pages of late-fifteenth and sixteenth-century literature. When women stepped outside the door of their homes, moved (however slightly) into the public realm, writers and audiences quickly and firmly shoved them back in. In particular, the texts considered here use witch-figures to punish both pre- and post-maternal women (single women and widows), the very same women who gained the greatest opportunities to move outside the home in the shifting economy of late medieval England. Be a mother or be a witch!

Discourses about witches emphasize a connection to a particular kind of maternity: the "witches' sabbath" typically involves sexual intercourse with a demon (or the devil himself), after which the witch gains control of an imp or familiar (a demonic spirit in the form of an animal), who comes to suckle at her "witch's mark" or "witch's teat," which Deborah Willis describes in *Malevolent Nurture* as a "third nipple by which [the witch] feeds her familiars" (33). When the witch acts, "her witchcraft is frequently directed against the children of her neighbors and almost always against domestic activities associated with feeding, nurture, or birth" (34). Maternity thus structures 1) the way the witch gets her power (through her sexual liaison with the devil, she obtains a child-substitute in the form of the suckling familiar) and 2) the way she exerts it (the domestic nature of the conflicts themselves). Witches are maternal, but their maternity is inverted—they suckle demons and harass human children. Witches are anti-mothers, not-mothers, women who have rejected traditional motherhood in favor of a demonic alternative. Stigmatizing women who are not mothers works to reaffirm the primacy of motherhood as the essential female role. Not a mother? Must be a witch. At the same time, these writers abject actual maternal figures, erasing any space for a positive notion of motherhood, for a good mother. The battlefield of this ideological war is Arthurian legend—the magical, mystical world where men and women are ideal and villains are monstrous. Women, the legends say, beware.

Beauty is the Beast: Love Magic and Lusty Witches

In *The Wizard of Oz*, Judy Garland's Dorothy can't believe it when she hears that Glinda is a witch. When asked by Glinda, "Are you a good witch or a bad witch?" Dorothy replies, "I'm not a witch at all! Witches are old and ugly!" The Munchkins begin to giggle, and the young Miss Gale, unaware of her *faux pas*, asks Glinda, "What was that?" Glinda smiles affectionately at Dorothy, the way a mother smiles when she humors a child: "The

The Lady is a Hag   111

Munchkins. They're laughing because I am a witch. I'm Glinda, the witch of the north." When Dorothy hears this, she's completely abashed, and she protests that she's "never heard of a beautiful witch before." Glinda instructs Dorothy gently, "Only bad witches are ugly." This exchange reveals an important difference between the way Dorothy and the residents of Oz view magic. For the denizens of Oz, Dorothy is naïve and uninformed, as they know what English authors have known for hundreds of years: some witches are beautiful.

In the late fifteenth and sixteenth centuries, the figure of the beautiful witch (a vision borrowed in part from classical authors) began to appear in Arthurian literature where she had not been before. Unlike the very maternal Glinda, these witches are described as physically beautiful and sexually alluring, and certainly not "good," as they seek to ensnare knights by any and all means. One of the defining characteristics of the beautiful witch, the pre-maternal witch, is that she craves sex, and much her of deceptive magic works towards arranging and executing extra-marital affairs. Her desire for sex is a function of her pre-maternal nature—her sexuality is not directed toward procreation. She does not make the connection between sex and motherhood; instead, her beautiful allure works to garner sexual power over men. For these writers, non-procreative sexuality is tainted sexuality, beauty misdirected. We know it's tainted beauty because it is merely a façade. Underneath, hidden away, the beautiful temptresses are wicked witches, just like their crone counterparts: they are loathly on the inside. The medieval loathly lady shows us that people who seem loathly can actually be good and beautiful: sometimes loathliness is only skin deep. The late medieval and Renaissance writers of Arthurian stories respond to that figure with a question: if an ugly woman can be beautiful on the inside, then why can't a beautiful woman be ugly on the inside? Maybe beauty can sometimes be skin deep as well, Malory and Spenser say: each author constructs a beautiful temptress-witch whose sexual allure is both her power and her undoing.

Malory's most famous beautiful witch is the nefarious Morgan le Fay. Arthur's three half-sisters make their first appearance in the *Morte* at the wedding of Uther and Igrayne, where the elder two, Margawse (Gawain's mother) and Elayne were married to Lott and Nentres, respectively. The young Morgan did not marry, but "was put to scole in a nonnery, and there she lerned so moche that she was a grete clerke of nygromancye" [was put to school in a nunnery, and there she learned so much that she was a great scholar of necromancy] (5). Before we learn anything else about her, we learn that Morgan is a necromancer, a practitioner of a kind of magic commonly associated with witches in the fifteenth and sixteenth centuries.[21] She's quickly married off to Uriens, and we don't see her again until her mother brings her to court. At this point in the text, we learn that Morgan "was a fayre lady as ony myght be" [was as fair a lady as any might be] (30). It is not until after these brief introductions, which highlight her magic and

112 *Crafting the Witch*

her beauty, that we learn the truth about Morgan. When the eternal meddler sends a knight to the home of King Mark, bringing with him a horn that exposes women's infidelity, the fact that the horn indicts all but four of the ladies present is dismissed because of Morgan's reputation: "[the barons] would not have tho ladyes brente for an horne made by sorcery that cam 'from the false sorseres and wychhe moste that is now lyvyng'" (270). They do not take Morgan seriously because they already know she is a witch—she is the "moste" notorious witch living, in fact. This episode characterizes Morgan well: when we see her, Morgan is usually in action, and boy is she busy.

Morgan le Fay is bad. She seduces Accolon, tries to murder both the king and her husband, imprisons Lancelot and assaults him sexually, tricks Tristram into becoming her delivery-boy, drugs Alexander so that his wounds won't heal, tortures an innocent woman, steals Arthur's sword and scabbard, and perpetuates a custom at her castle of forcing single knights into combat against two or three knights (and imprisoning those who lose).[22] She's decidedly wicked. As we've seen, her malfeasance strays beyond the realm of the sexual, but true to her type (the temptress-witch), Morgan is also a very lusty woman.

The episode which most characterizes Morgan's attempts to deceive and imprison knights who refuse to "dally" is the abduction of Lancelot. The notorious knight goes to sleep under an apple tree, never a good idea in a romance (as *Sir Orfeo* teaches us), as the locale is notorious for making sleepers more vulnerable to magic (149). Sure enough, Morgan comes along with three other queens, The Queen of North Galys, the Queen of Estlonde, and the Queen of the Oute Isles (all of whom are repeatedly associated with Morgan and with enchantment generally, so that Malory provides Morgan with a community of female magic-users, or a coven). When the queens see Lancelot, they begin arguing amongst themselves, and each one says she "wolde have hym to hir love" [would have him as her love] (151). Morgan enchants Lancelot so that he will remain asleep for seven hours, and they take him back to her castle so that they can force him to choose among them. In this scene, the four women, led by a witch, become so overcome with lust when they see a sleeping knight that they feel compelled to kidnap and imprison him.

Lust drives Morgan even further. In her most ambitious and complicated scheme, Morgan tries to murder Arthur and install her lover, Accolon, in his place. Her plan involves much planning, requiring her to steal Excalibur, make a false copy for Arthur, give the real sword and magical scabbard to Accolon, capture Arthur and Uriens, and stage the fight (84–90). This episode in particular associates Morgan with demonic power. When Accolon awakens from his experience on the enchanted ship, he immediately realizes what happened and explodes into anger: "Jesu, save my lorde kynge Arthure and kynge Uryence, for thes damysels in this shippe hath betrayed us. They were fendis and no women" [Jesus, save my lord king

The Lady is a Hag 113

Arthur and king Uriens, because these damsels in this ship have betrayed us. They were fiends and no women.] (84). When he names the women "fiends," Accolon characterizes Morgan's magic as demonic, as the magic of a wicked witch. While the fight between Accolon and the king is winding up, Morgan attempts to murder Uriens with a sword. When Uwayne finds his mother wielding a sword over the head of his father, he also calls Morgan a fiend, saying, "Men seyde that Merlyon was begotyn of a fende, but I may sey an ertheley fende bare me" [Men say that Merlin was begotten of a fiend, but I may say an earthly fiend bore me.] (90). Her use of magic marks her and her associates as demons, fiends, just like the "devyl's son," Merlin. More importantly, her attempt to murder her son's father positions her as a very bad mother. She not only participates in extra-marital sexuality— non-procreative sexual behavior—but she endangers the life of her current child's father. We get the impression that she would do anything in her pursuit of sex—if she'd kill her husband, why not her son? Though Morgan is already a mother, her execution of maternal roles is at best faulty and at worst lethal. Morgan has a child, but she's barely a mother—she behaves as if she does not have (or want) a child. Morgan's witchy behavior is thus linked to her lusty, pre-maternal desires and bad motherhood; at the core of her evil is her rejection of the maternal role.

Malory still allows Morgan, despite her witchy nature, to play an important role in Arthur's death scene, a role which in some ways redeems (or at least mitigates) the negative characterization that comes before, and which certainly makes her character far more complex and paradoxical. Directly after the battle outside Salisbury with Mordred, the mortally-wounded Arthur tells Bedwer, "I muste into the vale of Avylyon to hele me of my grevous wounde" [I must (go) into the vale of Avalon (in order) to heal (lit. heal myself of) my grievous wound] (716). Immediately thereafter, Morgan le Fay and her group of witchy queens, this time the Queen of North Galys, the Queen of the Waste Lands, and Dame Nineve, float up in a mysterious barge (716). Her role here is positive: she comes to take Arthur to Avalon to be healed, and her bevy of witchy women bewail Arthur's death. But wait—is this the same Morgan who tried to murder her brother? Is this the same Morgan whose hatred of the Round Table is so extreme that she imprisons Arthur's knights simply because they're his knights? This is a different woman entirely, a woman we've seen before, in the twelfth and thirteenth centuries. Taken from the chronicle tradition in which Morgan's primary function is a healing one, and completely out of character for the figure Malory paints prior to this scene, this moment hearkens back to a kinder, gentler Morgan, a benevolent lady who loves her brother.

The difference between Morgan's characteristic wickedness and her appearance in the barge scene reflects a trend towards duality evident throughout the *Morte Darthur* (less evident in Spenser and Shakespeare). Malory treats his witches ambivalently: they can be good or bad, they can switch between evil and kindness without warning, and the results of their

114 Crafting the Witch

handiwork are often mixed. The duality in Malory's representation of the beautiful temptress is a manifestation of the divide between her moral character and her outward appearance: her beauty covers her wicked core. Morgan exemplifies Malory's construction of beautiful witches as paradoxical and ambiguous, sometimes helpful and alluring, sometimes revealing the hidden, frightening side.[23] Their beauty is an imperfect veneer, a gauze behind which the confusing and perhaps evil core can lurk.

Where Malory's lovely ladies perplex, Spenser's beautiful witches leave no room for doubt: they are evil, through and through. The list of Spenser's beautiful witches includes Duessa, Lucifera, Acrasia, Phædra, Ate, and Munera, all of whom fit the same profile as Malory's witches: they are beautiful (at least on the outside), they are pre-maternal, voracious sexual predators, and they use deceptive magic to ensnare knights. But Spenser adds an element lacking from Malory's figures: the revelation of the grotesque core hidden behind the beautiful exterior, the "Snow White factor." In *Snow White*, the beauty of the wicked queen hides her evil at first, but her transformative power soon betrays her, and she transforms herself into an ugly hag, a grotesque ancient. In this guise, she dies, making the hag her final form—her "true" form, the outside that can reflect her moral character through the medieval convention of the grotesque. But Snow White's evil step-mother follows in the footsteps of a delightfully wicked and devious witch who haunts *The Faerie Queene*, the "false sorceresse," Duessa (I.ii.34.8).

Upon introducing Duessa, the first wicked witch to appear in his epic poem, Spenser immediately sexualizes her, describing her "scarlot red" dress covered with jewelry and trinkets, "The which her lavish lovers to her gave," and noting the "courting dalliaunce" and "wanton play" between Duessa and her lover (I.ii.13.114, 14.118–121). This is Duessa's art, clothing herself in the trappings of beauty, disguising herself with tempting sexual symbols. After Redcrosse defeats Sans Foy, Duessa tells her story, and Redcrosse's response demonstrates the effectiveness of Duessa's beautiful mask—as Duessa narrates a story in which Sans Foy takes her prisoner, threatening her virginity, Redcrosse "in great passion all this while did dwell, / More busying his quicke eyes, her face to view, / Then his dull ears, to heare what she did tell" (I.ii.26.5–7). The story doesn't matter nearly as much as Duessa's beauty—his eyes are "quicke," but his ears are "dull." Enthralled by Duessa's physical charms, Redcrosse swears to be her knight, giving her ample time to begin the next step, seducing the naïve knight of Holiness.

And seduce she does! When they rest in the "coole shade," the flirting commences directly: "Faire seemely pleasaunce each to other makes, / With goodly purposes there as they sit" (I.ii.30.1–2), and she tries again later, fainting after Fraudubio's story so that Redcrosse runs to her side and "oft her [kisses]" (I.ii.45.8). Redcrosse moves from flirting to

The Lady is a Hag   115

kissing in this scene, building towards abandoning his Christian morality entirely. Duessa, "The Witch," triumphs when she gets Redcrosse to drink from an enchanted spring causing him to become "dull and slow" and "faint and feeble" (I.vii.5.8–9). Thanks to the landscape of the fairy world, Duessa finally leads Redcrosse into sin: "Yet goodly court he made still to his Dame, / Pourd out in loosnesse on the grassy ground / Both carelesse of his health, and of his fame" (I.vii.7.1–3). Duessa's sexual drive is typical of the beautiful witch, whose sexual appetite motivates her deceptions. Her sexual advances are not directed at a procreative purpose, as she moves from knight to knight without ever becoming pregnant.

Lest Duessa also seduce the reader, Spenser includes repetitive warnings or clues, such as Fradubio's baleful tale or the narratorial condemnation at the beginning of Canto 7 (Book I). Fradubio's entire story indicts Duessa. He begins by calling Duessa "a false sorceresse" whose favorite activity is bringing "knights" to "wretchednesse," and goes on to hint that her beauty is false, saying that the "faire Lady" guise "did fowle Duessa hyde" (I.ii.34, I.ii.36.9). Fradubio tells of how at first he could not decide who was more beautiful, Duessa or his prior love, Fraelissa. His story reveals that Duessa has power over the appearance of others as well herself, when she uses her "hellish science" to raise a fog which turns the beautiful Fraelissa into a "foule ugly forme" (I.ii.38). Finally, Fradubio's story presents us with a glimpse of Duessa's "true" form, the ancient witch-hag. All the witches in Spenser's fairy-land must "do penance for their crime" about once a month, which apparently involves being unable to use their powers of illusion on the day of "Prime." Fradubio catches sight of Duessa "in her proper hew," and finds that she is "A filthy foule old woman" whose "neather partes" are "misshapen, monstruous," and "more foule and hideous, / Then womans shape man would beleeve to bee" (I.ii.40–41). Behind the façade of beauty lies the grotesque hag, the woman whose sexual organs are not alluring, but monstrous. For Spenser, the most frightening aspect of Duessa's character is her precious secret, her monstrous femininity. What men think should be beautiful transforms into something more horrifying than they ever imagined. Spenser uses the beautiful witch to construct feminine magic as both deceptive and sexual, (re)casting femininity with the same mold used by generations of male writers to disparage women. This is the virgin and the whore rolled into one, the lady who can first be worshipped for her beauty and then reviled once her sexual desire is revealed, a perfectly constructed example of the anti-feminist villainess. Duessa is the kind of witch we love to hate.

In fact, Duessa's character, explained so fully early on in *The Faerie Queene*, serves as a model for our encounters with the other lovely witches who populate the Spenserian fairy-land. Spenser provides an explicit warning describing Duessa's magical power at the beginning of Canto VII:

116 *Crafting the Witch*

> What man so wise, what earthly wit so ware,
> As to descry the crafty cunning traine,
> By which deceipt doth maske in visour faire,
> And cast her colours dyèd deepe in graine,
> To seeme like Truth, whose shape she well can faine,
> And fitting gestures to her purpose frame,
> The guiltlesse man with guile to entertaine?
> Great maistresse of her art was that false Dame,
> The false Duessa, clokèd with Fidessaes name. (I.vii.1)

This description works to free knights from responsibility for falling victim to deceptive magic—who is wise enough to avoid the power of illusion? There are a few levels of meaning created here: ironically, Spenser asks the audience "who could know?" with a giant wink, as we turn to one another and whisper, "I knew!"; he also alludes to the devil's relationship with the Christian, marked by Satan's constant attempt to deceive and manipulate innocent souls. Spenser links femininity with deceit and devilishness, rationalizing men's sin in terms of the always-already sinful woman, and he implicates magic as the tool of hell's minions, the foes of Christian virtue and the marital union.

Duessa, like Morgan le Fay, uses her beauty to achieve sexual power over men, sex that has no maternal consequences for women. Rather than being exchanged between men, these women pick and choose the men with whom they interact, circulating between the male partners they have selected. Duessa has no husband and no children, no one to restrict her movement, and this places her firmly outside the ideal feminine roles of wife and mother. She is the pre-maternal witch, the beautiful temptress, using sex against the system. Duessa is a woman who has found a way to evade male control (if only briefly), and in this way she is reminiscent of the growing number of English singlewoman who found ways (albeit limited ones) to achieve a small level of independence. Ultimately, both Malory and Spenser represent beautiful witches as single sexual predators, unmarried women who deceive men to achieve their own mysterious goals. If singlewomen were in danger of becoming beautiful wicked witches, their widow counterparts faced a slightly different fate in the figure of the post-maternal witch-hag. Though also a maternal figure, the hag takes us from before conception, when sexuality is critical, to after the child has matured, when the maternal impulse has outlasted its purpose. Her asexuality marks her as different from the beautiful temptress, but we know that she's really the same thing.

Wicked Old Witch: The Invasion of the Hags

When the wicked Queen of Disney's *Snow White* transforms herself into the hag, a few major alterations take place: she ages significantly, she curls into a stooped hunchback, her dress turns black and ragged, her facial features become large and exaggerated, her body loses its "feminine" shapeliness, and her voice deepens to a raspy cackle. Aside from the color of her skin, which in *Snow White* is pasty grey, the hag-queen looks a lot like the Wicked Witch of the West from the film version of *The Wizard of Oz*: she, too, is an older woman, who frequently stoops, wears a ragged, black dress, has large facial features (namely her warty nose), few signs of conventional femininity, and a raspy cackling voice. This is the witch little girls mimic on Halloween, with pointy hats and fake warts, the witch on Halloween stickers, paper plates, and specialty candy. This is our wicked witch. But we borrowed her from the Renaissance.

Early Arthurian romance had plenty of room for older, care-giving maternal figures: Chrétien's Thessela, who helps her mistress keep her virginity and feign death, is perhaps the most fully-developed example from the texts considered in this study, but Marie de France features the helpful aunt from Salerno in *Les Deux Amanz*, and the Middle English romances specialize in older, advice-giving women, especially in the form of the loathly lady. These women are witchy, practicing domestic forms of magic, especially healing and love magic, but they are not wicked. They generally assist the protagonists of the story, as we've seen, and their representations are often positive. By the sixteenth century, though, the space available in literature for what we might today call a "good witch" vanished, leaving the wicked, older, advice-giving witchy-woman—the hag—in her place. Malory's Brusen, an enchantress, demonstrates well the characteristics of the medieval "good" witch, while Spenser's unnamed witch of Book III (maker of the false Florimell) and Shakespeare's Weird sisters provide examples of the pervasive Renaissance witch-hag.

Though Malory's beautiful enchantresses never approach the hag type as closely as do the witches in the Renaissance texts, his elderly nurse-witch, Brusen, is a half-remembered great-aunt of the hag-witch. During the century after Caxton published the *Morte Darthur*, representations of the wicked witch drifted far away from this type of benevolent maternal witch. In a few important ways, the Renaissance writers build on the model of the elderly care-taker who does whatever she must to protect her mistress: 1) they emphasize her age and post-reproductive condition (often by visually marking her body as post-maternal), 2) they increase her malevolence (especially by associating her with demons or hell), and 3) they emphasize the destructive nature of her domestic magic. These changes create a hag-witch who functions as a condemnation of feminine power seeping outside the realm of the maternal: the hag is too old to bear children and thus gain the limited maternal authority associated with child-rearing, but she uses her power anyway, outside the domestic sphere. Her uncontrolled magical power is the threat here—with no male figure to channel that power, whether a husband or a son, the hag is loose, avoiding the circumscription of gender convention, avoiding the roles of mother,

118   *Crafting the Witch*

wife, or sexual object. Mitigating her threat in the narrative is the fact that both Spenser and Shakespeare adopt a strategy of marginalization when constructing their hag-witches, so it's clear that they are never in complete control of their magic.

Malory introduces dame Brusen as "one of the grettyst enchaunters that was that tyme in the worlde" (479). He eschews all physical description of the witch, preferring to allow her actions to speak for her (Malory's trademark). Both Spenser and Shakespeare, on the other hand, spend time describing the physical appearance of the witches in their work, emphasizing their age and their grotesqueness. Spenser's nameless "witch," referred to variously as "the Hag," "the wicked Hag," or "the vile hag," mother to the lazy churl who falls in love with Florimell, lives in a "gloomy hollow glen," where she resides alone so "that her deuilish deedes / And hellish arts from people she might hide" (III.vii.6). She dresses in "loathly weedes" and makes "ghastly" faces, staring "with fell looke and hollow deadly gaze" (III.vii.6.4, 14.6, 7.6). Spenser emphasizes her age and her post-reproductive status together: "This wicked woman had a wicked sonne, / The comfort of her age and weary dayes, / A laesie loord, for nothing good to donne" (III.vii.12.1–2). Not only is she an older woman, whose maternal necessity has passed (her child is grown, a "lord" now), but her maternal skills are impugned by the fact that her son is a lazy man who refuses to work or do anything at all (III.vii.12). Spenser's witch is an old hag, whose impoverished solitude reflects her evil nature, as are her Shakespearean sisters.[24]

Shakespeare's Weird sisters, the notorious witches from *Macbeth*, offer directors a wonderful opportunity in representation: they can choose what kind of witches they want the sisters to be, and the many versions of *Macbeth* on film attest to the diversity of witch-tropes that exist in addition to the hag with whom I am concerned in this study.[25] Despite this diversity, there are specific textual suggestions for the witches' appearance, as Banquo describes them in Act I:

> What are these
> So wither'd and so wild in their attire,
> That look not like th' inhabitants o' th' earth,
> And yet are on't? Live you? or are you aught
> That man may question? You seem to understand me,
> By each at once her choppy finger laying
> Upon her skinny lips. You should be women,
> And yet your beards forbid me to interpret
> That you are so. (I.iii.39–47)

Banquo is specific: the figures are "wither'd" and "skinny," suggesting their age, and "wild in their attire," and though they are "women," they have "beards." He specifies age, strange clothing, and lack of femininity—the classic hag figure. Later, Macbeth calls the women "secret, black, and midnight hags," confirming their witch-hag status verbally (IV.i.48). In both Spenser's and Shakespeare's visual representations of the hag-witch, her outward signs of difference (marked by her age, clothing, and use of gender conventions) reflect her inner malevolence. As we shall see, the hag-witch is visually marked because of her association with the demons who give her magical power.

The medieval good witch does not use demonological magic. Brusen, for example, employs love-potions, simple lies, and secret knowledge to assist King Pelles in his quest to make Lancelot sleep with Elayne, Pelles's daughter. The look-alike ring and drugged "kuppe of wyne" (which charms Lancelot so that he becomes "so asoted and madde that he myght make no delay but wythoute ony let he wente to bedde" [so besotted and mad that he could endure no delay, but without any hesitation he went to bed]) work to trick the knight into having sex with Elayne (480). Brusen's ploy does not involve demonic spirits or hellish powers; instead it remains strictly within the domestic sphere, featuring intimate knowledge of Gwenevere and Lancelot's habits, a potion creating tremendous sexual desire, and lies. Ultimately, Brusen assists a father in managing the sexual life of his daughter, taking over for Pelles in arranging the tryst and stepping into a parental role with Elayne (who is never consulted about the matter). While Pelles retains the paternal authority to choose the daughter's sexual (and usually, marital) partner, Brusen has authority over the bedroom, becoming the manager of the practical aspect of the sexual economy. Brusen's domestic magic is characteristic of the medieval good witch, someone non-threatening because her role is essentially maternal—she works within a family for procreative purposes (Galahad is the holy offspring of this union). Though the Renaissance hag-witch borrows Brusen's methods, she mixes them with the power of demons and employs them for different ends.

Spenser's "Hag," from Book III, uses domestic love-magic. When her son desires Florimell so much that he goes mad with woe, the witch pities her son's condition, and tries in vain to heal him "With herbs, with charms, with counsell, & with teares" (III.vii.21.2). Spenser distinguishes these approaches, so similar to those used by Brusen, as distinct from the "deuilish arts" to which the Hag turns next, after "all other helpes" have failed (III.vii.21.6, 9). The Hag sends her "hideous beast" to fetch Florimell or eat her, if things don't work out (III.vii.22.2). Though Spenser does not explicitly call the monster a demon, his introduction of the beast as the Hag's use of "deuilish arts" and his language when describing the beast—it has a "hellish gorge" and feels "deuilish despight" (III.vii.29.2, 28.7)—argue for its demonic origins. Domestic magic fails the Hag, so she moves outside the domestic realm, conjuring a weapon to use against Florimell.

When her "Monster" fails, despite the magical "charmes" which protect the beast against weapons, the Hag must use more demonic magic (III. vii.23.6, 35.9). This time, she brings hell into the home, using a demonic

120   *Crafting the Witch*

"Spright" as the basis for her creation: as she is post-reproductive, with no ability left to create a child through the power of her body, she must conjure spirits from hell to provide herself with creative power (III.viii.4–8). Spenser robs her of what is almost always an important attribute of conventional femininity, her fertility. First, she consults the "Sprights," who are the "maisters of her art," for advice about how to heal her love-sick son, and they suggest the false Florimell ploy—one we've already seen Archimago use when he fashions a demon into a false Una (III.viii.4.4–5). Then she gathers materials with which to mold the body, including conventional romance markers of beauty like "two burning lampes / In siluer sockets" for eyes and "golden wyre" for hair, and places "A wicked Spright yfraught with fawning guile" in charge of animating it (III.viii.7.1–2, 7.6, 8.1). This Spright is identified overtly with Satan, one of the many spirits who fell "with the Prince of Darknesse" into damnation and hell (III. viii.8). The Spright is a master of "counterfeisance," with "all the wyles of wemens wits" at his disposal—hell is the perfect place from which to learn the art of deception, for Spenser (III.viii.8.8–9). The Hag's demonic magic works to pacify her son, and he is pleased with his false lady (until Braggadocio snatches her away). The Hag gains her magic by harnessing the power of spirits, and she generally uses those spirits in the service of her undeserving son.

Shakespeare's witches are also tied to the power of hell and its demons. The Weird sisters meet with Hecat, or Hecate, the goddess of sorcery and enchantment.[26] A pagan deity, in the Christian schema, is a kind of demon, a false spirit, and Hecate even tells the witches to meet her "at the pit of Acheron" (III.v.15). Like Spenser's Hag, Hecate has control over demonic spirits, as she announces to the sisters: "I'll . . . raise such artificial sprites / As by the strength of their illusion / Shall draw him on to his confusion" (III.v.25–29). Likewise, the Weird sisters control spirits, as they reveal when they offer Macbeth the opportunity to hear the relevant prophecies from their "masters'" mouths. These masters turn out to be visual apparitions, spirits, who appear in various forms to tell Macbeth of his inevitable downfall. Through their association with Hecat and with prophetic spirits, the Weird sisters reveal that their magic, too, is drawn from the power of the spirits. The witches show no obvious signs of Christianity throughout the play, and in fact, their beliefs appear to be diametrically opposed to those of the Christian God, as I discuss below. As the witches have no access to Christian spirits, the late sixteenth-century structure of spiritual power dictates that they must be using infernal spirits.

During the play, we see the Weird sisters use their control over spirits to gain prophetic knowledge (which they tell Macbeth and Banquo) and to torment Macbeth with apparitions. But the manner in which the witches contact the spirit-world is derived directly from the domestic magic of the medieval good witch: the sisters brew their magic. The play offers one famous scene, in particular, which represents the magic of the witches as

The Lady is a Hag   121

domestic, "kitchen" magic, similar to that used by Thessela when brewing charms for Fenice. This scene is, of course, Act IV, Scene I, where the Weird sisters await Macbeth's return visit by preparing a magical potion in a cauldron, a characterization directly descended from medieval domestic magic. For example, Chrétien's domestic witch, Thessela, prepares her charms in two scenes from *Cligés* (both discussed in Chapter Two): first, she grinds the potion, using "spices in abundance" (162), and then she blends and mixes the draught with unspecified ingredients gathered "well in advance with everything she knew was needed for the potion" (193). Both Chrétien's designation of spices as key ingredients and his generalized descriptions of grinding, blending, stirring, and mixing work to create the image of a cook in a kitchen, preparing a meal. Shakespeare's witches invoke exactly this kind of culinary convention in the cauldron scene.

Act IV begins with the witches' appearance: "'Tis time" to begin brewing "the charm," as one witch calls the contents of the cauldron (V.i.3, 38). The women take turns adding ingredients to the "charmed pot," simmering them over the fire until the charm is ready and then cooling it rapidly to make it "firm and good" (Vi.9, 38). This is not an unusual domestic scene, women cooking together, but unlike Chrétien, Shakespeare describes the recipe in rich detail. His strategy in this scene mirrors the strategy of Spenser in representing witches—both authors emphasize the malevolence of the witch, the result of her involvement with the devil. She is evil because she seeks out the devil to gain his power; but she seeks out the devil because she is evil. It's a revolving door, a two-sided coin, a Möbius strip. What makes the witches worse is that their domestic actions are not directed toward nourishing children, but work to destroy families.

To emphasize their wickedness, Shakespeare gives the Weird sisters a cauldron full of increasingly more frightening and offensive ingredients. The first sister begins with the "poison'd entrails" of a "toad" who lay under a stone for thirty-one days, a foul-smelling but otherwise not horrible choice (IV.i.5–6). The second sister takes a step further, adding a mix of creature-bits that includes many denizens of the night or the underground, such as the oft-repeated favorite "eye of newt" or its lesser-known cousins "wool of bat," "blind-worm's sting," or "howlet's wing" (IV.i.14–17). She links the witch-brew with the underworld explicitly when she chants, "For a charm of pow'rful trouble, / Like a hell-broth boil and bubble" (IV.i.18–19). The third sister's ingredients most clearly establish the witches as transgressors of social boundaries. The third witch moves from mythology ("scale of dragon" IV.i.22) and traditional magical herb lore ("root of hemlock" IV.i.25) to murder ("liver of blaspheming Jew," "nose of Turk and Tartar's lips," "finger of birth-strangled babe / Ditch-deliver'd by a drab" IV.i.26, 29, 30–31). Her murder victims come from social groups commonly villainized in late medieval and Renaissance literature, including both local indigents (the prostitute) and the inhabitants of the Middle East and Asia (the "Jew," "Turk," and "Tartar," who are, of course, not

122 Crafting the Witch

Christian). Not only is she guilty of murder, but she uses body-parts from people marginalized and denigrated by mainstream society as key elements in her charm. The dead baby is particularly significant, as it demonstrates the anti-maternal instinct in these three women. The witches of *Macbeth* find themselves awash in blood, from the "baboon's blood" used to cool the charm to that of the unfortunate Duncan and Banquo (IV.i.37).

The Weird sisters don't seem to have any reason for offering Macbeth the prophetic knowledge they possess. Shakespeare leaves aside the question of motivation, an issue over which he usually lingers, allowing the witches simply to be evil. They don't require motivation—they are wicked witches, who use their association with fate to torture a man and his wife. Perhaps their intervention is "necessary" to promote the founding of the Stuart line (through Fleance), perhaps they are merely an embodiment of the temptation of the devil, but the witches of *Macbeth* are strictly functional—they embody evil. As in Spenser's *Faerie Queene*, the allegorical nature of wicked witches (hags and temptresses alike) precludes reasons or motivations: Shakespeare's witches target Macbeth because they are wicked; Spenser's witches attack the Faerie knights who wander through their land because they *are* pride (Lucifera), duplicity (Duessa), sexual desire (Acrasia), discord (Ate), envy (Enuie), and slander (Detraction). They have no purpose beyond that of their function—they embody all motivation towards evil.

Though Spenser and Shakespeare provide their witches with all the power of hell, they curtail the expression of that power within their texts. Their witches are often marginal to the main action, and their power is frequently weak or ineffectual against their primary targets. Spenser's Hag, for example, lives "far from all neighbors" so that she can "hurt far off vnknowne, whom euer she enuide" (III.vii.6). Her "herbs" and "charmes" fail the first time she tries to use them, when attempting to heal her son's love-sickness, as does the monster she sends after Florimell (though his mutilation of her horse does cause a few problems). Her fake Florimell works to satisfy her son until the ruling spirit flees the scene with Braggadocio—the Hag can't maintain control over the spirit she conjured. Though the false Florimell does cause trouble for the knights of Book IV, she does not accomplish her primary mission (the healing of the son). None of the Hag's actions affects the story-line until her magic frees itself from her control, and only then, once her power has been removed, can the spirit work for discord. Likewise, the two hags, Enuie and Detraction, don't frighten Arthegall, who "seem'd of them to take no keepe," continuing on to "Faery Court" without further ado (IV.xii.42.9, 43.9). Spenser's hags operate ineffectually, and they pose only a limited threat, one knights can easily overcome.

Shakespeare's marginalization of the *Macbeth* witches is a more complicated affair, as attested by the mountains of prose attempting to explain their presence and function in the play. The appearance of the Weird sisters in the first scene of the play places them in what appears to be a central position: they introduce us to the main conflicts and tell us about the

The Lady is a Hag 123

central character in the story, Lord Macbeth. Marina Favila, for example, argues that the witches clearly "provide the impetus for all action" in the play by presenting Macbeth with temptation (10), a position commonly presented in *Macbeth* criticism.[27] Most critics agree that the witches have some power, often connecting the "wayward" or "weïrd" sisters to various European representations of the three fates.[28] If the witches are not exactly the fates, they are at least prophets, as they accurately predict what will happen (whether or not they control it).[29] For critics and directors, the witches are not only prophets or fates, but also variously pure evil, voodoo priestesses, weather-workers, a Greek chorus, old hags, grotesques, three stages of woman (maiden, mother, crone), Scandinavian Norns, ambiguous figures, androgynes, or heroines revealing the hypocrisy of patriarchy.[30] As the play continues, it becomes more clear that while the sisters influence Macbeth's mental state, it is impossible to determine whether that influence derives from the efficacy of magical power possessed by the sisters or from Macbeth's own ambitious desires.[31] The majority of critics, even those who see the witches as possessing real power, do not see them as a causative force in the play. In other words, they are marginal to both the action and the moral dilemmas on which the play focuses. As the tradition of skepticism regarding witchcraft did not begin in the sixteenth century, but represents a continuous arc from Augustine through Reginald Scot and beyond, we can't say with absolute certainty whether the actors playing the witches (or the play's author) would have believed the sisters powerful or deluded, central or marginalized.

For Shakespeare, of course, Sycorax is the quintessential marginalized witch. Sycorax is always already absent: she is dead before the play begins, yet the overwhelming memory of her previous presence drives characters to invoke her story repeatedly. Caliban's version of the story has already figured in my discussion, when he reminds Prospero that he is heir to the island: "This island's mine by Sycorax my mother, / Which thou tak'st from me" (I.ii.331–2). Sycorax left her son a parcel of land, doing her duty as a single mother (well before *Murphy Brown* and *The Gilmore Girls*) to provide for her offspring. Caliban fails in this scenario, offering his mother's legacy to an abusive surrogate when her absence leaves him alone. To Caliban, Sycorax is "my mother," but to Prospero, she is "the foul witch Sycorax" and "this damn'd witch Sycorax" (I.ii.331, 258, 263). Prospero gives us the only piece of information we learn about Sycorax's physical appearance, calling her a "blue-ey'd hag" (I.ii.269). Though the editors of the Riverside Shakespeare gloss this phrase as "with dark circles around the eyes," it also recalls the gray-eyed heroines of medieval romance (1615n). A blue-eyed hag seems to be exactly the figure lacking in the works of Malory and Spenser—a combination of the beautiful temptress and the grotesque hag, but one who tried to protect her child, who tried to be a good mother. Such a figure defies possibility, it seems, because her body must be completely absent for this characterization to be possible. Sycorax's imagined body

124   *Crafting the Witch*

represents both the pre- and post-maternal, but she functions as neither; her disappearance allows her to stay a mother forever, avoiding the trap of the Renaissance witch. The absent Sycorax can be anything the characters want her to be—Prospero's hag, Caliban's mother, Ariel's original master and imprisoner. If the absent maternal body in Shakespeare's *The Tempest* is a generative screen onto which figures can be projected, the uniquely Spenserian figure of the "present" maternal body is quite the opposite, an over-determined grotesque, a pregnant hag.

"Her fruitfull cursed spawne": Magical and Monstrous Mothers

Less than eleven stanzas into the first Canto of Spenser's *Faerie Queene*, Book 1, Redcrosse Knight and Una find themselves at the mouth of Errour's cave. We catch but the briefest of glimpses of the "Gentle Knight" and his "lovely Ladie" before they rush headlong into danger's path. What leads them here? How is it that our hero, full of the best intentions, finds himself faced with his first enemy, and what is the nature of that enemy exactly? Spenser tells us that "as they past, / The day with cloudes was suddeine overcast, / And angry Jove an hideous storm of raine / Did poure into his Lemans lap" (I.i.6.4–7). The violence of the rainstorm in this passage signals a kind of rape, and the earth becomes the victim of a sexual assault, perpetuated by a masculine god who relentlessly pours a "hideous" fluid into his feminized victim's lap. The viciousness of the attack sends "every wight to shrowd," and Redcrosse and Una likewise seek cover in "a shadie grove" so bountifully full of vegetation that it hides "heavens light" (I.i.6.8, 7.5). Once inside, they are entranced by the many birds and the vast variety of trees, catalogued carefully in two full stanzas; they are "led with delight" to travel further and further within (I.i.10.1). The pathways multiply, creating "so many pathes, so many turnings" that they soon become hopelessly lost (I.i.10.8). "Amid the thickest woods," our hero and heroine find a "hollow cave," in which Errour lives (I.i.11.6–7). In this scene, a violent sexualized encounter forces the pair to proceed through a landscape of generative excess, with a surplus of birds and trees and paths, and leads them to a pregnant womb, a womb bursting with a monstrous, threatening evil. And this evil, we discover, is a mother.

Maternal femininity characterizes most of the female monsters Redcrosse encounters throughout Book 1, but Errour's maternity is the most readily discernible. Our first introduction to her is unequivocal; she is "A monster vile, whom God and man does hate" (I.i.13.7). She is half-serpent, half-woman, a coupling described as "Most lothsom, filthie, foule, and full of vile disdaine" (I.i.14.9). Her grotesqueness, Spenser reveals, is directly related to her generative maternity, magical in its extreme fecundity: a thousand babies suckle on her "poisonous dugs," and she uses "her fruitfull cursed spawne" as a weapon, spewing her progeny at Redcrosse when threatened (I.i.15.6, 22.6). Errour is, in fact, an embodiment of maternal abjection.

The Lady is a Hag 125

Lacanian psychoanalytic theory suggests that the abject is also the pre-object, the thing we hold near yet separate, that which allows one to begin delineating a discrete self, an ego separate from the other. The mother, as the first object, is also the first abject. The mother is abject not because she is other, but because the fantasy of her absolute power threatens to overwhelm the burgeoning, not-yet-fully-differentiated ego. Lacan calls the period in which this fantasy arises "alienation," and uses the term "phallic mother" to signify her apparent omnipotence. As Julia Kristeva explains in *Powers of Horror*, caught within the ambivalence of alienation, wherein the ego and object (the self and the other) have not yet been delineated clearly, the pre-subject fears its "very own identity sinking irretrievably into the mother" (64), and it is this fear that motivates abjection of the maternal body. For Kristeva, "fear of the archaic [or phallic] mother turns out to be essentially fear of her generative power" (77). What is fearsome about Errour is her generative power, her ability to consume, a skill highlighted when her ill-fortuned children creep into her mouth and disappear—Errour eats her children, who "suddain all [are] gone" (Spenser I.i.15.9). Errour threatens to overcome the identity of all who encounter her; she's clearly a phallic mother, who must be abjected to protect the self. Spenser's description of Errour, and of the other monsters that populate *The Faerie Queene*, situates monstrosity firmly within a discourse of abjection, inextricably linked to the abject maternal body and to the fertile sexuality that engenders it. This representation of the maternal is Spenser's way of expanding the indictment of maternity from the witch-figure, which marginalizes pre- and post-maternal bodies, to include abjection of maternity proper, moving from the corrupt sexual temptation of the temptress and the ancient, asexual body of the hag to the grotesque body of the mother.

Despite Spenser's ostensible concern with holiness in Book 1, *The Faerie Queene* notoriously circles around the problem of chastity, and its nemesis, sex. Critics have long argued that, throughout the poem, Spenser's malevolent women are associated with sex and sexuality. For example, Sheila Cavanagh describes the world of *The Faerie Queene* as one where "nightmarish women largely attempt to seduce men away from the field and from virtue, using sex as their primary weapon" (317).[32] The characters in *The Faerie Queene* are, quite frankly, obsessed with sex. The Errour episode of the first Canto functions as an introductory metaphor for Spenser's fascination throughout Book 1 with the corrosive power of sexuality and its resultant maternal generativity. In this sequence, Spenser foregrounds an equation that becomes the model on which he builds with each new malevolent creature: sexual union mandates excessive fertility, which is itself abject. Errour, who seems to be the classic phallic mother, threatens to engulf Redcrosse, wrapping him in her voluminous tail, smothering him, and prompting Una to shout, "Strangle her, else she sure will strangle thee" (I.i.19.4). To save his own subjectivity, Redcrosse must abject Errour, and the materiality of that abjection is highlighted in this scene. Redcrosse's

126 *Crafting the Witch*

touch spawns more generative excess, prompting Errour to vomit, a fertile bile likened to the excessive fertility of the Nile, and it isn't until Redcrosse castrates Errour, chopping off her head, that he is able to escape her threat. In Spenser's fantasy, castrating the mother poisons her, reversing her generative power: when she dies, Errour's offspring feast on her blood, gorging themselves to death. Her fluidity thus brings death, in opposition to the most maternal of fluids, milk, which sustains life. Generative excess, dangerous because it cannot be controlled, devours itself. Read in this way, the Errour encounter marks sex as both threatening and corruptive and characterizes maternity as the necessary (and monstrous) consequence of the sexual relation.

As we have seen with both Errour and Duessa, castration reveals the way in which fertility hides lack, robbing Errour of her brood and Duessa of her transformative power, and it is precisely this secret lack that is monstrous to Spenser. Redcrosse encounters repeated demonstrations of this principle, but consistently fails to recognize its implications. Sumptuous excess characterizes the house of Pride, domain of Lucifera: the building is "bravely garnished," covered in "golden foile," with "many loftie towers . . . goodly galleries . . . faire windowes, and delightful bowres" (I.iv.2.6, 4.4, 6–8). "Great troupes of people" travel towards the house, and "Infinite sorts of people abide" within (I.iv.3.1, 6.7). What Redcrosse does not realize, but we suspect, is that behind this fertile façade, the "hinder parts, that few could spie, / Were ruinous and old" (I.iv.5.8–9), and Spenser's description here echoes his description of Duessa's nether regions. When the Dwarfe discovers the "huge numbers" of "caytive wretched thrals" in Lucifera's "dongeon deepe," we see that her generativity is decayed, and therefore monstrous (I.v.45.8–9). The womblike dungeon produces creatures "that [waylè] night and day," like children born into death (I.v.45.9). Pride generates naught but sin, turning people into nothing but "carkases of beasts in butchers stall" (I.v.49.2). Here again, carefully contrived excess covers a lack, a poisoned fertility.

Castration and decay also characterize Night, whom Duessa calls "most auncient Grandmother of all," identifying her as the wellspring of all maternity (I.v.22.2). Duessa invokes "great Nightès children," trying to goad her into avenging the death of Sans joy and the defeat of Sans foy (I.v.23.8). Night, however, as Duessa learns, does not really possess this power; though she goes with Duessa to retrieve Sans foy, she cannot save him, and the two must bring him to the underworld, to death. Night's description reveals her as one of Spenser's abject mothers: "her abhorrèd face" is "so filthy and so fowle" that even wolves and owls, creatures of night, shriek to see it (I.v.30.9). Her children, like those of the other castrated mothers I've discussed, are doomed, born into eternal death, as Night is the "mother . . . of falsehood, and root of Duessaes race" (I.v.27.6–7). Her legacy is duplicity and façade, signifying the way in which maternal presence masks phallic absence. Mothers are monstrous because they are mothers.

The Lady is a Hag   127

There are several other examples of Spenser's consistent conflation of sex with generative excess and monstrous, reversed maternity: Orgoglio's exaggeratedly large body becomes nothing more than "an emptie bladder" when Arthur defeats him, and his castle floor is covered in the "bloud of guiltlesse babes" (I.viii.24.9, 35.6); Despair's womb-like residence furnishes a space in which he can work to promote death, echoing Redcrosse's experience in Orgoglio's lair (I.ix.33–54); and the final foe, the dragon, is "monstrous, horrible, and vast . . . swolne with wrath, poyson, and with bloudy gore," and possessed of a serpentine tail reminiscent of Errour's (I.xi.8.7–9). Spenser's gendering of the dragon as male should strip him of visible signs of femininity, but the swollen, fluid-filled body marks him as pregnant. The dragon, Redcrosse's ultimate challenge, therefore presents the most convincing and impenetrable pretense of phallic omnipotence, thwarting each of our hero's efforts to pierce its gargantuan, swollen body, and nearly killing Redcrosse twice. It is not until Redcrosse uses the dragon's excess against it, ramming his sword down the huge opening of its "darksome hollow maw" (another womb) that he is able to defeat the beast (I.xi.53.8). The dragon is so threatening, its façade so convincing, that people worry, even after its death, that "in his wombe might lurke some hidden nest / Of many Dragonets, his fruitfull seed" (I.xii.10.5–6). His fertility is so monstrous, so excessive, that even death seems too weak to counter it. In this example, grotesque maternity encompasses the masculine body as well.

Spenser's *Faerie Queene* is the most extreme example of the construction of maternity as a monstrous, threatening force, but the works of Malory and Shakespeare also address the issue of monstrous maternity. In particular, one Shakespearean example from *Macbeth* demonstrates the underlying fear that motivates representations of monstrous maternity. When Lord Macbeth begins to share his misgivings about the intended murder with Lady Macbeth, she questions his masculinity, telling him that he will be "a man" only if he dares to go through with the plan (I.vii.49). In this conversation, she uses a striking example to make it clear to her husband how loyal she is to her oath:

> I have given suck, and know
> How tender 'tis to love the babe that milks me;
> I would, while it was smiling in my face,
> Have pluck'd my nipple from his boneless gums,
> And dash'd the brains out, had I so sworn as you
> Have done to this. (I.vii.54–59)

Lady Macbeth conjures the most frightening image, a murderous mother, to illustrate the depth of her commitment to her word. In particular, she pinpoints one of the most tender moments, when the mother provides nourishment to her child, and emphasizes that, if needed, she would turn that nourishment into death. Avoiding monstrous maternity is not worth

128   *Crafting the Witch*

breaking an oath. The image of a mother killing her child is so powerful because it highlights the true relationship between mothers and children: because mothers have the power to sustain their children's lives, they also have the power to end them. Our response to murdering mothers comes from deep within, from the childhood terror of being consumed by the all-powerful mother—the murdering mother is that nightmare come true.

In particular, the early modern period saw a heightened fascination with the image of the murdering mother. Susan C. Staub analyzes the representation of "child murder" in early modern pamphlets and "street literature" in England.[33] Not only does Staub document the popularity of murderous mothers in "early modern dramas, broadsheets and news pamphlets," but her analysis reveals a tendency in these literary genres to characterize the murdering mothers as "decidedly unnatural, monstrous, and sexually promiscuous" (333, 335). The conflation of improper maternity with sexual promiscuity is an equation we have seen before, in the predatory witches lurking throughout Malory's and Spenser's texts, and its appearance here is simply an extrapolation of the same logic. Richard Kieckhefer reveals the medieval ancestry of the Renaissance interest in child-murders, arguing that fifteenth-century European witchcraft trials show a tendency to accuse witches, in particular, of abducting and eating children.[34] In the wake of economic change, maternity could no longer be taken for granted, a fact emphasized by the widespread representations of maternity gone wrong. This image was so powerful that the invocation of the murderous mother in Lady Macbeth's speech allows Shakespeare to conjure an entire legacy of monstrous maternity and to tap into the popular interest of his audience in just a few lines.

Both the anti-maternal representations of witches and other strategies for demonizing maternity in the texts discussed in this chapter reflect a more widespread concern with maternal roles in the sixteenth century. Scholars working on mothers and maternity in the Renaissance suggest a number of strategies of representation.[35] Deborah Willis, for example, who writes about the connection between witches and mothers in *Malevolent Nurture*, says, "Witches were women, I believe, because women are mothers: witchcraft beliefs encode fantasies of maternal persecution" (6). Willis cites changing familial and legal conditions as part of the reason for anxiety about maternity: specifically, tension over the management of finances in elite families where mothers might act "in ways that disadvantaged their male heirs" and developments in law allowing married women and widows "the significant right to file suits on their own behalf in Chancery court—suits that often brought them into conflict with their children" (17). As more research becomes available, it is increasingly clear that many representations of maternal power glorify rather than villainize, but the wicked witch (and the other kinds of monstrous mothers related to her) explores the maternal "dark side."

If witches are all anti-mothers, and all mothers may be witches, then the space for good mothers is remarkably small and tenuous. Anxiety about maternity permeates the discourse of early modern England, manifesting in both literary and non-literary texts. Mothers are everywhere—we all have one—and it is therefore no surprise that witches seem to be everywhere in the texts produced during the sixteenth century. Turn a corner, and there lurks a witch; bother your neighbor, and you might find she's a witch; even your wife might be a witch. And your mother, too!

IV. THIS WITCH IS MY WITCH, THIS WITCH IS YOUR WITCH

Shadowy shapes slip through the woods, some in the air, some on the ground. One by one, they materialize at a clearing where the dewy grass glistens in the moonlight. They dance together, and as the movements become more frenzied, the cry of a baby lingers high in the breeze. There's a fire, and the women take turns adding ingredients, chanting and dancing until a dark shape appears. The ladies' dancing becomes erotic, and it is not long before the movements become sexual. The sounds of passion, of prayers and songs to the night, of laughter and howling, continue until just before dawn, when the figures melt away, one by one, back through the forest and the skies, back to their homes.

The scene I have just described is a composite picture of the set of elements which became the "witches' sabbath" in the late fifteenth century: flying, nightly meetings, cannibalism (especially of children), naked dancing and orgies, sexual intercourse with the devil representative of a demonic pact, and ritualized magical spells. These elements pervade clerical and literary representations of magic, in particular, implicating witches as participants in a communal society of transgressive women in league with the devil. But there is another version of witchcraft, described by Deborah Willis:

> The "typical" witchcraft case began when an older woman had a falling out with a neighbor—often another woman, usually a younger one. The older woman tended to be poorer, and frequently the falling out occurred after she had gone to her neighbor with a request for food or some domestic item or for access to land, and the neighbor refused her request. The woman went away, cursing her neighbor openly or muttering under her breath. Later, some misfortune happened to the neighbor or her family. A child fell sick, a wife or husband died, cattle or sheep died, a freak storm destroyed the crops, the milk went sour, the butter would not turn. The neighbor recalled the cursing of the old woman and suspected the misfortune was the product of her witchcraft. (31–32)

This description is a generalization derived from sixteenth- and seventeenth-century witchcraft trial records and related pamphlets. This domestic conflict is the polar opposite of the erotic, exotic representation above—the

130   Crafting the Witch

time changes from night to day, the bodies turn from naked and sexualized to clothed and asexual, the community of women morphs into conflict between women, and the magic moves from a general desire for evil to a specific instance of malevolence. What a change is here!

Both versions of witchcraft represented above had currency in the cultural milieu of sixteenth-century England, but these narratives originate in two very different sets of documents: 1) the writing of theological men such as Nicolas Remy, Francesco Maria Guazzo, Pierre de Lancre, Heinrich Kramer, Jean Bodin, and even King James VI of Scotland,[36] and 2) the statements made by the accusers and accused (*not* the inquisitors and witchhunters) in extant trial documents. The theological writing, produced by erudite, religious men with authority and power, concocts a world where lusty, wild women worship a male figure whose violent sexual encounters bind his lovers to him. The women receive small children-substitutes, familiars, who suckle at the witch's "teat" or mark. This fantasy is clearly about motherhood, but a threatening motherhood, connected to an evil male father-figure, a powerful man behind the pawns who do his work. Motherhood is threatening here because it represents the power of a male adversary, a masculine threat to the power of Christianity and the church. Such specific and violent sexual imagery (including representing Satan's penis as ice-cold and sex as painful) paints sex as firmly within male power, something that the woman does not enjoy, but which she seeks to gain access to the power offered by the male. Sexuality here is only threatening insofar as it is connected to men. If men are in control of sexuality, then they are in control of motherhood, and this equation negates the threat of women who control their own sexuality, women like Duessa or Morgan le Fay, pre-maternal witches. The temptress witch of literature is sister to the sexual witch of theological writers.

On the other hand, the temptress witch does not fit the role assigned by the trial documents. The witch of the trial documents is typically older, often a mother, a member of a community of women engaged in domestic exchange.[37] In the trials, women most commonly accuse other women, moving within a world that does not often include men, a world of recurrent, never-ending domestic chores and conflicts. Just as the hag-witch of Renaissance literature seems to escape the control of male authority, moving throughout the narratives as she pleases, creating small moments of domestic havoc, the witches of Renaissance trials negotiate domestic problems with other women without male interference. In this world, witches were not overly sexualized, mystical figures; they were real women whose magical knowledge gave them an edge when responding to real problems. Accusers often resorted to male governmental authority only when those problems were unsolvable, as in the case of Elizabeth Sawyer; Sawyer was accused after she hit Agne Ratcliffe's sow (which had eaten some of Sawyer's soap), and Ratcliffe fell ill the same night.[38] The conflict here is typical—a domestic dispute between two women—and certainly not the kind of problem that the courts would be interested in adjudicating. Ratcliffe's illness

The Lady is a Hag   131

stymied the doctors, eventually causing her death. The unsolvable problem resulted in an appeal to the authorities as traditional domestic conflict-resolution did not work. The trial documents reveal a witch almost antithetical to the clerical fantasy-witch: instead of lusty and wild, trial witches are busy and ordinary; instead of sexual slaves to Satan, trial witches are mothers, wives, and widows who rule a female, domestic world; instead of plotting to overthrow male Christian authority, trial witches plot what they will cook for dinner.

The disparity between accused witches and the clerical fantasy was clearly great, but authorities were so invested in the idea of Satanic witch-craft that questioners went to great lengths to secure confessions that corroborated clerical beliefs. The following excerpt from the trial of Elizabeth Sawyer demonstrates a common method for eliciting details from accused witches:

> *Question.* How long is it since the Devil and you had acquaintance together, and how oftentimes in the week would he come and see you and you company with him?
> *Answer.* It is eight years since our first acquaintance and three times in the week the Devil would come and see me, after such his acquaintance gotten of me. He would come sometimes in the morning and sometimes in the evening.
> *Question.* In what shape would the Devil come unto you?
> *Answer.* Always in the shape of a dog and of two collars, sometimes of black and sometimes of white.
> *Question.* What talk had the Devil and you together when that he appeared to you, and what did he ask of you, and what did you desire of him?
> *Answer.* He asked me when he came unto me how I did and what he should do for me, and demanded of me my soul and body, threatening then to tear me in pieces if that I did not grant unto him my soul and my body which he asked of me. (qtd. in Levack 195)

The pattern is readily apparent: an interrogator asks a question indicating to the accused what he would like to hear, and the accused replies accordingly, sometimes adding the kind of embellishments that were often publicized in pamphlets and broadsides about trials. The details of the confession seem to have very little relation to the material evidence presented. In the case of Elizabeth Sawyer, the material evidence consisted of the following: 1) a "great and long suspicion" that Sawyer was a witch, 2) a test involving the burning of thatch from her home, which caused her to appear, indicating that she was the cause of wicked "mischief," and 3) physical deformity (including a "most pale and ghost-like" face and a "crooked and deformed" body). The facts of the case were circumstantial at best—Sawyer hit a sow, and Ratcliffe fell ill. Nevertheless, a substantive causal connection clearly existed in the minds of the accusers.

132 *Crafting the Witch*

Just as the clerical fantasy eclipsed the apparent evidence about accused witches in the Renaissance, literary representations inherited from the sixteenth century (especially the figure of the hag-witch) still overshadow the extant textual evidence. This happens even in learned circles, as with this example taken from Kieckhefer's *Magic in the Middle Ages*:

> The safest generalization [about those accused of witchcraft] is that fingers would point most quickly at someone who had established a reputation for being a bad, disagreeable neighbor. Dorothea Hindremstein, tried by a municipal court at Lucerne in 1454, is a perfect example. Some time earlier her mother had been burned for sorcery in Uri, and if Dorothea had not fled she would have been burned as well; in the meantime she had been made to swear that she would not return to Uri. Her neighbors and even her husband at Lucerne eventually concluded that she had inherited her mother's power to lay curses on people. One neighbor woman told the court how her child had gotten into a fight and shoved Dorothea's child into the mud. Dorothea came out and angrily threatened that the witness's child would never forget this offense. Within twelve hours the offending child began to grow ill, and he lay sick for three weeks. Who could doubt that Dorothea's curse had taken effect? Another neighbor told how he had been careful not to antagonize Dorothea because of her ill repute. Yet he told how other people had quarreled with her and had soon suffered the consequences: illness of half a year's duration, death of a fine cow, or blood instead of milk from a cow. How had Dorothea done all this? The man could not explain—indeed, the witnesses were generally unconcerned about the precise mechanism of the supposed sorcery—but he feared that if she and her family were allowed to live they would inflict still more damage. Then he said no more, fearing that he might be ill repaid for his testimony.
>
> In many ways Dorothea fits the stereotype of the "old hag." Many of the women prosecuted for sorcery seem to have been old women who had no family to support them, or who received no support from the family they did have. Doubtless they tended, like Dorothea, to be ill-natured sorts, who bore resentment toward those about them and inspired resentment in return. (192–3)

Dorothea Hindremstein, Richard Kieckhefer tells us in the above excerpt, is a perfect example of the witch-hag. She is a real-life embodiment of the kind of witches who figure prominently in Renaissance literature, it would seem. Or is she? Let us consider the above passage. Dorothea suffers accusations of witchcraft because she is a bad neighbor, according to Kieckhefer's reading here, a view consonant with many other historians.[39] Robin Briggs argues that the conflicts precipitating witchcraft accusations arose from long-standing, localized tensions needing an outlet for resolution, and

The Lady is a Hag   133

the specificity of those conflicts is not suited to overarching generalized explanations (such as those made by most scholars when discussing the witchcraft phenomenon). Thus, people who lived in close contact with one another for decades might end up embroiled in witchcraft accusations—this seems a bit like Kieckhefer's "ill-natured" neighbors.

But Kieckhefer's example doesn't really fit this explanation. Dorothea is not a long-time bad neighbor whose constant irritations drive those around her to protect themselves: Kieckhefer says she moved to Lucerne from Uri, where her mother was burned for practicing magic. Dorothea was an outsider with a reputation for witchcraft inherited from her mother, not a long-term member of the community. Kieckhefer's description of Dorothea's practice of witchcraft defies his summative explanation that so assuredly tells us Dorothea "fits the stereotype of the 'old hag'" (193). Dorothea had children who played with those of the accusing mother in the first example Kieckhefer notes, which suggests that she was not "old," but probably around the same age as her accuser. Dorothea is not a woman "with no family to support her," as Kieckhefer mentions both her husband and at least one child in his description of her offenses. Finally, though Kieckhefer accuses Dorothea of being the one who "inspired resentment" because of her "disagreeable" nature, his examples both tell the reverse story. In the first instance, the accusing mother's child pushes Dorothea's child into the mud, at which point Dorothea intercedes to chastise the offending child. In the second example, the male witness attests to Dorothea's reputation for witchcraft (her unfortunate dowry), and then recites the local gossip about the accused woman. In both of these cases, Dorothea is the recipient, not the initiator of the aggression. My point here is simple: the literary stereotype of the witch-hag can easily eclipse the specificity of the individual people actually accused of practicing witchcraft.

This is a problem endemic to scholarly work on witchcraft, a point Diane Purkiss makes convincingly in her deconstruction of the "the myth of the Burning Times."[40] Although she focuses on the figure of the healer-witch associated with certain feminist appropriations of fertility mythologies, the effect is similar: critics, historians, theorists, and other scholars often disregard the details in search of the bigger picture, the larger ideological issues at stake. This fact is surely frustrating to someone looking for the truth about the identities of the real women and men accused of being witches, but it is also demonstrative of the remarkable power of narrative to structure perceptions and thus transcend everyday life. The reason we continue to study magic and witchcraft in particular results just as much from our ability to mold medieval and early modern discourses to suit the needs of contemporary culture as it does from a desire for information about those time periods.

My own work is surely no exception. I am certain that my readings of the development of magical figures in Arthurian literature are colored by my understanding of similar figures currently popular in American film

134 *Crafting the Witch*

and literature. In fact, it is because of contemporary representations of the witch-figure that I believe this study to be especially important. Witchcraft is no longer a viable threat to most residents of Europe and much of North America, largely because of disbelief in its efficacy, yet we continue to use figures popular in the medieval and early modern periods (when the percentage of the population who believed in magical power was much higher) to villainize and patronize women in popular media. Perhaps the best example of our witchy Renaissance inheritance is the Wicked Queen from Disney's *Snow White*.

The Wicked Queen of *Snow White* possesses the power to transform herself, from sinister beauty to cackling hag. Presumably, she has the power to change back, but she never gets the opportunity to use it, as the dwarves chase her over a cliff and she falls to her death. Her power is fascinating, and the Disney artists linger over the details in the potion-brewing scene, my favorite cinematic representation of the domestic magic of the witch. This scene, which takes place in a dungeon-like kitchen complete with hollow skulls and a large black cauldron, highlights the domestic nature of the magic. The Queen has a recipe-book from which she works, adding a drop of this and a dram of that, and the products of her toil are a potion and a poisoned apple, domestic artifacts. The attack itself is domestic: an older woman offers a younger woman apples for baking. The domesticity of the magic throws its malice into sharp relief; such malevolence seems out of place in a setting we associate with nurturing care. In many ways, the Wicked Queen typifies the Renaissance literary witch: she embodies both manifestations of the anti-maternal figure, the beautiful, evil temptress and the ugly, old hag; she's a monstrous (step)-mother who threatens the stability of the nuclear family when she tries to kill her husband's daughter; and in the end of her story, she receives her punishment (death!). The hag overwhelms and completes the representation—the temptress is always a veneer for the hag, who is the true form of the creature. As a stereotypical example of the wicked witch, she seems to leap right out of the sixteenth century, perfectly preserved for modern audiences by the artful animators at our most popular magic shop, the wonderful world of Walt Disney.

The Queen's domesticity is connected to her particular brand of anti-maternal evil, a reversed domestic space where nurture turns dangerous. Specifically, the Queen is a would-be murdering mother—one who tries to kill a child. The figure of the murdering mother is perhaps one of the most disturbing images we continue to produce. She was certainly a popular figure in the Renaissance, and though she does not appear frequently in contemporary film, we do see her commonly enough in other forms of media. Unfortunately, where she appears most is the news, as we gape in awe at sensational accounts of women who have killed their children, whether by driving them into the water or leaving them in a hot car. This seems the

The Lady is a Hag   135

most monstrous of paradoxes—that someone who can create life should be willing then to kill what she created. We continue to marginalize this kind of figure, blaming the actions on mental illness, extreme poverty, or even on lack of education.

Despite such grim representations of "real" mothers in the news media, twentieth-century cinema has produced less pessimistic representations of maternal hostility. For example, a fantasy film from the 1980s, *Labrynth*, offers a contemporary look at the instinct towards monstrous maternity, resolving that instinct through a magical fantasy quest that simulates the murderous instinct in an otherworld not unlike that of medieval and early modern romance. Sarah (played by a young Jennifer Connelly), the daughter of a quasi-wicked stepmother, must watch her younger half-brother; she is forced into the role of surrogate mother, a role she rejects as violently as she does her step-mother's comments about her tardiness. She expresses aloud the desire of a murderous mother, that her child be taken away from her (in this case, through its symbolic death, transformation into a goblin). Her expression of this desire makes it true, and the Goblin King (David Bowie in super-tight tights) snatches her brother away to his castle, where he will turn the baby into a goblin after a ritual amount of time. Once she enacts her desire in the fantasy world, she regrets it, and the rest of the movie follows her journey to rescue her brother from the otherworld (the underworld?). In the end, of course, she regains possession of Toby, the baby brother, and returns to accept the maternal role she's clearly meant to play. Though the film's restrictive construction of femininity as maternity can frustrate a female viewer, its creation of a fantasy space in which hostile feelings about maternity can be explored and resolved without horrible consequences promotes needed tolerance of a range of relationships to maternity available for women. Sarah must love and care for her brother, but he is just her brother, after all, and not her child. The movie ends with her recognition that her hostile feelings are ok (she lets her fantasy-world friends enter the real world, bringing her explorative space back like a souvenir from her journey), and as the credits roll, we can imagine she is free to make her own choices from now on.

Contemporary representations of maternity such as this one work towards mitigating maternal hostility towards children without recourse to the trope of the monstrous mother. In this film, there are no witches, though there is a shrill-speaking step-mother who complains that Sarah treats her "like a wicked step-mother in a fairy story." This film's initial solution to the problem of the step-mother is akin to Shakespeare's: it erases her. As the story develops, *Labrynth* offers an alternate solution in the figure of Sarah, who works out her maternal hostility in the course of a traditionally masculine quest narrative. The generally positive tenor of the movie is largely due to the magic of Jim Henson's puppets, but relies also on the fact that magic, the operative force in the world of the Goblin King,

136   Crafting the Witch

is no longer perceived by the audience as an immediate or viable threat. The sheer joy of the puppetry almost disguises the fact that Sarah decides she does love her brother (and the normative domestic world), as long as she can dream about a space where she can reject those choices. The story is clearly a fantasy, a harmless children's story, not the description of what many feared was a real threat to their lives. That fear no longer permeates mainstream discourses about magic, but the wicked witch has not disappeared along with belief. She still remains, cackling and riding her broomstick across countless autumn skies, a wicked crone. Why is the witch *still* wicked? Let's find out.

5 Hags on Film
Contemporary Echoes of the Early Modern Wicked Witch

In this project, my purpose was to describe and analyze trends in the literature (favoring literary evidence over social, cultural, anthropological, or historical studies), and that task occupies the bulk of the preceding pages. What we have seen is that, in Arthurian literature, male magical threats transform over the course of five centuries into female magical threats. I identified a few of the most salient social factors for the authors and representations of gendered magic considered—from feudal violence and economic disaster to nascent capitalism (and the resulting extreme gender anxiety)—but my discussion is by no means an exhaustive one, and the complex web of power structures which comprise societal relations cannot be explained adequately in as short a space as I have devoted to them. My analysis of Arthurian witches adds one more perspective to the ever-growing conversation about literary and cultural representations of magic. I have argued that while twelfth- and thirteenth-century writers utilized magic to construct a normative gender binary, emphasizing the threat of male violence, writers producing Arthurian narratives after the fourteenth century began to represent female magical power as threatening, a shift which resulted in the re-appropriation of the wicked witch-hag. Specifically, the witch-hag assuages a profound cultural anxiety about the position of women within the shifting economic pressures of nascent capitalism (i.e., mercantilism) by stigmatizing and punishing (both symbolically and actually) women who do not conform to an idealized maternal norm.

The Renaissance hag still bewitches contemporary American audiences. We watch her in Disney films and extravagant musicals (old and new), read about her in fantasy fiction and neo-gothic horror stories, dress up like her on Halloween, and evoke her iconic image with a mere cackle. We write about her—legions of us!—still fascinated with her appeal, still interested in why, for about 200 years, she became so important and dangerous that she required quick, decisive, and widespread extermination. The European witch-craze, in particular, has been the subject of an extraordinarily large amount of writing, as scholars from just about every discipline have taken on such queries as why witch persecutions dramatically increased after about 1500, why they varied by region yet were so maddeningly pervasive,

138   *Crafting the Witch*

and, more recently, why women were accused and prosecuted over eighty percent of the time. Theories abound: groups of women secretly worshipped a horned god and sought to reclaim matriarchy in a patriarchal world;[1] narrow-minded misogynist, heterosexist, patriarchal (and perverse!) clerics foisted elite demonological beliefs onto a naïve and needy populace, who happily utilized the church-provided scapegoats (women, mothers, homosexuals, the poor, and so on);[2] long-festering village-level domestic conflicts between women escalated when unexplained tragedies coincided with a particularly nasty quarrel;[3] real practitioners of magic or ignorant rubes rubbed psychotropic ointments on their skin or ate fungus-filled rye bread, resulting in hallucinatory visions about night-flying, orgiastic sex, and strange twitchy fits;[4] and early modern Europe fell prey to record numbers of mental and physical illnesses, from mass hysteria to syphilis.[5] And that's only a few of the theories in circulation! Even when critics privilege one particular causative factor, most ultimately acknowledge the need for a multi-causal approach (as do I); surely a huge variety of factors combined to create and sustain the cultural milieu in which the early modern witch-hunts flourished. One factor often addressed by critics is the question of belief in magic, and more specifically, in witches.

The reason that the nexus of religious change, scientific experimentation, economic crisis, sexist backlash, and local politics coalesced around the witch figure (rather than landing on an Amazon, an elf, or a dragon) is that early modern people believed in witches. Not all people, but a lot of people. The majority of people, it seems, believed that things sometimes happened because *someone* (a witch) desired them to happen, because *someone* used secret magical power to transform reality. They inherited belief in witches from ancient sources—Europeans, North Africans, and Middle Easterners all had vibrant traditions of magic featuring various kinds of witches. Their beliefs were specifically inflected for different individuals and different groups (as are all beliefs), depending on such factors as socio-economic status, gender, ethnicity, religion, sexuality, and nationality—and resulting in such radically different figures as the devil's whore of clerical fantasy, the grotesques of romance, and the crabby village mom of the trial documents—but there was a fundamental cultural agreement in magic's efficacy that allowed government officials to prosecute successfully the crime of being a witch.

There are as many theories of why belief in witches (and thus the prosecution of witches) ended as there are about why it began, and they are equally as plausible and, ultimately, as unsatisfying. The general consensus seems to be that forces like scientific rationalism, urbanization, and secularization simply became too powerful to ignore. But nobody can say why with any certainty. Why do paradigm shifts happen? Why do beliefs change? They do so slowly, with no easily pinpointed spot—there it is, the moment people stopped believing in witches, the minute they began believing the world was round, the second when people stopped believing that

Hags on Film   139

Christopher Columbus was a hero. It's fairly easy to document changes of belief—as I have done here—creating complex narratives about when a particular idea entered the discourse and when another idea displaced it. But to explain *why* the change happened, why individual humans (and large groups) change their minds, their speech, their beliefs, we can speculate, if we wish, narrate precise timelines, even—but how can we know? There's no way to determine definitively what people actually believe (let alone why that belief should change) in any period, including our own. We know what we believe (perhaps), and we know what others tell us they believe (whether over a cocktail or with a keyboard), and we can observe people's behaviors (which may tell us something about their beliefs)—but we cannot know with certainty what they believe. In lieu of certainty, we can at best hope to explore and interpret the evidence (whatever we consider that to be). Two types of evidence seem especially relevant to the question of belief: legal and literary.

Why is the analysis of a legal system potentially useful to the question of belief? Because generally we don't bother to go through the ponderous processes of the legal system unless we believe the grievance is serious. Though people with money can surely take advantage of legislation more easily than those without (and this must have been even more true for those who lived in the highly stratified society of England from the twelfth to the sixteenth centuries than it is today in the U.S.), bureaucratic procedure prevents most of the frivolous cases from bothering the authorities (although some might argue that's no longer true). Even when people abuse the judicial system by making unfair accusations, they must provide a charge likely to be believed by a judge or jury. Analysis of the legislation against witchcraft and the circumstances of specific cases thus offers some insight (though limited) into what was considered threatening enough—and believable enough—to demand legal action. In the Renaissance, the multitude of witchcraft cases that reached the inquisitors demonstrates deep-seated fear of (and therefore belief in) witches and witchcraft.

Literary evidence is also useful to understanding how a culture's discourses construct and maintain particular beliefs. Literary production is generally understood by both creator and consumer as imaginative—that is, as representing events and characters that do not necessarily exist. Literary evidence can't tell us whether or not the things represented actually happened, but it can tell us how a figure or plot functioned mythically, psychologically, and socially: literature performs cultural work, assigning certain representations privilege while divesting others of importance, constructing certain sets of behaviors as normative or as other, and negotiating social tensions by resolving them within a safe narrative space. Literary evidence can't tell us what people in a particular culture believed, but it can tell us something of what they believed *in*. Literature can show us what people find honorable and reprehensible, what fascinates them and what they find uninteresting or unimportant, and what latent assumptions and

140   *Crafting the Witch*

biases color their daily lives. If the law can show us what behaviors people found intolerable, literature can show us what they found acceptable, exciting, tragic, or ridiculous.

As we might expect, when we compare the literary representation of magical users with prosecution and punishment histories for the twelfth through the sixteenth centuries, we find a strong correlation: generally, in times when the law is relatively relaxed, when few cases of magic-use or witchcraft are prosecuted, the literature tends to represent magical characters as less threatening, but when legislation becomes more strict and cases come to trial more frequently, the literature tends to feature representations of magical figures which are more extreme and sinister. In other words, the cultural resonance of certain figures—wicked witches—is greater at certain times than at others. Early medieval English writers and readers did not find the witch-hag as powerful a figure as did later writers, whose villainization of female magical figures provided an ideological justification for accusing and punishing real women (who may or may not have been magic–users).

Many scholars have analyzed the legislation about and prosecution of witches and witchcraft. I cannot possibly hope to add original scholarship to the monumental works produced in this field in just a few pages, nor do I attempt such folly.[6] Rather, I would like to highlight a few major aspects of the development of magic- and witchcraft-related law in England to illustrate the manner in which the literature and the law influence one another.

In medieval England, secular courts usually prosecuted magic-users only if the magic was both heretical and harmful, and the method of prosecution was accusatorial. Kieckhefer outlines accusatorial procedure as follows:

> Until the late Middle Ages . . . municipal courts retained what is known as "accusatory" procedure: a trial would begin only when an aggrieved party pressed charges in court and took responsibility for proving them; if the accusers did not prove the allegations, they would typically be liable to the same punishment that the accused would otherwise have suffered. (189)

In light of the consequences for accusing someone else of using harmful magic, it's no surprise that few cases against sorcerers and witches appear in legal records.[7] Anglo-Saxon laws were generally lenient towards magic use, and prosecution generally occurred only when the magic was used for harm or destruction.[8] In fact, when it came to night-flights, a precursor to the more fully developed witch's sabbath of early modern witchcraft, the attitude of the court was often one of skepticism.[9] In this time of few prosecutions and significant skepticism about the actual ability of women to possess harmful magic, the magical figures who appear in the texts surveyed in this study are represented in positive (though hegemonic) ways, as Chapter Two demonstrates. The early narratives construct magical giants and

Hags on Film 141

churls as the most prominent threats (although usually easily dispatched) while the records of prosecution suggest that violent men were prosecuted in secular courts far more often than were magic-users of either gender.[10] During a time when state prosecutions of violent male behavior were on the rise, the knights of Christian romance rode around valiantly, lopping off the heads of those dangerous super-men, symbolically castrating those who did not conform to the dictates of the chivalric ethos, whose masculinity is too violent.[11] While the representation of violent masculinity was relatively simple (follow the rules=good; break 'em=bad), the most complex and ambiguous representations of magic in the early Arthurian material involve prophetic power, a kind of magic important to Christian doctrine and thus probably more widely believed in than other forms of magic less connected to or disparaged by the church (like medicine or necromancy). Here, skepticism about certain magical figures (e.g., witches) provides space for playful use of those figures, but writers embedded the more familiar, commonly-practiced magical behaviors (e.g., wizardly prophecy) within a matrix of ambivalence and fear.

At some point after the thirteenth century, English secular courts began to adopt an inquisitorial procedure influenced by both ecclesiastical and secular law in continental Europe. I say at some point because different scholars support a variety of opinions about when inquisitorial practice really came to England: Richard Kieckhefer and Alexander Murray name Pope Gregory IX's appointment of inquisitors for heresy from 1227 to 1241 as the beginning of inquisitorial procedure,[12] but Michael Bailey cites the decree of Pope John in 1326 (*Super illius specula*), which condemned all sorcerers to excommunication and "other appropriate penalties" (967);[13] others, such as Pennethorne Hughes, point to Pope Innocent III's 1484 bull, *Summis desiderantes affectibus*, which condemned magical practices as heretical;[14] and still others maintain that inquisitorial practice didn't fully set in until the sixteenth and seventeenth centuries, when the parliaments of Henry VIII (in 1542), Elizabeth I (1563), and James I (1603) each passed successively more strict acts punishing the crime of witchcraft.[15] What this timeline suggests is that from about the middle of the thirteenth century, church officials and inquisitors increasingly conflated magic-use and heresy. The slow, constant build-up of anxiety about magic is demonstrated by the regular reiterations of its prohibition.

If it is difficult to indicate precisely when the legal system institutionalized certain practices (even though it is in this area that we have some of the most extensive, clearly dated records), it is even trickier to pinpoint the moment in a cultural tradition when a paradigm shift has happened—in this case, when anxiety about women's roles grew enough to demand the villainization of women through the wicked witch figure. What is clear is that the series of economic and social crises that dominated the fourteenth century had an immediate and lasting impact on the literary and legal traditions. The crises of the fourteenth century exacerbated the growing fear

142   *Crafting the Witch*

of demonic magic, and the end of the century brought increased numbers of witchcraft trials. Kieckhefer documents the number of trials in Europe from 1300–1500, arguing that after 1375, there was a "steady increase" in witchcraft trials, from the fourteenth-century rate of "roughly one each year" to the mid-fifteenth-century rate of over twenty trials per year ("Witch Trials" 25–30). The rising presence of witches as trial defendants collided with the country's need for economic scape-goating, and in the aftermath, writers adapted the familiar Arthurian stories and characters to do a new kind of cultural work. Rather than villainizing giants and super-manly masculinity, writers dredged up that ancient staple, the wicked witch, polished her off, and dropped her smack in the middle of the medieval family. Specifically, she appeared as a step-mother, a figure of domestic intrusion, a dispossessing, (step) child-hating, scheming representation of all that was wrong with the new estates-threatening, money-oriented economic system. The witches of the late-fourteenth and fifteenth centuries reinforce an ideological commitment to land ownership as the fundamental class determinant; upstart women with new money might enjoy certain benefits, but they are easily revealed as power-hungry monsters whose destruction sets the feudal hierarchy back to rights.

In the courts of late medieval and early modern England, fear grew that all magic might actually be the result of traffic with demons, and this judicial climate soon permeated a variety of genres featuring representations of magic (most notably, drama).[16] As scholars have exhaustively documented, the sixteenth and seventeenth centuries saw prosecutions (and executions) for witchcraft in record numbers.[17] Here, where belief is strongest and the criminal witch is the most threatening, the literary wicked witch also reigns queen, experiencing perhaps her greatest interlude of popularity in what's been far more than fifteen minutes of fame throughout the history of western literature. The fifteenth century saw the rise of writing specifically designed to link women, witchcraft, and diabolic activity (the quintessential work of this nature is Jacob Sprenger and Henry Kramer's *Malleus maleficarum*), and some of the most influential authors of the fifteenth and sixteenth centuries participated in the conflation of femininity with demonology and monstrous maternity. The witch figure, in both legal and literary contexts, functioned as a warning to all women: stay in the home, caring for children, or risk becoming a wicked hag. This warning was particularly ominous because it was, in effect, backed by the legal system. Literature told women what behaviors were witchy, and the courts punished them if they didn't toe the line.

But belief went away. In England, witch persecution officially ended with George II's repeal of penal laws against witchcraft in 1736, and suddenly, instead of it being illegal to practice witchcraft, it became illegal to feign the possession of magical power.[18] Across Europe and into the U.S., prosecutions for witchcraft stopped. Belief simply disappeared, crushed by the weight of that growing behemoth, Rationality, which was to replace

Hags on Film 143

the church as the state weapon of repression and control. Why science, reason, and Enlightenment rationality should come to dominate culture at the moment they did is a question for someone else to answer. What's far more interesting to me than why belief in witches stopped is why, once belief had vanished, the wicked witch remained.

In particular, contemporary American media keeps utilizing wicked witches—and in almost exactly the same ways as the Renaissance authors did—even though the majority of people in the U.S. don't believe in magic. There are many differences between the culture of medieval and Renaissance England and that of the contemporary U.S., but the salient difference here is simple: in the early modern period, people believed in magic, but now, we don't. Some people do—like my Wiccan student, like children before they learn there's no Santa, like those of us reading about that indefatigable Potter boy—but the majority of people do not believe that things sometimes happen because *someone* desired them to happen and used secret magical power to transform reality.

If we have any witchcraft legislation still existing in the U.S. (and we might), it is not enforced.[19] As Christina Larner puts it in *Witchcraft and Religion*, "the truth is that nobody cares" about practicing witches these days (83). Larner overstates the case here—people who practice witchcraft today probably care very much about what they do. But mainstream attitudes about witches in England and the U.S. are no longer comprised mainly of fear. We indulge modern witches, with some notable exceptions.[20] Perhaps with contemporary witchcraft manifestations like the Satanic cults analyzed by Larner or with some groups engaged in religious or spiritual practices called "witchcraft" by white Americans, there may be fear (especially about rituals and sacrifices), but the women associated with neo-pagan witchcraft practices don't suffer accusations of cannibalism and night-flights. Instead, they are accused of relatively benign things such as dancing, self-help, or gullibility. Perhaps the most culturally loaded charge is that of lesbianism, which of course carries its own complex matrix of social signifiers. Generally, though, mainstream U.S. society treats people who self-identify as witches as I treated my student, with affectionate (or for some, perhaps, irritated) contempt. The contempt reflects the widespread lack of belief. Most contemporary Americans don't worry about witches hurting us because we simply don't believe they can.

From 1939 to 2008, U.S. witches have appeared frequently in two related genres, children's literature and fantasy literature, and the witch-hag especially enjoys showing her ugly face when these two combine, in children's fantasy literature. What this suggests is that modern audiences view witches as suitable for art forms that are overtly representing imaginary, not-real spaces. Literature of the fantastic (written for whatever age) makes no claim to verisimilitude—rather, quite the opposite, as the fantasy world makes impossible things possible; thus, within fantastic literature we find it completely acceptable to represent figures (like witches, dragons,

144 *Crafting the Witch*

hobbits, house-elves, and talking Beasts) which do not conform to modern biological norms. Children's and fantasy literatures reflect the things audiences want to believe, but don't, things like "love is all we need," "presents and candy can magically appear in your home overnight," or "good triumphs over evil"—the things that we want our children to believe in for as long as they can, preserving the magic until the day when Santa and the Tooth Fairy become gaping holes in the fabric of reality. Evidence from fantastic literature can show us what people don't believe.

The two evidential records (legal and literary) for 20th-century U.S. culture show that despite the absence of prosecution and the normative lack of belief (a complete 180-degree-turn from Renaissance culture), the witch figure persists—and in almost exactly the same form. Writers and directors in the U.S. continue to represent and resolve anxieties about women and femininity in the spaces of popular literature and film. The gnarled, cackling Renaissance crone still has meaning for us—but what's amazing is that she still has predominantly the same meaning. Why is the witch figure still here if we no longer believe in or persecute witches? Why do we still find her so fascinating, her threat to children so terrifying, and her demise so satisfying? If belief has changed, what has stayed the same? In short, what's stayed the same is capitalism.

The shift away from land and toward capital as the primary determinant of wealth altered women's social function. In the land-oriented feudal estate system, people could not easily alter their socio-economic and gendered positions: peasants stayed peasants, aristocrats stayed aristocrats, women stayed in the private sphere and men in the public, with few notable exceptions. While the church offered an alternate path, and the working classes had some mobility within their own estate, individual agency was severely circumscribed by governmental and religious institutions, which regulated land ownership. The pervasive ideology of a divinely-ordained microcosmic hierarchy rested on the solid foundation of the land: if you owned it, you were powerful. The primacy of the land, however, did not remain. Growing regional, national, and international trade increased the utility of owning production materials and the importance of what they represented—capital. The population buckled to the pressures of plague, war, and climate, and the lack of workers rendered land a far less valuable commodity. Population loss coupled with the increasing role of international exchange meant that ownership of goods and labor for trade production was potentially more valuable than a large estate in the country. Merchants were lending nobles money, towns were becoming independent, self-governing, and prosperous, and the third estate was developing a new and powerful group of wealthy families who could buy land (and the accompanying titles) if they wished. Capital changed everything.

The effects of this economic paradigm shift on women were less radical than they were for men, yet still profound. Opportunity knocked. Women could live without husbands and outside the church, supporting themselves

Hags on Film   145

(albeit barely). Single women were still ghettoized anomalies, creatures to be explained and suspected, but they were able to take jobs as domestic servants, as weavers and seamstresses, laundresses, victualers, field-workers—even, for a brief period, guild-members. The upshot of all this: women could engage in paid labor, giving them opportunities to both expand and reject outright the maternal feminine norm. These opportunities, while certainly slim in comparison with modern freedoms, nevertheless represented a remarkable gain in agency for medieval women. The chance to refuse motherhood (without becoming a nun) had materialized. The neat system whereby women were controlled by husbands (wife) or church officials (nun) opened a loophole, one which, despite Herculean efforts on the part of governmental and religious institutions over the next three centuries, never quite closed.

Today, women in the U.S. have a wealth of opportunities—we can head large, multi-national companies, fight in combat, and serve in Congress and Presidential Cabinets, for example (each of which would have been unthinkable for a medieval woman). There are still institutionalized restrictions, of course—we can't be professional football players or President of the U.S.A., apparently. The threat (and reality) of women moving further and further away from an idealized maternal role has only intensified over the years, prompting countless backlashes and sometimes violent attempts to contain female-ness within the domestic sphere. In the twentieth and twenty-first centuries, there are so many ways for women to avoid being mothers, it's dizzying (as evinced by my female students' frequent remarks to that effect). Reinscription and reinforcement of rigidly defined gender roles (especially in relation to maternity) therefore remains a primary ideological agenda in hegemonic cultural representations. Renaissance writers used the witch-hag to push women back towards the home, and contemporary writers and filmmakers do exactly the same thing. Lack of belief in witches as efficacious magic users does not impair their functionality as warnings to women.

In the twenty-first century, witches are still anti-mothers. The version of the anti-maternal witch-hag which impacted current representations of witches most indelibly is the iconic Wicked Witch of the West in *The Wizard of Oz* (1939, dir. Jack Haley, Jr.), as played by the remarkable Margaret Hamilton. The Witch is physically marked as post-reproductive: her body is hidden in a shapeless dress, lacking conventionally maternal signifiers such as large breasts or corseted waist; her face is both warty and green, deemphasizing her lips and eyes (so enticing to romance writers and directors) and contrasting the pale skin of most 1930s film heroines (and Glinda); and her nose is exaggeratedly large, a grotesque capstone to the erased sexuality of the Wicked Witch. She wields a broom, symbol of domestic power, but instead of removing dirt and mess, the Witch's broom creates chaos and fire—here, domestic power has gone terribly wrong. Not only does the Witch menace the sweet, blue-eyed orphan Dorothy, threatening

146 *Crafting the Witch*

to kill her, but her sister, the Witch of the East, was the tyrannical ruler of an entire land of child-like Munchkins. In Oz, witchcraft is a family heritage, an evil bond allowing the two women to hurt children instead of nurture them. Property rights (those pesky slippers!) prompt the Witch to take action against Dorothy, bringing her in conflict with another female figure, Glinda, recalling the village-level conflicts between Renaissance women which ended in accusations of witchcraft.

Glinda represents idealized femininity: her conventional feminine markers include her pink dress—cinched tightly at the waist, low-cut to expose the bosom slightly, and adorned with sparkling jewels—and her face—ivory surrounded by a cloud of golden hair, with blue eyes, small nose, and red lips, all of which are reminiscent of conventional western aesthetics. An idealized mother-figure, Glinda protects Dorothy from the Wicked Witch of the West, guides her on her quest, and confirms the meaning of Dorothy's experiences in Oz: "there's no place like home!" Glinda is all the things the Witch is not: she cares for Dorothy and the Munchkins (saving the girl's life in the poppy fields), she wishes to return the girl to her family, and she floats in and out of Dorothy's life in her own protective womb, a beautiful pink bubble.

An early scene in Munchkinland emphasizes the opposition between the Wicked Witch and Glinda, between anti-mother and idealized mother: just after she arrives, the Wicked Witch approaches Dorothy. The Witch dominates the left side of the screen, leaning in toward Dorothy, broom at ready, curled into the now-familiar gnarled silhouette. Glinda and Dorothy occupy the other side of the frame together, connected by both proximity and Glinda's arm, which is wrapped around Dorothy, pulling her away from the Witch and into her own bosom. Highlighting her moral superiority, Glinda's hat reaches to the very top of the frame, far above the Witch's pointy black chapeau, making Glinda the tallest figure on screen. Dorothy's face reflects the horror we are supposed to feel, the terror of the anti-maternal crone's challenge to the make-shift mother-daughter pair.

Dorothy herself is a motherless child, an orphan whose aunt doesn't provide her with the type of nurturing she wants: her Aunt Em and Uncle Henry shoo her away at the very moment she desires their attention the most. Her dilemma is motivated by a stereotypically feminine desire to protect her dog (a child-surrogate, practice for the future), and it places her into conflict with a powerful single woman with lots of money but no children. Gulch's solution to the problem is typically witchy—she wants to have the dog (child-surrogate) killed—and it is this threat that motivates Dorothy's decision to abandon the only home she has. Here, a small town suffers when an anti-mother threatens a child, a situation so unnatural it spawns a tornado. Like the Renaissance conflicts between women which were mediated by male authorities via witchcraft trials, the supernatural events that follow the conflict between the Gales and Miss Gulch eliminate the problem of over-reaching female agency and restore hegemonic domesticity.

Hags on Film   147

Dorothy leaves home in revolt against what she perceives as a lack of domestic nurture: Aunt Em doesn't pay her enough attention. Told to "find a place where [she] won't get into any trouble," Dorothy dreams of a place she "heard of, once, in a lullaby" where "troubles melt like lemon-drops." Details such as the lullaby and the lemon-drops evoke early childhood, an idyllic time when distractions like broken incubators did not intrude upon maternal attentiveness. Dorothy is no longer simply a child, but she's also not yet an adult, a fact emphasized by her fall into the pig-pen, necessitating her rescue. Her domestic frustration is confirmed when Prof. Marvel cold-reads Dorothy, saying "They don't understand you at home; they don't appreciate you." Dorothy is amazed; it is as if he can "read what was inside of [her]." Dorothy's resistance to moving toward adulthood (and her own maternal role) prompts the journey to Oz, which, in turn, catalyzes the journey into the home.

The entire world of Oz is designed to demonstrate that there really is "no place like home," that the domestic world is the only proper place for a young woman to be. In Munchkinland, Dorothy sees firsthand an example of rejection of maternal norms: she meets the Wicked Witch of the West, anti-mother extraordinaire. She also meets the perfect mother, Glinda, who provides her with the kind of nurturing she always wanted. Dorothy is caught between these two poles, the Good Witch and the Wicked, the perfect mother and the perfect anti-mother, and it is no coincidence that she confronts this particular choice at this particular moment. Just as Dorothy is on the verge of becoming an adult, she must choose between motherhood and the alternative, witch-hood. Unlike Kansas, where the world is black and white but the moral dilemmas aren't, the Technicolor world of Oz makes choices easy. Hmmm, will you follow the menacing "other" trying to kill you or the pretty lady with the magic wand? Dorothy's presence in Munchkinland has already killed one anti-mother, setting her on the journey that will lead toward her adulthood, towards the home. Does the Witch of the West ever stand a chance?

Dorothy continues her journey to adulthood by consulting the top patriarchal authority, the Wizard of Oz, following the yellow-brick road to find the answers she needs. The Wizard of Oz confirms what we have suspected all along: to get home, Dorothy needs to kill the Wicked Witch, the anti-maternal model. Once the option for non-mother no longer exists, where can Dorothy be but "home?" Even Dorothy's companions emphasize the gendered nature of the yellow-brick road quest: while the Scarecrow searches for brains (intellect), the Tin Man for a heart (faith), and the Lion for courage (courage!), Dorothy searches for home. Male quests can be varied and involve developing one's character, but female quests are focused steadfastly on the one place women can claim for themselves, the home. Little girls may think they desire adventure and freedom, but once they leave the protective domestic space, they soon realize that the land of freedom and Technicolor is a dangerous place, and there truly is "no place like home."

148   *Crafting the Witch*

The Wizard of Oz relies directly on the witch-hag developed in the Renaissance, using the figure, exactly as sixteenth- and seventeenth-century writers did, to frighten women back into domestic roles. The film's communication of domesticity as normativity is reliant upon the changes made to the original story by the writers, directors, and producers: the film version adds the entire Gulch scenario (and the beautiful song that attends Dorothy's desperate straits, of course) and the first meeting between Dorothy and the Wicked Witch of the West in Munchkinland; it alters the Wicked Witch's appearance, turning the one-eyed lady of the book into the classic Renaissance witch-hag in all her glory; and where in the book Dorothy asks the silver shoes to "take [her] home to Aunt Em" (Baum 217), the film girl chants "There's no place like home" over and over again. While these changes are relatively subtle, they reflect the radically altered economic situation in the U.S. Baum wrote the story at the turn of the twentieth century, but the filmmakers adapted it during the late 1930s, at the end of the Great Depression. It is no coincidence that during a time of extreme economic hardship, the filmmakers turned Baum's story into a warning about the dangers of rejecting traditional roles, about the way in which home may seem bad at first, but really is the best place to be (especially for young girls). Just as the medieval writers adapted existing figures to suit new narrative needs (e.g., Morgan le Fay turns from good to bad), so modern filmmakers freely shape their sources to more effectively satisfy audiences. As far as I can tell, in the case of *Wizard*, the changes work pretty well: friends routinely explain how their children couldn't watch the entire movie the first time, because the Witch frightened them so effectively. She is a powerful Witch indeed. Children easily recognize her physical markers as "other," so embedded are the cultural conventions of femininity, and respond to them with fear and loathing. Clearly the Witch represents a choice we should not make, and both adults and children receive the message with ease. Really, the Witch tells us, for women, there's no place BUT home.

While Margaret Hamilton's Wicked Witch is perhaps the most iconic of the twentieth century, Disney's animated films feature a long line of wicked witches who function in extremely similar ways. *Snow White and the Seven Dwarfs* (1937), *Alice in Wonderland* (1951), *Sleeping Beauty* (1959), *101 Dalmatians* (1961), *The Sword in the Stone* (1963), *The Rescuers* (1977), *The Little Mermaid* (1989), and *The Emperor's New Groove* (2000) all feature hag-crone "witches" who threaten little children. *Snow White*, the first and the most explicit in its adherence to the witch-hag icon, sets the stage for the rest of the wicked witches who will terrorize Disney's innocent, beautiful heroines for years to come. As we all know, the wicked Queen in Snow White begins as a beautiful woman.

The Queen is known for her beauty, and it is no coincidence that Snow White is beautiful too. In a world dominated by the male gaze (which reaches even into animated spaces), women are judged by our beauty, by adherence to culturally-specific norms.[21] It is beauty that attracts men so

Hags on Film   149

that women can be what we know we're supposed to be, mothers. The Queen is a mother, of sorts—she's that especially frightening beast who reared her nasty head in the loathly lady romances in Middle English, the step-mother. We have already seen the danger presented by step-mothers to their non-biological children: step-mothers in romance are likely to dispossess their children, stealing land and resources from their unlucky new spouse's offspring. The Queen acts true to form, but her immediate motivation is no longer merely possession of land (though she does get the castle all to herself); instead, the Queen wants to be the most beautiful, to have the most power to attract the male gaze. What makes her desire for beauty poisonous is its competitive nature—if she didn't have to be the most beautiful woman in all the land, the Queen could have let Snow White live in peace.

Beauty and competition within patriarchy are so intimately connected that we all know what will happen when two beautiful women get together: they'll fight. Inevitably, one will envy the other. How can she help it? The male gaze evaluates females against an ideal set of beauty conventions, ranking them as pretty, prettier, and prettiest. Naomi Wolf analyzes the late twentieth-century operation of "the beauty myth," or the false assertion that "the quality called 'beauty' objectively and universally exists. Women must want to embody it and men must want to possess women who embody it" (12). In the beauty myth (currently perpetuated largely by advertising, cosmetics, and pornography industries), beauty is the only way women can access the scraps of power thrown to them by male-dominated institutions. The Wicked Queen's obsession with beauty presented in Disney's film is just one of many manifestations of the beauty myth, which Wolf suggests began as early as the fourteenth century (59–61).[22] Snow White, a younger, and therefore better, beauty, must be eliminated for the Queen to win the (beauty) contest.

In *Snow White*, Walt Disney began a trend he and his animators would perfect over the course of the next eight or nine decades: they marked a particular kind of beauty as dangerous, lethal, and deviant, as indicative of an evil anti-mother, a wicked witch. The Wicked Queen created an aesthetic type: tall, so thin as to lack the conventional secondary sex markers of femininity (like breasts and/or hips), with pallid, chalky skin, bright red streaks as lips, and lots of black eye make-up, wearing a shapeless black dress. While on the one hand this figure adheres to certain norms of beauty, including the use of make-up and high heels, on the other she deviates from the most important rule for women: she refuses to be contained within the roles assigned to her within patriarchy. The Wicked Queen has no male master, no husband or father to reign her in, to make her submit. The lack of male control is a defining marker of Disney's wicked witch villains: *Alice*'s Queen of Hearts repeatedly screams "cut off his head" while her physically and symbolically miniscule husband sputters ineffectively; *Sleeping Beauty*'s Maleficent works entirely on her own, to the dismay of the

150   *Crafting the Witch*

entire kingdom; *Dalmatians'* Cruella de Vil buys everyone and everything, including all the men around her; *The Sword in the Stone*'s Mad Madame Mim openly fights Merlin, the only man on the planet who could hope to curtail her wild agency; *The Rescuers* Madame Medusa uses and abuses a "soft" male goon in her search for a gigantic diamond; *Little Mermaid*'s Ursula threatens everyone under the sea, seducing and using males as she wishes; and *Emperor's* Yzma uses a male thug to threaten the male king.

The story marks the women as free (and thus dangerous) agents in a patriarchal world, and the film marks the women visually as witches through one of the two options set out in the blueprint of *Snow White*: 1) a beautiful grotesque, marked by extreme thinness, pasty skin, and stark make-up (ala the Queen before she takes the potion) or 2) the classic hag-crone, marked by round, shapeless body, exaggerated (or deformed) facial features, and wild hair (the Queen after she takes the potion, as the Hag). The figures are connected, two sides of the same coin, tainted beauty signaling the true ugliness within. The appearance of the iconic witch-hag in *Wizard of Oz* one year after *Snow White* connected her to the Wicked Queen solidified the connection between tainted femininity and anti-maternity. The beautiful grotesque is dangerous because she is the witch-hag.

Malificent, Cruella de Vil, and Yzma are all examples of the beautiful grotesque. While not stooped with age, each woman's beauty is nevertheless mature, over-ripe with stark redness and the pallor of age, contrasted with the soft pastels and nubile bodies of heroines like Aurora, Belle, and Ariel. The angularity of the witches' bodies also starkly differentiates them from the matronly curves of Disney's "good" mothers, like the three good fairies of *Sleeping Beauty* (Flora, Fauna, and Merryweather) or *Dalmations'* Nanny. Emphasizing their anti-maternal function, Maleficent, Cruella, and Ymbra directly threaten children (Cruella symbolically, of course, through the puppies). In each case, it is the children who are able to neutralize the threat, the children whose actions rid the world of the bad mother. It's up to children, Disney tells us, to stop wicked witches, to choose maternity.

The Queen of Hearts, Mad Madame Mim, Madame Medusa, and Ursula all conform to the conventions of the witch-hag.[23] Their bodies are large and lack the conventionally feminine hour-glass shape, their faces have exaggeratedly large features (noses, mouths, and chins, especially), and their hair is wild and unkempt. Like Snow White's Queen in disguise, these women are visibly recognizable as non-maternal, as witchy. Unlike Disney's matrons, who are plump but maintain recognizable feminine markers like breasts, waists, and hips, these women resist being defined by gender conventions (recalling the androgynous Weird sisters), shifting and seeming to change size at any moment; in both Mim's and Ursula's cases, the changing is literal, as they possess shape-shifting magic. As hags, they are post-maternal women who threaten children like their thin, pasty counterparts, and children play important roles in neutralizing them. Children are clearly the intended audience of Disney's messages—the marketing, if

Hags on Film   151

nothing else, makes that fact apparent. Messages about gender roles are especially important to children, who are engaged in the complex processes of identity-formation, and Disney's use of wicked witches targets young girls, in particular.

Why does it matter that Disney and MGM represent witches as barren, anti-maternal hags? Witches, especially wicked ones, are steeped in a patriarchal ideology that essentializes women as mothers, a "compulsory maternity" which is in some ways the logical extension of what Adrienne Rich so insightfully called "compulsory heterosexuality."[24] In this centuries-old story, a daughter (future mother) rids herself of the barren hag preventing her from participating in hetero-normative behaviors so that she can end up married to the prince, safe at home, the epicenter of a patriarchal, capitalist economy. Just like medieval and Renaissance writers, contemporary Americans are invested in the maintenance of censures against child-less women, especially ones who possess power and autonomy, as do each of the witches in these films. When they watch films like these, children learn that older, single women are anomalies, monsters who need to be tamed or perhaps chased off a cliff.

The investment in an essential maternal female identity grounds even the more positive representations of witches popular in the late twentieth century, especially those witches appearing on television. Two U.S. shows, in particular—the quaint 1960s sit-com *Bewitched* (1964–1972) and the late 1990s cult "drama," *Charmed*—provide excellent examples of positive, yet ultimately hegemonic witch-figures. Let's start with *Bewitched*. Samantha (Elizabeth Montgomery), beautiful housewife to Darrin Stephens (Dick York, 1964–1969, and Dick Sargent, 1969–1972), is a good witch, but her husband prefers that she not use her witchcraft. Witchcraft, to Darrin, is innately dangerous. The admonition against witchcraft happens in the first episode of the show ("I, Darrin, Take This Witch Samantha"), where an otherwise "typical American" couple meet trouble in the form of Samantha's magic use. After Darrin learns that his "wife is a witch," a phrase he repeats a few times throughout the episode, he makes a pact with Samantha to try to make it work as long as "there's not going to be any more" witchcraft. Darrin can't even say the words "witchcraft" or "magic"; he simply waves his hand in a vague evocation of conjuring, a tactic he employs twice in the episode. Samantha promises to try not to use witchcraft from then on, but breaks that promise in the next scene, a pattern which will provide the conflict in every episode throughout the rest of the series: Samantha routinely attempts to avoid magic-use, but often finds herself with no other choice (frequently because of Darrin's thick-headedness).[25] Samantha is circumscribed by domesticity; she rarely leaves her house, she's responsible for all the cleaning and cooking, and her tasks center around supporting Darrin (who is often supporting his boss, Larry Tate). The show argues that witchcraft belongs in the domestic space, an idea also emphasized by Samantha's mother and daughter. Whenever Sam's mother, Endora (Agnes

152   Crafting the Witch

Moorehead), uses magic or encourages Sam to use magic, havoc ensues.[26] Domestic tranquility is ripped apart by the unmarried mother-in-law, who, while extremely mischievous, stops just short of being wicked. Tabitha (Erin Murphy), Samantha and Darrin's daughter, inherits her mother's magical abilities, and Samantha's role as mother includes shepherding and containing her growing powers. Samantha's connection to domesticity situates her firmly within a matrix of conservative television families like the Cleavers who preceded her and the Keatons who would follow. Each of these families privileges heterosexual marriage, the primacy of children, and above all, the importance of the mother as primary care giver and unpaid domestic worker.

A more recent show which updates, yet still inscribes, the message of domesticity is *Charmed*. On the surface, the show appears to offer a post-feminist alternative witch: three unmarried sisters gain magical power, and use it to right wrongs and end injustice, eventually saving both the magical and human worlds from destruction. Prudence (Shannen Doherty), Piper (Holly Marie Combs), Phoebe (Alyssa Milano), and Paige (Rose McGowan, who joined the series when Doherty left) Halliwell are hot sisters who kick demon butt! Is this female agency or what? A closer inspection, however, reveals that this series, despite its promise and charm, produces an essentialized female domestic identity. The premise of the show suggests that the Halliwell sisters are special, the Charmed Ones, a prophesied group of witches who will save the world, and the show presents the sisters very positively, emphasizing not only their conventionally feminine beauty, but also their compassion, intelligence, and willingness to stick together when the going gets tough. We're supposed to like the sisters, just as we're supposed to hate wicked witches.

While the representation of the *Charmed* witches is overwhelmingly positive, it is also overwhelmingly domestic. The physical home—the Halliwell Manor—sits on a nexus of magical power, and all their magical endeavors begin and end there. Their own magical powers come to them through their maternal line: their mother and grandmother were both powerful witches. Though each sister possesses different powers (like the ability to blow things up or telekinesis), they all share the responsibility of brewing potions. Potion brewing happens frequently in the kitchen itself, especially at the beginning of the series, when Piper, a chef in her non-magical life, makes the connection between brewing and cooking explicit, complaining that she'd like to get back to brewing soup instead of potions. Piper is not only a cook, she is also a mother, and her maternal role structures her character's narrative arc.[27] Throughout the series, Piper repeatedly reminds us that she would rather be exclusively a mother, and not a witch—she wishes for domestic tranquility and only leaves her homey oasis when demonic activity forces her to act.[28] While Piper is maternity realized, her sisters represent women on the journey to motherhood.

Hags on Film 153

Phoebe and Paige are overtly sexualized, wearing tight, revealing clothing and heavy make-up; the men in their lives all behave as if they are extremely sexually appealing, and the Halliwell sisters engage in a constant process of rejecting dating only to find themselves, well, dating. For most of the series, Phoebe overtly desires male companionship, marriage, and children, whom her prophetic knowledge assures her will exist.[29] She says things like, "How am I supposed to find true love if I'm busy fighting demons?" or "I'm committed to the search for true love, even if it takes a while." Phoebe's obsession with love is emphasized when she takes a position as a relationship advice columnist for the local newspaper in Season Five, and when Cupid (Coop, played by Victor Webster) takes on the task of finding Phoebe's true love (which turns out to be him, of course). Phoebe's even-sexier sister, Paige, joins the family when Prudence, the oldest sister, dies in a demonic brawl; Paige is perhaps the most sexualized of all the sisters, a fact consistently reasserted with such details as the belly-baring clothes she favors and her bright red lipstick. She does not yearn for true love, as Phoebe does, but her attempts to abandon dating and relationships and focus exclusively on her career as a witch eventually lead her to the man she will marry, Henry (Ivan Sergei).[30] The allure of these women recalls the beautiful temptresses of Renaissance literature like Duessa, but is really more akin to the earliest incarnations of Morgan le Fay, whose beauty and power were used in service of a patriarchal system. The Halliwell sisters work in service of "Good," or a set of values that embraces heterosexual, nuclear families, domesticity as a defining characteristic of women (even career-oriented ones), and upholding the status quo. The character who has the most fraught relationship with domesticity is the oldest sister, Prudence (Prue).

Prue is the least sexualized of all the sisters except Piper, but as the oldest, she functions in a maternal role toward her younger siblings. Prue is uncomfortable with the role of older sister precisely because of the maternal elements which somehow innately obtain. Not only is she angry at the deaths of both her mother and grandmother (who leave her in the maternal role), but she rejects her magical power at first, only becoming a witch reluctantly.[31] She complains about her situation, highlighting many of the same factors that second-wave feminists railed against: the unfairness of the automatic expectation that she should be the one to take care of the family, the pressure of being responsible for everyone else but never getting any time for herself, and her desire to focus on her career. Her character dies at the end of Season 3 ("All Hell Breaks Loose"), leaving the younger sisters in despair (and opening the door for a new sister); even though the character's death surely had more to do with Doherty leaving the series than with any original intent of the writers to kill her, the effect is remarkable. The one witch who challenged the compulsion to be domestic dies violently, replaced by someone who embraces her (hetero)sexuality and domesticity (giving up everything else to focus on magic). While the Charmed Ones are

154   *Crafting the Witch*

charming and powerful women, the show ultimately confines femininity within the domestic space, essentializing women as mothers.

Television programs like the ones I've described work alongside films, such as *The Witches of Eastwick* and *Practical Magic*, which represent witches in positive ways. Like their small-screen counterparts, even the "good" silver-screen witches ultimately reinforce hegemonic constructions of femininity as maternity. In *The Witches of Eastwick*, for example, the three witches transgress the normative conventions of their small New England town, with what are ultimately disastrous results. The women physically evoke the three "types" of Euro-centric, feminine beauty—the blond (Suki, played by Michelle Pheiffer), the brunette (Alex, played by Cher), and the red-head (Jane, played by Susan Sarandon). In the first scene with all three women, the director demonstrates a connection between the repressive culture of New England (and thus, by extension, the U.S.) and the women's desperate resort to magic. After enduring the singing of a local goody-goody, Felicia, our three witches look terribly annoyed as the sexually-harassing school principal prepares to make a long-winded speech. Through quick cuts from the women to the sky, the editing suggests that the three women call up a violent thunderstorm through some form of unified wish-magic, forcing the empty ceremony to a quick end. This scene promises a story of transgressive power, a protective magic which will disrupt patriarchal norms and free the women from societal expectations. For a while, it does.

As the women sip martinis later in Alex's home, apparently successfully freed from the obligation of their children, they talk of their relationships (ended by "death, divorce, and desertion"), their lack of sex, and their unfulfilled desires—in short, their dissatisfaction with the hetero-normative lifestyle demanded by the town. That this behavior is transgressive is demonstrated by Jane's shock at some of the things Alex says, as when Jane tells Alex she's "over-simplifying" when Alex points out that the other two women's marriages were reduced to procreation: "[Suki's] husband leaves her because she has too many kids. [*To Jane*] Your husband leaves you because you can't have any." Alex has pointed out an important truth, however, one which the women will learn by the end of the film: patriarchy views women primarily *vis a vis* their reproductive power, it over-simplifies femaleness to a maternal function.

Ultimately, the promise of transgression offered in the thunderstorm scene remains unfulfilled. The witches' major act of communal magic—their first "intentional" magical act—conjures up, not an alternate reality where women are freed from patriarchal essentialized maternity, but a dream-guy. They create "the perfect man," playing into the exact set of expectations they expressed frustration with only moments before. This scene posits the solution to patriarchy as another man, albeit a unique one. When Jane asks Suki and Alex, "Who should we be looking for?" the qualities mentioned in response include, in summary: nurturing tolerance ("someone nice, someone you could like"; "someone you could really be yourself with"; "someone you

Hags on Film   155

could talk to"), sexualized body ("handsome," "not too handsome," "nice eyes," "nice ass," "huge" [said of his penis], "who cares—as long as it works" [also]), and a mysterious, unknowable quality ("a stranger, interesting," "a tall, dark prince traveling under a curse," "a foreign prince on a big, black horse"). What they want is a man with feminine qualities, a female with the phallus. What they get is the devil.

The relationship between Daryl and the women evokes the discourse of Renaissance witch-hunting. The devil figures prominently in Renaissance texts, sealing his demonic pacts by fornicating with a coven of prospective witches, and this is precisely what Daryl van Horn accomplishes when he arrives. He seduces Alex, Jane, and Suki one after the other, playing on their frustrations with mundane life, sexual repression, and the responsibilities of motherhood, respectively. Their sexual liberation marks their cultural liberation: they no longer care about the rules of Christian morality, abandoning monogamy and heterosexuality for sexual freedom and experimentation, and for a time they experience an Edenic world where they slowly become more cognizant of their magical abilities. Though the women are certainly happier with Daryl, their "transgression" is strictly sexual and, frankly, not transgressive at all. While it appears that Daryl is satisfying all their needs (sexual, emotional, financial, etc.), what results is that the three women's lives revolve around the whims of one man. As they interact with Daryl, the women become more and more overtly sexualized, wearing bigger hair, bolder make-up, higher heels, and fewer clothes, until they all conform to the same male-centric notion of feminine beauty.

The turning point comes when Daryl encourages the three witches to focus their anger on another woman, employing an ancient trick of patriarchy designed to prevent female solidarity. The film seems to reject patriarchy at this moment: when the women stop seeing Daryl in the aftermath of Felicia's death, he employs force (psychological torture) to punish them for their disobedience. We are clearly meant to sympathize with the suffering women, and not with Daryl's sudden resort to aggressive patriarchal strategies, which literally turn him into a monster. Patriarchy, we learn in these scenes, is mean and monstrous. But then the women employ the same tactics, finally killing Daryl by means of a wax doll, which they have stabbed with pins, thrown around, and finally burned in their pursuit of Daryl's demise. The same violence which was so condemned in Daryl is lauded in the women—as a reward for their efforts, they receive possession of the lush mansion and nature conserve Daryl owned. Why is force acceptable for the women when it was condemned for Daryl? Because they are protecting the demon-babies they carry in their bellies.

The final trick of the film is to cap the entire story off with the birth of three babies (blond, brunette, and red-headed, of course), including one from the previously barren Jane. Daryl's parting gift was the most momentous, placing all three women squarely within the maternal role and reversing the potentially subversive elements of their sexual freedom. The final

156   *Crafting the Witch*

scene of the film emphasizes the importance of the maternal function, the way it provides the perfect ending for the women's stories. The women tend their baby boys (Daryl's brood), looking happy and loving in the communal utopia (Daryl's old house). Alex, Suki, and Jane appear to have discarded the lifestyle that asked them to find male partners, instead banding together in a supportive community of women. This community successfully replaces the need for witchcraft, we are shown: in this utopian space, the women work and tend their children together, free from the hassles of their prior lives—like jobs, sexually harassing bosses, and judgmental ladies. The female community seems to resolve the problem of patriarchy by replacing it with an egalitarian democracy, and this makes feminine magic unnecessary. It is in this moment that the film takes the biggest step towards a transgressive view of women; though cooperation between women can only exist in relation to maternity, at least it exists, which is more than most texts representing magical women allow. The moment is short indeed, as the film quickly reminds us, with a final image of van Horn (who is never really gone), that patriarchal appropriation of maternity is never far away, and, in fact, is always already there.

Twentieth- and twenty-first-century visual representations of witches, which link women securely to reproduction, work in service of patriarchy. Representations like these, whether positively or negatively presented, have negative ramifications on women who do not conform to this particular feminine identity, whose particular racial, class, national, religious, or sexual circumstances differ from those demanded by the normative maternal ideal. They have consequences for little girls playing "good fairies" together in a park, for little boys watching endless Disney films showing them how bad (non-maternal) women are, and for any little children who wish to reject mainstream thinking and transcend the paradigms of today, imagining endless tomorrows. Contemporary representations of magic no longer bring with them the power of law or science, as they did during the early modern period. While magic has lost its efficacy in these fields, it has retained its ideological power through its relationship to gender. What brings Renaissance and contemporary witch-stories together is their joint insistence that women who do not marry or who marry without bearing children have access only to a false power, one easily overthrown if young women will simply reject any lifestyle or familial arrangement except the nuclear, hetero-normative, white western family. In the contemporary world, witches are still anti-mothers.

Witches became strictly anti-mothers in the late medieval period, eclipsing the more positively constructed healing maidens of early Arthurian legend, and have remained as anti-mothers throughout centuries of literary and (now) cinematic productions. If the figure of the witch is so pervasive and so consistently configured, as I have argued, how can we possibly hope to reclaim her for modern feminists? One answer to that question perhaps lies with my shy Wiccan student, the one who hoped

Hags on Film 157

(only for a moment) that I might share her belief in witches, her desire to live in a magical world.

Writers like Margaret Murray and Gerald Gardner developed some of the early narratives that ground the beliefs of many neo-pagan witches, like the people who practice Wicca, feminist witchcraft, and other forms of feminist spirituality.[32] Murray, in particular, suffered virulent critiques based on her anti-academic methodology and lack of traditional historical evidence to support her claims about the secret survival of an ancient pagan fertility cult lead by a horned god.[33] There are many elements of modern feminist and neo-pagan spiritual practices, which I'll call witchcraft, that are problematic at best. One of the most significant problems with modern witchcraft is, as Diane Purkiss explains, "its insistence on an identity grounded in the maternal body" (33). It is true that modern witchcraft practices often essentialize women as mothers, as Purkiss documents, or construct idealized female identities which neglect material realities, as Susan Greenwood observes (129–31).[34] Just as the films and television shows which present positive witch figures nevertheless reinforce patriarchal ideology, so some of the positive discourses of neo-pagan witchcraft fall prey to essentialism.

When even discourses which attempt to reconfigure positively constructions of the wicked witch collapse under the pressure of normative heterosexual maternity, what are folks like myself and my Wiccan student, who want to believe in a world where witches (and other women who don't conform to patriarchal norms) can be good, where little girls (and boys) can indulge in positive self-fashioning using models that don't circumscribe their options before they've even started? Is there power to be found by seizing the production of discourse and telling new stories? As someone who analyzes literary production for a living, I clearly believe that there's something useful, something potentially transgressive, and more importantly, something transformative about analyzing and constructing discourses.

Discourse is a tricky subject. Perhaps one of the most influential writers to address discourse is Michel Foucault, who describes the operation of power and its connection to discourse. For Foucault, power is not only a hierarchical, top-down force; instead, "power is employed and exercised through a net-like organization" (*Power/Knowledge* 98). Janet Jakobsen described Foucault's description of power memorably in a formulation something like this one: it's not just Power (capital *P*), but lots of small moments of power, or little *p*s.[35] Power relations are not simply monolithic, in other words, but the operation of power happens in small moments between individuals as well as in large ways through governmental and other institutions. While some progressive tasks, like divesting corporations and multi-national conglomerates of economic power or white men of political power, seem impossible because of the enormous amount of resources devoted to the maintenance of inequity, there are myriad simple, local, and individual opportunities for progressive change. Foucault says

158 Crafting the Witch

power "traverses and produces things, it induces pleasure, forms of knowledge, produces discourse. It needs to be thought of as a productive network which runs through the whole social body" (*Power/Knowledge* 119). If power "runs through the whole social body," then there are moments when each of us possess power. Individuals, Foucault says, "are always undergoing and exercising this power" (98). We have economic, sexual, intellectual, racialized, physical, discursive, and myriad other forms of power to varying degrees at any given moment.

The operation of discourse, and its relationship to power, is complicated. Foucault argued that, as the phrase now goes, "nothing has any meaning outside of discourse."[36] As many have pointed out, Foucault doesn't mean that material objects do not exist, but that their meanings are dependent on discourse. Discourse is the way we assign meaning to the things and concepts we encounter. Stuart Hall explains it this way: discourse is the "group of statements which provide a language for talking about—a way of representing the knowledge about—a particular topic at a particular historical moment" (44). Both language-use and social interactions are discursive, because both "entail meaning, and meanings shape and influence what we do—our conduct"; in fact, "all practices have a discursive aspect" (44). Discourse is the medium through which knowledges are generated and disseminated. Knowledge, the saying goes, is power, but that's only true because, as Hall explains, "knowledge linked to power, not only assumes the authority of 'the truth' but has the power to make itself true" (49). Discursive formations generated by corporate, governmental, religious, and educational institutions are exchanged so frequently and with such connection to power they dominate many cultural spaces. But they are not the only spaces in which discourse can be generated, adapted, manipulated, and deployed—opportunities to harness discursive power exist in the "little *p*" ways as well.

Foucault's radical assertion that the subject is produced through discourse (i.e., the subject is forced into a particular subject-position by discourse) seems to eliminate the individual subject's potential agency—if we are produced by discourse, how can we turn around and create it? One way of approaching this question is to analyze discursive change. Discursive formations do not stay the same; Foucault's own work focuses far more on the breaks and shifts between cultures than on their continuities. As Foucault indicates, often he "confine[s himself] to describing the transformations themselves" in the hope that identifying the change would be a first step towards developing a theory of "change and epistemological causality" (*The Order of Things* xiii). Discursive change happens. If we extrapolate logically from Foucault's own analysis of the architecture of power, which disperses the operations of oppression and agency through a web of individual discursive power relations, we find that change must happen individually. Each tiny nexus of power and agency, each moment when one individual asserts power over another, requires the individuals engaged in the power struggle to make choices—to assert agency or not assert it, to resist or not resist another's attempt to curtail agency, to oppress or be oppressed or compromise. A subject is subjected to discourse, but must also utilize that discourse, construct it individually, and deploy it in daily interactions. A subject must internalize an external discursive formation as a prerequisite to subject-hood, but once the subject has dived into the sea of discourse, she alone can choose how to use it, to sink or swim.

The operation of discourse reminds me, in a way, of a child playing with Legos. The little plastic blocks pre-exist the child, and the child can't change the basic block formations (rectangles and squares, mostly), but each child playing with Legos will create something unique, something that uses the blocks in a distinct way. Sometimes, particularly creative or spatially-oriented children will even use the blocks to make things that the Legos creators didn't anticipate or expect, creating constructions that make the original shapes (rectangles and squares) unrecognizable. Discourse pre-exists the subject, but the subject can use the "building blocks" of discourse to construct ideas and realities that may not even seem possible, at first. Where discourse outperforms the Legos is in the potential for change; whereas plastic building blocks retain their original shape under a great deal of pressure, language responds to pressure by changing, by altering sounds, words, meanings, and significations. An individual speech or writing act may not constitute a change in discourse, but eventually, millions of individual speech and writing acts will. Each of those acts happens when an individual chooses how to deploy the blocks at her disposal.

Hélène Cixous famously described the process of seizing discursive power as "writing the body": "Women must write through their bodies, they must invent the impregnable language that will wreck partitions, classes, and rhetorics, regulations and codes, they must submerge, cut through, get beyond the ultimate reserve-discourse, including the one that laughs at the very idea of pronouncing the word *silence*" (256). We must "invent" our own "impregnable language[s]," telling ourselves new truths about our lives and our positions in the world. Creative use of language, reclaiming positive meanings for negative words, retelling ancient stories and writing new ones, telling our own stories: these are powerful tools. Our lives are narrated for us, our subject-positions interpellated by the overwhelming crush of discourses, a phenomenon often described as "the media" by people who recognize the discursive pressure but perhaps don't have the theoretical language to describe it. As we take control of narrating our own lives, one person at a time, we engage a profound resource for change.

Modern neo-pagan witchcraft practices, like Wicca, feminist witchcraft, Gaians, Goddess-worshipers, and so on, often focus energy on self-transformation. In particular, the transformation sought by many witches is the replacement of internalized misogyny with self-love. Elinor W. Gadon describes Goddess-worship, a common form of modern witchcraft, as helping women "be healed of the destructive psychological impact of our culture's pervasive negative image of the female" (261). Gadon focuses on the

160   *Crafting the Witch*

potential for psychological change offered by witchcraft, and Cynthia Eller has a similar explanation for its transformative power: "feminist spirituality is the attempt to transform handicaps into blessings, to take negative identities that have been imposed on one and convert them into positive identities that have been freely chosen" (215). Again, individual self-transformation is the goal, to alter "identities." The process of transforming the self is a discursive process, the construction of a new "group of statements" to describe (and thus alter) the self. Wendy Griffin argues that Goddess-worship can "transform gender identity by subverting traditional meaning and representation of what it means to be female, simultaneously creating new definitions of appropriate gendered behavior for women. This process redefines the boundaries of what is acceptable" (85). "Creating new definitions" of femaleness and femininity and "subverting traditional meaning and representation" involve self-consciously altering discursive formations. I do not mean simply that the spells or rituals utilized to achieve desired results use language as a locus of power, though that does happen in many of the spells. The discursive transformation process involves a multitude of tactics, from the myriad performative and collaborative acts of practicing witches to the engendering of countless books, journals, and publishing houses dedicated to sharing women's stories.[37] Women and men achieve transformative change—they become witches—by reading and hearing stories about witches, by writing and creating narratives about themselves and their relationship to the world, and by sharing those new discursive formations with others.

Discursive generation is a particularly powerful attribute of neo-pagan and feminist spiritual practices. Purkiss explains: "the entirety of modern witchcraft offers a unique opportunity to see a religion being made from readings and rereading of texts and histories. No one person is in charge of the process, so modern witchcraft is not a unified set of beliefs; every interpretation is subject to reinvention by others" (31). While Purkiss goes on to critique the way in which modern witchcraft discourses often boil down to "a male fantasy about what femininity should be" (39), her description of the process through which modern witchcraft discourse is generated is worth analyzing more fully. Here, new meaning is created by multiple "readings and rereading of texts and histories," or by expropriation of previously male-dominated narratives about women. Within the religious literature, there's not one privileged text that hierarchically trumps all other texts, but a variety of interpretations each "subject to reinvention" at any given time. Witchcraft discourses offer practitioners a space where not only can they write their own stories, but they can rewrite the stories handed down to them by centuries of men. Sparhawk argues that "true social change can only come about when the myths and symbols of our culture are themselves changed" (213). Modern witchcraft creates a space for women to seize discursive power and use it to change the stories told about women by changing the stories women tell about themselves.

Hags on Film   161

The most transgressive aspect of the generative discourse encouraged by modern witchcraft is the way in which it allows women to transform themselves. Much like 1960s-70s feminist consciousness-raising groups which provided spaces for women to rethink oppressive paradigms, many witchcraft groups overtly address issues of patriarchy and gender inequity; in particular, Greenwood suggests feminist witchcraft emphasizes that "witches must work actively to change patriarchal society" (130). While all consciousness-raising and feminist endeavors must carefully negotiate a complex web of power dynamics to achieve change without simultaneously further disenfranchising people whom economic and ethnic inequities have already marginalized, practices like feminist witchcraft, which both implicitly and explicitly seek progressive change through discursive rejection of patriarchy, offer critical opportunities for personal transformation. Personal transformation is the first stone thrown into the deceptively placid patriarchal pond; its ripples move outward in ever-widening rings, expanding to local, regional, national, and international proportions. This is the lesson taught by feminist activists seeking the vote in the late nineteenth century, by civil rights activists in the middle of the twentieth, and by the variety of twenty-first-century programs dedicated to one-on-one mentoring of "at-risk" children today: transforming individuals is transforming culture. My Wiccan student was on the path of transformation. If I had listened more closely, she might have told me how she got there.

I'm listening now. Throughout my academic career, I have seen that personal transformation comes in many ways, and one of the most powerful transformative tools, despite its problems, is discourse. Discourse helps construct reality: we tell stories about our pasts, our presents, and our futures, and, eventually, those stories become truth. If I want Morgan le Fay to be a positive, non-sexualized, not-necessarily-maternal figure who rejects patriarchal norms and works in harmony with the women and men around her, then I need to write her that way. Witches teach us that the past is a story we tell about ourselves. I need to tell Morgan's story, to tell my version of her story, which is really a story about me. We can rewrite the past, and we should. I'll start with that conversation I had with my Wiccan student. Here's how it should have gone:

> A young woman with intelligent eyes approached me after class one day. "I really enjoyed your lecture on medieval magic," she said. "I'm Wiccan, you know."
>
> "Really?" I asked, excited. "How did you become a witch?"
>
> "Well," she began, her whole face brightening into a smile. "It all started when I read this book. . . ."

Rewriting the past is a way of beginning again. Writing our own beginnings can be powerful, even if some of them get appropriated by patriarchy and some reinforce stereotypical norms, because they allow us to change our world. Writing and rewriting stories gives women and girls agency, at least one way to choose not to be mothers without fear of becoming wicked witches, at least one opportunity to begin again. I must admit that I like these beginnings, these bids for a new kind of acceptance, which whisper to me that next time I meet a witch, I should try not to scare her away. I like these beginnings very much indeed.

Notes

NOTES TO CHAPTER 1

1. While writers of texts within the traditions of feminist spirituality and anthropology often reference personal experiences with magical practices, I've seen few literary critics or historians who admit to knowing anyone who believes in magic. One literary critic I've encountered who discusses practicing witches at length is Diane Purkiss, whose shrewd analysis in *The Witch in History* nevertheless maintains an attitude of scholarly disbelief.
2. This is Gower's phrasing of the question as it appears in the "Tale of Florent," from the *Confessio Amantis*.
3. All etymological information in this paragraph taken from the *Shorter Oxford English Dictionary* in two volumes.
4. From Old French *alkemie, astrologie, nigromancie, prophecie,* and *sorcerie,* respectively.
5. The arguments of Richard Kieckhefer, Jeffrey Burton Russell, Valerie Flint, and Keith Thomas support these categories, for example.
6. None of the charms in the Anglo-Saxon *Leechbook* or *Lacnunga* feature all of these elements combined together in this way, but G. Storms's *Anglo-Saxon Magic* provides examples of all of the techniques described here— sometimes the elements appear discretely but other times they appear in various combinations. See especially pages 49–106 and 132–311.
7. The five romances by Chrétien are *Erec et Enide, Cligés, Le Chevalier de la Charrete* (*Lancelot,* or *The Knight of the Cart*), *Le Chevalier au Lion* (*Yvain,* or *The Knight with the Lion*), and *Le Conte du Graal* (*Perceval,* or *The Story of the Grail*).

NOTES TO CHAPTER 2

1. This quote appears in *The Witch in History*.
2. I recently got the chance to play the Wicked Witch in a community theater production of *The Wizard of Oz*. My performance as a child was not so different from my adult interpretation of the role, I imagine.
3. See Purkiss's *Witch in History* (especially Part II) and Deborah Willis's *Malevolent Nurture* (especially Chapter Two) for documentation of witches as neighbors who threaten children.
4. All citations from Chrétien's romances come from William Kibler's edition. The translations are Kibler's for all the romances except *Erec and Enide,* which was translated by Carleton W. Carroll.

164 *Notes*

5. When I discuss "masculinity" or "femininity" in this chapter and throughout this project, I am referring to the conventionally coded markers—physical, behavioral, psychological, social, and so on—which members of a particular culture recognize as signifying gender, and not to a biologically determined set of definitive gender truths. I find there is no concise way to refer to the historically-specific, shifting processes which comprise gender construction and identification without risking a certain naturalization of gendered markers, however unintentional; despite this risk, for the purposes of brevity and readability, I offer the terms "masculinity" and "femininity" as a shorthand for the complex and ongoing debate about gender.

6. See, for example, Ad Putter's essay in *Becoming Male in the Middle Ages* for a reading of transvestitism in European chivalric romance as reflecting an anxiety about the mutability of gender roles, and his essay in *Arthurian Romance and Gender* for discussion of the rhetoric of effeminacy in Arthurian material. Judith Weiss argues in "The Power and the Weakness of Women in Anglo-Norman Romance" that representations of women in Anglo-Norman romances are "ambivalent and inconsistent," and that the women sometimes take on a masculine role (7).

7. See Krueger's essay, "Beyond Debate: Gender in Play in Old French Courtly Fiction," in *Gender in Debate from the Early Middle Ages to the Renaissance* (ed. Fenster and Lees), for evidence of the fact that courtly fiction was a literary space devoted to gender play, and her chapter, "Questions of Gender in Old French Courtly Romances," in *The Cambridge Companion to Medieval Romance* for a discussion of gender mutability in the Old French romances.

8. Quotations from Marie's *Lais* come from Glyn S. Burgess and Keith Busby's edition; for Geoffrey's *Historia*, I use the Lewis Thorpe edition; and for Laʒamon's *Brut*, all citations come from the W. R. J. Barron and S. C. Weinberg edition (translations of the *Brut* are mine).

9. For women described upon first appearance in Chrétien's romances, see pages 42, 128S, 156, 309, and 404; in Marie's *Lais*, see pages 56, 86, 105, 111, and 114; in Geoffrey's *Historia*, see pages 159, 205, and 221; in Laʒamon's *Brut*, see lines 1105–9, 2488–2500, 5502–4, 7131–41, 9248–50, 9616–19, and 11090–8.   For descriptions of the beauty of heroines, see pages 42, 46, 56, 128, 133, 156, 309, and 404 for Chrétien; for Marie, see 56, 64, 80, 86, 97, 105, 114, and 120; for Geoffrey, see pages 159, 205, and 221; for Laʒamon, see lines 1105–9, 7131–41, 9248–50, 9287–9, 11090–8, and 14283–5.

10. For descriptions which include reference to conventionally feminine physical features, see pages 42, 56, 133, 136, 313, 325, and 404 (Chrétien), pages 56, 74, and 80 (Marie), and lines 2488–2500 (Laʒamon).

11. Chrétien's ladies who share these qualities include Enide, Saredamors, Laudine, and Blancheflor. Marie replicates Chrétien's conventional description in her brief descriptions of Equitan's lady and Lanval's lady. Geoffrey and Laʒamon both draw on the romance tradition in their even briefer descriptions of Guinevere (Gwenevere), Renwein (Rouwenne), and Ygerna (Ygerne).

12. For descriptions including racial and class markers like white skin or expensive clothes, see pages 42, 56, 67, 133, 136, 313, 325, and 404 (Chrétien), pages 56, 64, 74, 80, 86, 97, 105, 111, and 121 (Marie), page 221 (Geoffrey), and lines 2488–2500, 7131–41, 9348–60, 11090–8, and 12229–42 (Laʒamon).

13. For example, another strategy for romance writers in particular involves alluding to the creative power of Nature and God to help validate the beauty of the heroine. Making Nature responsible for the beauty of whiteness provides a biological basis for a racist and classist aesthetic; mentioning God's

Notes 165

involvement adds to the force of biology that of divine ordinance. Attributing beauty to God or Nature removes responsibility for beauty from the lady herself—certainly she cannot be responsible for her own loveliness—and situates her passively in relation to her own body. References to Nature and God occur on pages 42, 133, 156, 313, and 404 in Chrétien's romances, and pages 56 and 64 for Marie's *Lais*. Another strategy for reinforcing conventions of passive feminine beauty in Chrétien's work is the explicit objectification of the lady through comparison to objects and animals. Chrétien compares ladies variously to flowers (42, 74), mirrors (42, 133, 313), gems (133, 313), an arrow (133), birds, (156, 404) and a carving (404). Characterizing the heroine as another object belonging to the knight reinforces her position as the passive recipient of the male gaze, as a figure in tableau.

14. For examples of descriptions including references to a reputation for valiant or noble acts, see page 38 (Chrétien), pages 44, 68, 97, 105, and 111 (Marie), pages 55, 66, and 212 (Geoffrey), and lines 9896–9901 (Laȝamon).

15. There is an extended description of Arthur's armor in Laȝamon's *Brut*, lines 10542–10562, for example, and Chrétien's romances describe knights arming on pages 46, 395, and 399.

16. For example, Cligés and Guigemar both fear to speak of their feelings for their beloved (Chrétien 185, Marie 49), Elidus cries over his swooning lover (Marie 119), and Lancelot faints when he sees Guinevere's comb (Chrétien 225), as does Yvain when Laudine withdraws her love (Chrétien 330).

17. In Chrétien's *The Knight of the Cart*, the ladies organize a tournament (273), and Meleagant's sister rescues Lancelot when he's trapped in a tower (288). There are many examples of ladies manipulating lovers, including pages 186–8, 263, and 277 in Chrétien's romances, and pages 50, 69, and 115–6 in Marie's *Lais*.

18. See pages 54–55 of Feinstein's article, "Losing Your Head in Chrétien," and 31–33 of Alexander's "Women as lovers in early English romance." Judith Weiss also makes a similar argument about love affecting gender transgression (7–23).

19. There were many women who worked in religious orders as healers, and some learned women wrote about medicine—Hildegard von Bingen, who wrote a medical treatise, is the most famous example.

20. In a note about Odysseus's boar injury, Robert Renehan argues that "the combination of 'rational' medicine and 'irrational' magic in the treatment of an injury" was a practice dating from before the Indo-European diaspora (2). Bandaging was not effective without the corresponding chant; magic and medicine were not necessarily discrete practices. The Anglo-Saxon *Leechbook* provides additional evidence that elements of healing which seem magical to modern scholars may have been part of standard healing practices.

21. Of the five heroines in Chrétien's Arthurian romances, four endure torture and extreme suffering (Enide, Fenice, Guinevere, and Laudine). Marie's *lais* are also filled with female suffering, a trend explored by Renée Curtis in "Physical and Mental Cruelty in the *Lais* of Marie de France." Kathryn Gravdal studies female suffering in *Ravishing Maidens: Writing Rape in Medieval French Literature and Law*, which traces "the naturalization of the subordination of women in medieval French culture by examining representations of rape" (1).

22. Marie's "Lanval," for example, features a lady who maintains strict secrecy in her liaison, though she actively seeks out Lanval's love.

23. There have been a number of recent studies which consider the social situation of Anglo-Saxon women, including Lisa Bitel's *Women in Early Medieval Europe*, Christine Fell's *Women and Anglo-Saxon England*, and Helen Jewell's *Women in Medieval England*.

166   *Notes*

24. See Jewell's *Women in Medieval England*, S. F. C. Milsom's "Inheritance by Women in the Twelfth and Thirteenth Centuries," and Linda Mitchell's *Portraits of Medieval Women* for discussions of dowry, dower, and inheritance in Anglo-Norman England.
25. See Chapter 4 of Ferrante's *To the Glory of Her Sex*.
26. Marie's *Lais* are not marked by the frequency of battle scenes—battles appear in only a few. This suggests perhaps a gendered breakdown of interest in representations of male violence.
27. Jeffrey Jerome Cohen's article, "Decapitation and the Coming of Age" surveys early models of giants.
28. If the larger structure of jousting in the romances helps create a controlled space for the aggressive physical violence integral to the construction of medieval masculinity, the pitched battles of the chronicles perform a related function: they offer an acceptable group of men—the foes—on whom pain can happily be inflicted. In fact, because the foes of the chronicles are most frequently rivals for the land, the heroes are obligated to fight, whether to secure the land from unfriendly giants (as does Brutus) or to protect it from being overrun by the greedy Saxon hordes (as does Arthur).
29. I thank Naomi Miller for her observation that prophecy can be read as birthing the future.
30. This passage appears in Genesis 1:3. As this reference is merely symbolic, I am simply using the language of the New International Version, rather than the Vulgate's wording.
31. See Fritz Graf's *Magic in the Ancient World*, especially Chapter 6, "Literary Representations of Magic," for a discussion of this trend drawing on Lucan's *Pharsalia* and Thoecritus's *Pharmakeutriai* (175–204).
32. Both Plato (in the *Republic*, among other places) and Aristotle (in *Nicomachean Ethics*, for instance) consider this problem, as do Augustine (in *City of God*) and Boethius (in *The Consolation of Philosophy*).
33. Keith Thomas discusses this tradition in *Religion and the Decline of Magic*, with an especially detailed section on the invocation of political prophecy during times of crisis from the fourteenth through the seventeenth centuries (113–150, 389–434); Karen Moranski corroborates his position in "The *Prophetie Merlini*, Animal Symbolism, and the Development of Political Prophecy in Late Medieval England and Scotland"; Jean Blacker analyzes "political apocalyptic" prophecy in "Where Wace Feared to Tread" (39–40).
34. For a detailed documentation of Merlin's presence within early Welsh literature, see A. O. H. Jarman's "The Merlin Legend and the Welsh Tradition of Prophecy" (117–46). For a discussion of the two Merlin traditions (Merlin Ambrosius and Merlin Celidonius/Silvestris), see also Jean Blacker's "Where Wace Feared to Tread" (36–52).
35. Chrétien also features prophets with gender mutability, such as the fool of *The Story of the Grail* (who predicts Kay's defeat) or the knight in *The Knight with the Lion* (whose body becomes a kind of prophetic sign).
36. There is still critical debate over whether or not Laȝamon used Geoffrey's text in addition to his primary source, Wace's *Roman de Brut*. Regardless of which position one defends (and there are many), Laȝamon's choices about retaining or altering Wace's text invest the entire text of the *Brut* with Laȝamon's approval. Whether following Wace or deviating from him, Laȝamon's text is a result of his own decisions; I therefore treat Laȝamon's text as a unique work in its own right, not as a "translation" of Wace's text.
37. For documentation of emotional sensitivity and affective spirituality as gendered feminine by medieval authors, see Caroline Walker Bynum's *Jesus as Mother*, especially Chapter Four, "Jesus as Mother and Abbot as Mother: Some Themes in Twelfth-Century Cistercian Writing" (110–169). Scholars

Notes 167

arguing that witchcraft is a feminine (or feminized) practice are so numerous as to defy summary, but a few I rely heavily on are Diane Purkiss's *The Witch in History*, Robin Briggs's *Witches & Neighbors* (especially pages 257–86), and Keith Thomas's *Religion and the Decline of Magic* (especially pages 435–586).

38. Judith Weiss argues in "The Power and the Weakness of Women in Anglo-Norman Romance" that "learning, skill, and wisdom" are often attributed to the female characters in Anglo-Norman romance; she reads skill as a feminine trait when opposed to masculine strength (13).

39. Marie's hawk-knight, Muldumarec, also demonstrates the deadliness of pushing subjectivity beyond its limits. The extreme nature of his self-transformation goes too far; not only does he transgress gender conventions, but he also defies humanity by becoming a bird. As a bird, he receives his death-wound. His prophecy also outlasts his body, allowing his son to avenge him.

40. Mention of Merlin and/or his prophecies appears in lines 11490–506, 11898, 13530–8, 13964–5, 14200–2, 14288–97, 16064, and 16078.

41. His chronicle employs ambivalence in other thematic arenas as well. In "Laʒamon's Ambivalence," for example, Daniel Donoghue supports the claim that the *Brut* expresses "an ambivalence toward the past which Laʒamon demonstrates throughout his chronicle and which can be seen as part of a wider cultural ambivalence in twelfth- and thirteenth-century England" (537). This ambivalence creates a narrative space in which Laʒamon demonstrates that he "does not abhor his Anglo-Saxon heritage—he cherishes it, but he does so in a way that justifies its decline" (563). Laʒamon's ambivalence towards Merlin and transformative prophecy allows him to pay them a similarly ambiguous compliment.

NOTES TO CHAPTER 3

1. For versions using the fairy god-mother, see Disney's *Cinderella*, *Maid to Order*, and ABC's *Cinderella*; for versions using the rich man, see *Pretty Woman*, *Annie*, and *Ever After*.

2. All quotations from the churlish knight stories besides *Sir Gawain and the Green Knight* come from the edition of Thomas Hahn, which collects Gawain romances in a volume entitled *Sir Gawain: Eleven Romances and Tales*. Numbers refer to lines.

3. Quotations from "The Tale of Florent" come from the edition of the *Confessio Amantis* edited by Russell A. Peck; I have used *The Riverside Chaucer*, edited by Larry D. Benson, for citations from "The Wife of Bath's Tale"; citations from *The Wedding of Sir Gawain and Dame Ragnelle* and *The Marriage of Sir Gawain* come from Thomas Hahn's edition.

4. For a full discussion of this phenomenon, see Chapter 2. In summary, examples of heroes who exhibit aggressive masculinity include Erec (*Erec and Enide*), Alexander (*Cligés*), Cligés (*Cligés*), Lancelot (*The Knight of the Cart*), Yvain (*The Knight with the Lion*), and Perceval (*The Story of the Grail*). Their passive heroine counterparts include Enide (*Erec and Enide*), Soredamors (*Cligés*), Fenice (*Cligés*), Guinevere (*The Knight of the Cart*), Laudine (*The Knight with the Lion*), and Blancheflor (*The Story of the Grail*).

5. Heroes blamed for their love-driven passivity include Alexander (*Cligés*), Cligés (*Cligés*), and Yvain (*The Knight with the Lion*); heroines praised for their love-driven action include Enide (*Erec and Enide*) and Fenice (*Cligés*).

6. Dates for *Wedding*, *Marriage*, *Carle*, and *Carlisle* comes from Hahn's edition.

7. Christopher Dyer documents the enduring use of this concept in *Making a Living in the Middle Ages* (363).

168   *Notes*

8. Dyer also documents a fourteenth-century increase in trade (295–329).
9. Hudson discusses the rise of a gentry class (distinct from ancestral nobility) in the fourteenth and fifteenth centuries (81), corroborated by Alan Mac-Farlane (263–90), Dyer (339–40), A. J. Pollard (185), and M. M. Postan (157–63). The increase in trade and merchants is documented in Dyer (see note 6) and Pollard (188–9). The greater frequency of farmers with large landholdings after the fourteenth century is documented by Dyer (346–9) and J. L. Bolton (184–5).
10. All quotations from *Sir Gawain and the Green Knight* in this chapter come from the edition by William Vantuono, but the translations are mine. Numbers refer to lines, not pages.
11. The *Marriage* manuscript is missing a number of leaves; one of the omissions is the wedding night transformation scene.
12. See *The Middle English Dictionary* (Ed. Hans Kurath) for examples of these usages.
13. In the world of medieval romance, the hospitality shown by one aristocratic stranger to another is a central part of the story's action, allowing the long quests characteristic of the genre. In a world where settlements are farther apart and less easy to move between, where there are no hotels at every highway intersection, respect for the conventions of hospitality likely had more resonance than it may today. This is the same kind of hospitality lauded in Odysseus's journeys.
14. The Christian element in *SGGK* has been the object of much critical inquiry. See, for example, Robert W. Ackerman's "Gawain's Shield: Penitential Doctrine in *Gawain and the Green Knight*" or Thomas D. Hill's "Gawain's Jesting Lie: Towards an Interpretation of the Confessional Scene in *Gawain and the Green Knight*."
15. The standard discussion of the exchange of women by western men is, of course, Lévi-Strauss's *Elementary Structures of Kinship*; see also Gayle Rubin's "The Traffic in Women: Notes on the 'Political Economy' of Sex."
16. Chaucer's version is the only tale to deviate in this detail, a significant omission I discuss in section IV.
17. Dyer gives a thorough overview of the economic situation in Europe, arguing that the fourteenth century was one of crisis for England (228–63). This argument, made by many scholars, is so well-accepted now as to be included as a section (titled "The Crises of the Fourteenth Century") in the *Broadview Anthology of British Literature: Vol. 1: The Medieval Period* (ed. Black, et al).
18. Paston documents the population decline (27–31), as does Pollard (177).
19. Dyer (336–7), Paston (33–5, 95–7), Bolton (218–21), and Pollard (181–3) all corroborate the decline in land-value.
20. See Dyer (305, 313–29), Bolton (241, 346), and Pollard (185).
21. The only figure who deviates from this pattern is the Turk in *Turke*. Because of the manuscript damage, it is not clear whether or not the Turk, revealed to be Sir Gromer, owned land previously. He receives kingship over a castle when Gawain refuses it.
22. In addition to Henry Savage, Avril Henry and R. E. Kaske support this view, among others.
23. The poet draws our attention to her gaze explicitly, noting on each of the three days she visits Gawain that she sneaks in to watch him as he sleeps (see ll. 1193–94, 1476, and 1742–56). I call the gaze phallic to highlight the way this situation reverses the classic psychoanalytical masculine/feminine structure.
24. See Derek Pearsall's "Middle English Romance and Its Audience" for a thorough discussion of the problem of audience. Pearsall, Hahn (11–7), Hudson

Notes 169

(77), and Knight (114) all attest to the diversity of romance audiences, and Ferrante suggests that there were many female readers and listeners.

25. *Sir Gawain and the Green Knight*, *The Greene Knight*, and *The Turke and Sir Gawain*
26. *Sir Gawain and the Carle of Carlisle* and *The Carle of Carlisle*
27. Of course this is not true of those many gender theorists upon whose work my own discussion stands, especially those theorists in masculinity studies. I merely wish to point out that even today, it is often the category of femininity that demands investigation, which stands out as the other to be studied. Though I obviously believe strongly in the importance of attending to questions of gender, I do not think this necessarily means we must study "women's issues" exclusively (thus risking the "ghetto-ization" of "women's issues"). Women's issues are human issues.
28. The phrasing of this question comes from Chaucer's *Wife's Tale*.
29. As so many have detailed this issue, I will not rehearse it here.
30. P. J. P. Goldberg, Helen Jewell, Lisa Bitel, Claudia Opitz, Maryanne Kowaleski, Judith Bennett, and Kim Phillips each support some version of this narrative, though each differs about the degree to which these changes actually afforded women autonomy, economic success, or "better" lives.
31. See Claire de Trafford's "Share and Share Alike? The Marriage Portion, Inheritance, and Family Politics."
32. See Claudia Opitz's essay "Life in the Late Middle Ages" (especially pages 308–11).
33. See *Women, Work, and Life Cycle in a Medieval Economy*, in particular.
34. See Chapter 8 for a useful summary of Goldberg's findings (324–361).
35. See, for example, Judith Bennett and Amy Froide's *Singlewomen in the European Past, 1250–1800*, especially pages 1–37 and 236–69.
36. Helen Jewell's *Women in Medieval England* provides a detailed survey of women's employment, especially pages 102–114.
37. There have been a number of studies of prostitution in England—especially useful are Ruth Mazo Karras's *Common Women: Prostitution and Sexuality in Medieval England* and P. J. P. Goldberg's "Pigs and Prostitutes: Streetwalking in Comparative Perspective." Karras confirms the difficulty of analyzing records about prostitution, which are uneven and spotty at best, as well as frequently biased or ambiguous.
38. I must note here that the two "literary" versions of these stories, *SGGK* and *Wife's Tale*, do not feature a usurping step-mother figure, preferring to substitute a healing-goddess (Morgan le Fay) and a Christian moralist (the loathly lady), respectively. Rather than developing this distinction as an example of the problematic idea of a high-art/low-art schizm, I prefer to see the differences as strategies for influencing what were clearly highly specific audiences. Chaucer wrote for the court in London, and the *SGGK*-poet wrote for a limited audience at best, whereas the other romances—the popular romances—are "popular" because they were likely composed with a more general audience in mind.

NOTES TO CHAPTER 4

1. Naomi Wolf describes the beauty myth in her book, *The Beauty Myth*, which I discuss in Chapter 5.
2. In the interest of not ruining the films for those who haven't seen them, I'll address the villains only here in the footnote. Spoilers ahead! In *Psycho*, Norman Bates (Anthony Perkins) is an attractive man who turns out to be a

170 *Notes*

cross-dressing psycho; in *Kiss the Girls*, the villain is played by Cary Elwes, a cop who turns out to have "issues"; in *From Hell*, Johnny Depp shocks Victorian society with his revelation that Jack the Ripper was an aristocrat (played by Bilbo Baggins himself, Sir Ian Holmes). In *Scream*, the slashers are two popular high school boys, Billy Loomis (played by Skeet Ulrich) and Stuart Mocker (Matthew Lillard).

3. I have used Eugene Vinaver's edition, *Malory's Works*, for all citations from *The Morte Darthur*; quotations from *The Faerie Queene* come from Thomas P. Roche, Jr.'s edition; all Shakespearean quotes come from *The Riverside Shakespeare*, edited by G. Blakemore Evans.

4. See Chapter One of Richard Kieckhefer's *Magic in the Middle Ages* for a more thorough description of these two categories.

5. The list of scholars who support this thesis (in one version or another) spans decades and disciplines: see R. E. L. Masters (1962), Wallace Notestein (1968, esp pages 1–32), Mary Douglas (1970, especially Section 1), R. Trevor Davies (1972), Alexander Murray (1976), Rossell Hope Robbins (1978, see "Witchcraft: An Intro"), Richard A. Horsley (1979), Christina Larner (1981), Jeffrey Burton Russell (1984, esp. Chapters 2 & 10), Brian Levack (1987, esp. Chapters 2 & 3), Richard Kieckhefer (1989), Diane Purkiss (1996, see all chapters in Part II), and Michael Bailey (2001).

6. Notestein documents the increasing use of stringent penalties (including death) during the mid-16th century (11–32).

7. Christopher Marlowe's *Dr. Faustus* also participates in this trend.

8. See Levack's *The Witch-Hunt in Early Modern Europe*.

9. Sarah (played by a young Jennifer Connelly) hears this repeatedly in *Labrynth*, a classic fantasy film.

10. Merlin advises Arthur about military strategy on pages 13–15, 16–17, 47, 49, 58–59, and 61. He unsuccessfully discourages Arthur's marriage to Gwenevere on page 59.

11. Pages 35–6, 4 and 25, 29, 29, 5, and 34, respectively.

12. There are examples of similar expressions on pages 121, 142, 166, 186, and 313.

13. As *Macbeth* features female magic-users, I will discuss that play in a later section.

14. See I.ii.2.246–309, in particular, and V.i.4–7.

15. Prospero threatens Ariel with imprisonment in I.ii.296–300, dangles freedom in front of Ariel in I.ii.301–2 & 503–05, but then requires more and more of him in IV.i.33–50, 164–87, & 254–62, and V.i.30–32, 97–105, & 254–6.

16. The colonial (and post-colonial) implications of the relationship between Prospero and Caliban are well known and often discussed. Though the colonial relationship is both striking and important, a thorough discussion of the play's ideological investment in colonial power lies outside the scope of this study.

17. The first gloss here comes from Thomas P. Roche's edition (1079n), the latter two from the Norton anthology (Abrams, ed. 639n).

18. Another example of Archimago's non-magical deception occurs in Book II, when Archimago convinces Braggidochio and Trompart to attack Guyon and Redcrosse in revenge for Mordant and Armania (II.iii.11–18).

19. This is the central argument of his book, *Women, Work, and Life Cycle in a Medieval Economy*.

20. See Goldberg (Chapter 8 of *Women, Work, and Life Cycle* summarizes the results of his study), Jewel 100–1 & 113–4, Opitz 293, and the work of Marian Dale, Maryanne Kowaleski, Judith Bennett, and Barbara Hanawalt.

21. Michael Bailey traces the process by which witchcraft became linked with necromancy in "From Sorcery to Witchcraft: Clerical Conceptions of Magic in the Later Middle Ages."

Notes 171

22. In order, pages 88, 50 & 90, 151–2, 339–43, 392–6, 478, 49–50, and 367.
23. Nineve is another example of an ambivalently magical woman in the *Morte Darthur*.
24. Compare Spenser's description of the two hags, Enuie and Detraction. When Arthegall meets the pair, Spenser tells us they were "Two griesly creatures; and, to that their faces / Most foule and filthie were, the garments yet / Being all rag'd and tatter'd, their disgraces / Did much the more augment, and made most vgly cases" (V.xii.28.6–9). Of particular interest is Enuie's extended description, which includes details like "dull eyes," "foule heare," skinny lips like "raw lether, pale and blew," very "foule and durtie" hands, and which notes that she's holding a snake that she eats, w/ "bloudie gore and poyson dropping lothsomely" from her lips (V.xii.29–30).
25. Akira Kurosawa's *Throne of Blood*, for example, merges the three witches into one extraordinarily creepy woman.
26. While I am well aware of the debate over whether or not the Hecate scenes are truly Shakespeare's work, I am not convinced that they aren't his. Whether the Hecate scenes were originally created by Shakespeare is less important to me than the effect they have on the text when included. If someone else authored them, that person was clearly working within the same discursive framework as Shakespeare, a discourse which highlights the demonic nature of magic.
27. See, for example, L. C. Knights, Cleanth Brooks, Leo Kirschbaum, Herbert R. Coursen, Jr., Coppélia Kahn, Roland Mushat Frye, and Stephen Orgel.
28. Samuel Taylor Coleridge and Albert H. Tolman are early proponents of this argument, as are Canon J. A. MacCulloch and A. W. Crawford, as well as M. D. W. Jeffreys, and more recent adherents to this view include Charles J. Rzepka, Nicholas Brooke, and Paul Edmonson. Laura Shamas provides an exhaustive study of their relation to mythology, including the Fates.
29. See Claude E. Jones, Joe Ross, and Marina Favila.
30. Critics and directors utilizing these interpretations are as follows: J. Dover Wilson regards them as "the incarnation of evil in the Universe" (xxxi); Orson Welles presented them as voodoo priestesses in his 1936, all African American version of the play (see Susan McCloskey's review); Mary Floyd-Wilson sees them as powerful weather-workers; Ian Robinson proposes that their role in the beginning of the play is as a chorus; Joe Ross sees them as hags, and Akira Kurosawa represents them as one old, freaky woman in *Throne of Blood*; Albert H. Tolman believes they are vulgar and Felix E. Schelling, grotesque; Roman Polanski's version, *The Tragedy of Macbeth* (1971), offers three women of different ages, as does the 1982 BBC version directed by Jack Gold; Henry B. Wheatley connects the sisters to the Norns of Norse mythology; Giles E. Dawson doesn't know "just what sort of creatures the Weird Sisters were supposed to be" (255), and Peter Stallybrass emphasizes their deliberate ambiguity; Janet Adelman analyzes the witches' androgyny and Leslie Katz their "hybrid gender" (235); and Terry Eagleton famously characterized them as "the heroines of the piece." For a comprehensive survey of the Weird sisters' performance history, see the Introduction to Laura Shamas's *"We Three": The Mythology of Shakespeare's Weird Sisters*.
31. Critics argue both sides of this question. On the side of the witches as marginal and bereft of real power are H. W. Herrington, Giles E. Dawson, A. C. Bradley, Susan McCloskey, and Stephen Greenblatt; arguing that the witches have influential magic are William Hazlitt, Felix E. Shelling, Henry B. Wheatley, and Mary Floyd-Wilson.
32. This appears in "Nightmares of Desire: Evil Women in *The Faerie Queene*."

172 *Notes*

33. "Early Modern Medea: Representations of Child Murder in the Street Literature of Seventeenth-Century England."
34. This appears in "Avenging the Blood of Children: Anxiety Over Child Victims and the Origins of the European Witch Trials."
35. The kind of work being done in this field varies widely, from Diane Purkiss's analysis of maternal tropes associated with witchcraft in *The Witch in History*, to the collection of essays edited by Naomi Miller and Naomi Yavneh, *Maternal Measures*, which explores "a striking range of positive and negative constructions of female caregiving in the sixteenth and seventeenth centuries" (1).
36. See Brian Levack's *The Witchcraft Sourcebook* or Elaine G. Breslaw's *Witches of the Atlantic World* for excellent collections including these writers and others.
37. Diane Purkiss provides an extensive analysis of English witchcraft trials in Part II of *The Witch in History*, "Early Modern Women's Stories of Witchcraft" (91–176).
38. This trial is one of the ones included in Brian Levack's *The Witchcraft Sourcebook* (190–197).
39. Alan McFarlane, Keith Thomas, Robin Briggs, Diane Purkiss, and Deborah Willis all attest to the importance of village-level conflicts in witchcraft trials.
40. This phrase is part of the title of Chapter One, in *The Witch in History*.

NOTES TO CHAPTER 5

1. Margaret Murray is perhaps the most famous to argue for a surviving pagan fertility religion, but Jules Michelet and Carlo Ginzburg have made similar claims. Elliot Rose provides a thorough refutation of Murray's work in *A Razor for a Goat*.
2. Mary Daly rehearses the most radical version of this argument, also made less vehemently (and often in non-feminist iterations) by Wallace Notestein, Arthur Evans, H. R. Trevor-Roper, Richard Horsely, Christina Larner, Jeffrey Burton Russell, and Michael Bailey.
3. Alan McFarlane, Keith Thomas, and Robin Briggs have famously suggested village-level conflicts, and Diane Purkiss and Deborah Willis reread village-level conflicts to recover the female voices represented therein.
4. H. Sidky addresses the issue of psychotropic drug-use in European witchcraft (though does not argue that drugs *caused* the witchcraze), as does Michael J. Harner; Mary Matossian points to ergotism as a cause of the Salem panic; Chadwick Hansen and Linnda R. Caporael also cover the Salem context.
5. See Eric Ross's discussion of syphilis, John Demos's on repressed aggression being projected and displaced, and Edward Bever's on psychosocial disease, for example, or the studies of G. Zilboorg, G. Rosen, Chadwick Hansen, or R. P. Anderson.
6. There are many books with significant sections (and sometimes the entirety) devoted to analysis of the witch-hunts within a legal context, including Anne Llewellyn Barstow's *Witchcraze* (especially Chapters 2, 3, 4, and 7), Brian P. Levack's *The Witch-Hunt in Early Modern Europe* (Chapters 3, 6, and 7), Alan Macfarlane's *Witchcraft in Tudor and Stuart England* (Chapters 1–6), Edward Peters's *The Magician, the Witch, and the Law* (Chapter 6), and Keith Thomas's *Religion and the Decline of Magic* (Chapter 14).
7. Alexander Murray and Brian Levack both cite the *lex talionis* as the relevant code governing accusatorial procedure ("Medieval Origins of the Witch Hunt" 67 & *The Witchhunt in Early Modern Europe* 70).

Notes 173

8. R. Trevor Davies discusses Anglo-Saxon law in *Four Centuries of Witch-Beliefs*, arguing for English leniency until the reign of Elizabeth (13–15). Cf. Hughes's discussion of Anglo-Saxon law in *Witchcraft* (154–55) and Thomas's discussion in *Religion* (466–7).

9. Alexander Murray also provides evidence for skepticism towards aspects of witchcraft in both secular and ecclesiastical courts from as far back as the ninth century to as late as the mid-fifteenth century.

10. Richard Kaeuper, for example, argues that central governments in England and France were increasingly hard-pressed to control rising violence by the end of the thirteenth century; see also H. R. T. Summerson's description of the legal system, which implies that female crime was essentially nonexistent.

11. See R. C. Van Caenegem's discussion of the monarchy's growing role in the maintenance of order in twelfth-century England, especially the traditionally male crimes of theft, murder, and robbery (37–60).

12. Kieckhefer's *Magic in the Middle Ages* (190), and Murray's "Medieval Origins of the Witch Hunt" (68–9).

13. This appears in "From Sorcery to Witchcraft: Clerical Conceptions of Magic in the Later Middle Ages."

14. Hughes discusses this in Chapter Twelve of *Witchcraft* (166–7).

15. Brian Levack offers a comprehensive discussion of the legislative changes spanning the thirteenth through sixteenth centuries in Chapter 3 of *The Witchhunt in Early Modern Europe* (especially pages 69–76). Others who corroborate include Macfarlane (14–20), Thomas (442–3), H.C. Erik Midelfort in "Were There Really Witches?" (193), and Ronald Holmes in *Witchcraft in British History* (69–82). R. C. Van Caenegem suggests the shift happened as early as the twelfth century (1–36).

16. Keith Thomas's discussion of the development of demonic magic as a crime is comprehensive (435–65), and Levack, Davies, Murray, Bailey, and Midelfort all agree that fear of demonic magic as a pervasive threat developed in the late-fifteenth, sixteenth, and seventeenth centuries, as do Christina Larner and Russell Hope Robbins.

17. All of the scholars cited so far support this idea, though estimates about the number of witchcraft trials and executions vary widely.

18. See Thomas (443) and Hughes (178).

19. I did not conduct a thorough study of witchcraft legislation in the U.S., though I did come across a few studies of U.S. witchcraft which addressed the slow, eventual decline (with occasional resurgences) of prosecution and/or legislation: Richard Weisman explores the New England context, pinpointing 1693 as the end of witchcraft prosecution in that region (117–131, 160–183); Ramón A. Guitiérrez argues that eighteenth-century Spaniards used witchcraft accusations as a racialized tool to oppress Indian women; and Aline Helg throws light on witchcraft beliefs (or lack of them) in the U.S. South & Cuba in the late nineteenth century.

20. When members of marginalized groups, like Native Americans or African Americans in the U.S., participate in religious, spiritual, or magical practices termed "witchcraft" by white accusers (correctly or incorrectly), the danger for prosecution rises significantly (especially if a white person has been injured or killed). In these cases, though witchcraft is surely a motivating factor, prosecution focuses on the effects of the magic rather than on the use of witchcraft itself. One example of this kind of case occurred in New York in 1930; see Sidney L. Harring's description of the situation in "Red Lilac of the Cayugas: Traditional Indian Laws and Culture Conflict in a Witchcraft Trial in Buffalo, New York, 1930."

174   *Notes*

21. Naomi Wolf's *The Beauty Myth* describes the most recent manifestation of the social expectation of female beauty in the U.S. and Britain.
22. I think the myth began even earlier. Wolf mentions as evidence the fourteenth-century troubadours' use of "catalogs" of female body parts, but these appear at least as early as the twelfth century in the works of Chretien de Troyes and Marie de France (as documented in Chapter Two).
23. The *Rescuer's* Medusa is really a mix of the beautiful grotesque and the witch-hag: her body is amorphous and de-sexualized, but her sexy red dress, stockings, high heels, and stark make-up mark her as attempting to conform to conventional feminine beauty norms.
24. See "Compulsory Heterosexuality and Lesbian Existence."
25. See "Help, Help, Don't Save Me," "Love is Blind," or "Your Witch is Showing" in Season One, or "Fastest Gun on Madison Avenue" in Season Two, for examples of Darrin's actions necessitating witchcraft.
26. See, for example, the following episodes: "Mother Meets What's His Name," "Witch or Wife," "It Takes One to Know One," "A Change of Face," "Eat at Mario's" (from Season One), "A Very Special Delivery," "Trick or Treat," or "Junior Executive" (from Season Two).
27. During Season One, she meets Leo (Brian Krause), whom she marries at the beginning of Season Three; Piper is pregnant during Season Four, and she has a son, Wyatt, in Season Five, and another, Chris, in Season Six.
28. In "Once Upon A Time," for instance, Piper's focus on Leo endangers a child. Two especially interesting episodes which highlight Piper's desire to be a perfect mother are "Brain Drain" in Season Four and "Desperate Housewitches" in Season Eight.
29. See, for example, "Dream Sorcerer" or "The Fourth Sister," in Season One, "The Honeymoon's Over" in Season Two, or "A Knight to Remember," "Lost and Bound," and "The Three Faces of Phoebe" from Season Four.
30. See Season Eight's "Battle of the Hexes" for their first meeting and "Engaged and Confused" for their engagement and marriage.
31. See the first episode, "Something Wicca This Way Comes," Season Two's "Witch Trial," and Season Three's "Death Takes a Halliwell."
32. See Murray's *The Witch-Cult in Western Europe* & Gardner's *Witchcraft Today*, along with Sparhawk's *The Spiral Dance*, Mary Daly's *Beyond God the Father*, Elinor Gadon's *The Once and Future Goddess*, or Zsuzsanna Budapest's *The Holy Book of Women's Mysteries*.
33. See Elliot Rose's *A Razor for a Goat* for a full-scale refutation of Murray's argument.
34. See also Linda Jencson's analysis of misogynist uses of Goddess worship, "In Whose Image? Misogynist Trends in the Construction of Goddess and Woman."
35. She taught a class for the University of Arizona, "Queer Theory," in 1997, which I took. I'm rehearsing her explanation from memory and my class notes.
36. See *Archaeology of Knowledge*, especially pages 40–49.
37. See Sparhawk's *Spiral Dance* and Wendy Griffin's "Crafting the Boundaries: Goddess Narrative as Incantation" for examples of different approaches to transformation in Goddess spirituality.

Bibliography

Abrams, M. H., ed. *The Norton Anthology of English Literature.* Vol. 1B. 7th ed. New York and London: Norton, 2000.

Achterberg, Jeanne. *Woman as Healer.* Boston: Shambhala, 1991.

Ackerman, Robert W. "Gawain's Shield: Penitential Doctrine in *Gawain and the Green Knight.*" *Anglia* 76 (1958): 254–65.

Adelman, Janet. "'Born of woman': Fantasies of Maternal Power in 'Macbeth.'" *Cannibals, Witches, and Divorce: Estranging the Renaissance.* Ed. Marjorie Garber. Baltimore: Johns Hopkins UP, 1987. 90–121.

Alamichel, Marie-Françoise. "King Arthur's Dual Personality in Layamon's *Brut.*" *Neophilologus* 77 (1993): 303–319.

Alexander, Flora. "Women as Lovers in Early English Romance." *Women and Literature in Britain, 1150–1500.* Ed. Carol M. Meale. Cambridge: Cambridge UP, 1993. 24–40.

Alice in Wonderland. Dir. Clyde Geronimi and Wilfred Jackson. Disney, 1951.

Anderson, R. P. "The History of Witchcraft: A Review with Some Psychiatric Comments." *American Journal of Psychiatry* 126 (1970): 1727–1735.

Annie. Dir. John Huston. Perf. Albert Finney, Carol Burnett, Ann Reinking, Tim Curry, Bernadette Peters, and Aileen Quinn. Columbia, 1982.

Arden, Heather. "Chrétien de Troyes's Lancelot and the Structure of Twelfth-Century French Romance." *King Arthur Through the Ages.* Ed. Valerie M. Lagorio and Mildred Leake Day. Vol. 1. New York and London: Garland, 1990. 80–98.

Aristotle. *Nicomachean Ethics.* Trans. J. L. Acknill. London: Faber, 1973.

Augustine of Hippo. *City of God.* Trans. Gerald G. Walsh, et al. Ed. Vernon J. Bourke. New York and London: Image Book-Doubleday, 1958.

Bailey, Michael D. "From Sorcery to Witchcraft: Clerical Conceptions of Magic in the Later Middle Ages." *Speculum* 76.3 (2001): 960–90.

Bakhtin, Mikhail. *Rabelais and His World.* Trans. Hélène Iswolsky. Bloomington, IN: Indiana UP, 1984.

Barstow, Anne Llewellyn. *Witchcraze: A New History of the European Witch Hunts.* San Francisco: Pandora, 1994.

Baum, L. Frank. *The Wizard of Oz and The Marvellous Land of Oz.* London: Octopus Books, 1979.

Bennett, Judith. "Medieval Women, Modern Women: Across the Great Divide." *Feminists Revision History.* Ed. Ann-Louise Shapiro. New Brunswick, NJ: Rutgers UP, 1994.

———. "Public Power and Authority." *Women and Power in the Middle Ages.* Ed. Mary Erler and Maryanne Kowaleski. Athens: U of Georgia P, 1988. 18–36.

Bennett, Judith M. and Amy M. Froide, eds. *Singlewomen in the European Past, 1250–1800.* Philadelphia, U of Penn, 1999.

176   *Bibliography*

Bever, Edward. "Witchcraft Fears and Psychosocial Factors in Disease." *Journal of Interdisciplinary History* 30.4 (2000): 573–590.

Bewitched. Creator Sol Saks. Perf. Elizabeth Montgomery, Agnes Moorehead, Dick Sergent, and Dick York. ABC, 1964–1972.

Bitel, Lisa. *Women in Early Medieval Europe 400–1100.* Cambridge: Cambridge UP, 2002.

Black, Joseph, et al, eds. "The Crises of the Fourteenth Century." *Broadview Anthology of British Literature: Vol. 1: The Medieval Period.* New York: Broadview, 2005. 200–212.

Blacker, Jean. "Where Wace Feared to Tread: Latin Commentaries on Merlin's Prophecies in the Reign of Henry II." *Arthuriana* 6.1 (1996): 36–52.

Boethius. *The Consolation of Philosophy.* Trans. V. E. Watts. London: Penguin, 1969.

Bolton, J. L. *The Medieval English Economy, 1150–1500.* London: J. M. Dent, 1980.

Bradley, A. C. *Shakespearean Tragedy.* New York: St. Martin's, 1957.

Braswell, Mary Flowers, ed. *Sir Perceval of Galles and Ywain and Gawain.* Kalamazoo: Medieval Institute P, 1995.

Brennan, John P. "Rebirth of a Nation? Historical Mythmaking in Layamon's *Brut.*" *Essays in Medieval Studies* 117 (2000): 19–33.

Breslaw, Elaine G., ed. *Witches of the Atlantic World: A Historical Reading and Primary Sourcebook.* New York: New York UP, 2000.

Briggs, Robin. *Witches & Neighbors: The Social and Cultural Context of European Witchcraft.* New York: Penguin, 1996.

Bromwich, Rachel, A. O. H. Jarman, and Brynley F. Roberts, eds. *The Arthur of the Welsh: The Arthurian Legend in Medieval Welsh Literature.* Cardiff: U of Wales P, 1991.

Brooke, Nicholas. *The Tragedy of Macbeth.* Oxford: Clarendon, 1990.

Brooks, Cleanth. *The Well-Wrought Urn: Studies in the Structure of Poetry.* London: Dennis Dobson, 1949.

Bruckner, Matilda Tomaryn. "Strategies of Naming in Marie de France's *Lais*: At the Crossroads of Gender and Genre." *Neophilologus* 75.1 (1991): 31–40.

Bryan, Elizabeth J. "Truth and the Round Table in Lawman's *Brut.*" *Quondom et Futurus: A Journal of Arthurian Interpretations* 2.4 (1992): 27–35.

Budapest, Zsuzsanna. *The Holy Book of Women's Mysteries.* San Francisco: WeisnerBooks, 2003.

Bullough, Vern L. "On Being a Male in the Middle Ages." *Medieval Masculinities: Regarding Men in the Middle Ages.* Ed. Clare A. Lees. Medieval Cultures 7. Minneapolis and London: U of Minnesota P, 1994. 31–45.

Burgess, Glyn S. and Keith Busby. "Introduction." *The Lais of Marie de France.* New York and London: Penguin, 1986. 7–36.

Butler, Judith. *Gender Trouble: Feminism and the Subversion of Identity.* New York: Routledge, 1990.

Bynum, Caroline Walker. *Jesus as Mother: Studies in the Spirituality of the High Middle Ages.* Berkeley: U of California P, 1982.

Can't Buy Me Love. Dir. Steve Rash. Perf. Patrick Dempsey and Amanda Peterson. Buena Vista Pictures, 1987.

Caporael, Linnda R. "Ergotism: the Satan Loosed in Salem?" *Science* 192 (1976): 21–6.

"Carle." *The Middle English Dictionary.* Ed. Hans Kurath. Ann Arbor, MI: U of Michigan P, 2001.

"The Carle of Carlisle." Hahn 373–92.

Cavanagh, Sheila T. "Nightmares of Desire: Evil Women in *The Faerie Queene.*" *Studies in Philology* 111.3 (1994): 313–338.

Bibliography 177

Charmed. Creator Constance M. Burge. Perf. Holly Marie Combs, Shannen Doherty, Alyssa Milano, and Rose McGowan. WB Television, 1998–2006.

Chaucer, Geoffrey. "The Wife of Bath's Tale." *The Riverside Chaucer*. Ed. Larry D. Benson. 3rd ed. Boston: Houghton Mifflin, 1987. 116–22.

Chrétien de Troyes. *Arthurian Romances*. Trans. William W. Kibler and Carleton W. Carroll. London and New York: Penguin, 1991.

Cinderella. Dir. Clyde Geronimi, Wilfred Jackson, and Hamilton Luske. Walt Disney, 1957.

Cinderella. Dir. Robert Iscore. Perf. Whitney Houston and Brandy Norwood. ABC/Walt Disney Television. 2 November 1997.

City Slickers. Dir. Ron Underwood. Perf. Billy Crystal and Daniel Stern. Columbia, 1991.

Cixous, Hélène. "The Laugh of the Medusa." *New French Feminisms*. Ed. Elaine Marks and Isabelle de Courtivron. Trans. Keith Cohen and Paula Cohen. Amerherst: U of Massachusetts P, 1980. 245–64.

Cohen, Jeffrey Jerome. "Decapitation and the Coming of Age: Constructing Masculinity and the Monstrous." *The Arthurian Yearbook*. Ed. Keith Busby. Vol. 3. New York and London: Garland, 1993. 173–92.

Coleridge, Samuel Taylor. *Lectures and Notes on Shakespeare and Other Dramatists*. 1810–1820. London: Oxford UP, 1931.

Coursen, Herbert R., Jr. "In Deepest Consequence: Macbeth." *Shakespeare Quarterly* 18.4 (1967): 375–388.

Crane, Susan. *Insular Romance: Politics, Faith, and Culture in Anglo-Norman and Middle English Literature*. Berkeley: U of California P, 1986.

Crawford, A. W. "The Apparitions in Macbeth." *Modern Language Notes* 39.6 (1924): 345–50.

Curtis, Renee. "Physical and Mental Cruelty in the *Lais* of Marie de France." *Arthuriana* 6.1 (1996): 22–35.

Dale, Marian K. "The London Silkwomen of the Fifteenth Century." *Economic History Review* 1.4 (1933): 324–335.

Daly, Mary. *Beyond God the Father: Towards a Philosophy of Women's Liberation*. Boston: Beacon, 1985.

———. *Gyn/Ecology: The Metaethics of Radical Feminism*. 1978. Boston: Beacon, 1990.

Davies, R. Trevor. *Four Centuries of Witch-Beliefs*. New York: Benjamin Blom, 1972.

Dawson, Giles E. "The Catholic University Macbeth." *Shakespeare Quarterly* 3.3 (1952): 255–56.

De Trafford, Claire. "Share and Share Alike?: The Marriage Portion, Inheritance, and Family Politics." *Pawns or Players?: Studies on Medieval and Early Modern Women*. Ed. Christine Meek and Catherine Lawless. Portland, OR: Four Courts Press, 2003. 36–48.

Demos, John. "Underlying Themes in the Witchcraft of Seventeenth-Century New England." Breslaw 480–488.

Donoghue, Daniel. "Laȝamon's Ambivalence." *Speculum* 65.3 (1990): 537–563.

Douglas, Mary, ed. *Witchcraft Confessions and Accusations*. London: Travistock, 1970.

Drive Me Crazy. Dir. John Schultz. Perf. Melissa Joan Hart and Adrian Grenier. Twentieth Century Fox, 1999.

Duby, Georges. "The Courtly Model." *A History of Women in the West: Silences of the Middle Ages*. Vol. II. Ed. Christiane Klapish-Zuber. Cambridge, MS: Belknap P, 1992. 250–266.

Dyer, Christopher. *Making a Living in the Middle Ages: The People of Britain 850–1520*. New Haven and London: Yale UP, 2002.

178   *Bibliography*

Eagleton, Terry. *William Shakespeare*. Oxford: Blackwell, 1986.

Edmonson, Paul. "*Macbeth*: The Play in Performance." *Angles on the English-Speaking World* 5 (2005): 121–133.

Eller, Cynthia. *Living in the Lap of the Goddess: The Feminist Spirituality Movement in America*. New York: Crossroad, 1993.

The Emperor's New Groove. Dir. Mark Dindal. Disney, 2000.

Evans, Arthur. *Witchcraft and the Gay Counterculture: A Radical View of Western Civilization and Some of the People It Has Tried to Destroy*. Boston: Fag Rag Books, 1978.

Evans, G. Blakemore, ed. *The Riverside Shakespeare*. Boston: Houghton Mifflin, 1974.

Ever After. Dir. Andy Tennant. Perf. Drew Barrymore, Anjelica Huston, and Dougray Scott. Twentieth Century Fox, 1998.

Everett, Dorothy. *Essays on Middle English Literature*. Oxford: Clarendon, 1955.

Favila, Marina. "'Mortal Thoughts' and Magical Thinking in 'Macbeth.'" *Modern Philology* 99.1 (2001): 1–25.

Feinstein, Sandy. "Losing Your Head in Chrétien's *Knight of the Cart*." *Arthuriana* 9.4 (1999): 45–62.

Fell, Christine. *Women in Anglo-Saxon England*. New York: Blackwell, 1984.

Ferguson, Gary. "Symbolic Sexual Inversion and the Construction of Courtly Manhood in Two French Romances." *The Arthurian Yearbook*. Ed. Keith Busby. Vol. 3. New York and London: Garland, 1993. 203–13.

Ferrante, Joan M. *To the Glory of Her Sex: Women's Roles in the Composition of Medieval Texts*. Bloomington, IN: Indiana UP, 1997.

Flint, Valerie, I. J. *The Rise of Magic in Early Medieval Europe*. Princeton: Princeton UP, 1991.

Floyd-Wilson, Mary. "English Epicures and Scottish Witches." *Shakespeare Quarterly* 57.2 (2006): 131–61.

Foucault, Michel. *The Archaeology of Knowledge & The Discourse on Language*. Trans. A. M. Sheridan Smith. Pantheon: New York, 1972.

———. *The Order of Things: An Archaeology of the Human Sciences*. 1970. New York: Vintage, 1990.

———. *Power/Knowledge: Selected Interviews and Other Writings 1972–1977*. Ed. Colin Gordon. Trans. Colin Gordon, Leo Marshall, John Mepham, and Kate Soper. New York: Pantheon, 1980.

Freud, Sigmund. "Some Psychical Consequences of the Anatomical Distinction Between the Sexes." *The Standard Edition of the Complete Works of Freud*. Ed. and trans. James Strachey. London: Hogarth, 1953–1964.

From Hell. Dir. Allen and Albert Hughes. Perf. Johnny Depp and Heather Graham. Twentieth Century Fox, 2001.

Frye, Roland Mushat. "Launching the Tragedy of *Macbeth*: Temptation, Deliberation, and Consent in Act I." *The Huntington Library Quarterly* 50.3 (1987): 249–61.

Gadon, Elinor W. *The Once and Future Goddess: A Symbol for our Time*. New York: Harper & Row, 1989.

Gardner, Gerald. *Witchcraft Today*. London: Rider, 1954.

Geoffrey of Monmouth. *The History of the Kings of Britain*. Trans. Lewis Thorpe. New York and London: Penguin, 1966.

———. *Vita Merlini*. Ed. and trans. Basil Clarke. Cardiff: U of Wales P, 1973.

Gies, Frances and Joseph Gies. *Marriage and the Family in the Middle Ages*. New York: Harper and Row, 1987.

Ginzburg, Carlo. *The Night Battles: Witchcraft and Agrarian Cults in the Sixteenth and Seventeenth Centuries*. Trans. John and Anne Tedeschi. 1983. New York: Penguin, 1985.

Bibliography 179

Goldberg, P. J. P. *Women, Work, and Life Cycle in a Medieval Economy: Women in York and Yorkshire c. 1300–1520.* Oxford: Clarendon, 1992.

———. "Pigs and Prostitutes: Streetwalking in Comparative Perspective." *Young Medieval Women.* Ed. Katherine J. Lewis, Noël James Menuge, and Kim M. Phillips. New York: St. Martin's P, 1999. 172–93.

Gower, John. "Tale of Florent." *Confessio Amantis.* Ed. Russell A Peck. Toronto: U of Toronto P, 1980. 58–71.

Graf, Fritz. *Magic in the Ancient World.* Trans. Franklin Philip. Cambridge, MA: Harvard UP, 1997.

Gravdal, Kathryn. *Ravishing Maidens: Writing Rape in Medieval French Literature and Law.* Philadelphia: U of Pennsylvania P, 1991.

Greenblatt, Stephen. "Shakespeare Bewitched." *New Historical Literary Study: Essays on Reproducing Texts, Representing History.* Ed. Jeffrey N. Cox and Larry J. Reynolds. Princeton, NJ: Princeton UP, 1993. 108–35.

"The Greene Knight." Hahn 309–36.

Greenwood, Susan. "Feminist Witchcraft: A Transformational Politics." *Practising Feminism: Identity, Difference, Power.* Ed. Nickie Charles and Felicia Hughes-Freeland. London: Routledge, 1996. 109–134.

Griffin, Wendy. "Crafting the Boundaries: Goddess Narrative as Incantation." *Daughters of the Goddess: Studies of Healing, Identity, and Empowerment.* Ed. Wendy Griffin. Walnut Creek: Alta Mira, 1999. 78–88.

Guitiérrez, Ramón A. "Women on Top: The Love Magic of the Indian Witches of New Mexico." *Journal of the History of Sexuality* 16.3 (2007): 373–390.

Hahn, Thomas, ed. and trans. *Sir Gawain: Eleven Romances and Tales.* Kalamazoo, MI: Medieval Institute P, 1995.

Hall, Stuart. "The Work of Representation." *Representation: Cultural Representation and Signifying Practices.* London: The Open University, 1997. 15–64.

Hanawalt, Barbara. *The Ties that Bound: Peasant Families in Medieval England.* New York: Oxford UP, 1986.

Hansen, Bert. "Science and Magic." *Science in the Middle Ages.* Ed. David C. Lindberg. Chicago: U of Chicago P, 1978. 483–506.

Hansen, Chadwick. *Witchcraft at Salem.* New York: G. Braziller, 1969.

Harner, Michael J. "The Role of Hallucinogenic Plants in Europe." *Hallucinogens and Shamanism.* New York: Oxford University Press, 1973. 125–150.

Harring, Sidney L. "Red Lilac of the Cayugas: Traditional Indian Laws and Culture Conflict in a Witchcraft Trial in Buffalo, New York, 1930." Reis 183–199.

Hazlitt, William. *Characters of Shakespeare's Plays.* World's Classics series. London: Oxford UP, 1939.

Helg, Aline. "Black Men, Racial Stereotyping, and Violence in the U.S. South and Cuba at the Turn of the Century." *Comparative Studies in Society and History* 42.3 (2000): 586–604.

Henry, Avril. "Temptation and Hunt in *Sir Gawain and the Green Knight.*" *Medium Ævum* 45 (1976): 187–88.

Herrington, H. W. "Witchcraft and Magic in the Elizabethan Drama." *The Journal of American Folklore* 32.126 (1919): 447–485.

Hill, Thomas D. "Gawain's Jesting Lie: Towards an Interpretation of the Confessional Scene In *Gawain and the Green Knight.*" *Studia Neophilologica* 52 (1980): 279–86.

Holmes, Ronald. *Witchcraft in British History.* London: Tandem, 1976.

Homer. *The Odyssey.* Trans. Robert Fitzgerald. New York: Farrar, Straus and Giroux, 1998.

Horsley, Richard A. "Who Were the Witches? The Social Roles of the Accused in the European Witch Trials." *Journal of Interdisciplinary History* 9.4 (1979): 689–715.

180   *Bibliography*

Hudson, Harriet E. "Towards a Theory of Popular Literature: The Case of the Middle English Romances." *Journal of Popular Culture* 23.3 (1989): 31–50.

Hughes, Pennethorne. *Witchcraft*. London and New York: Longmans, Green, and Co., 1952.

Jakobsen, Janet. *ENGL 550/CCLS 550: Modern Theories of Cultural Studies: Queer Theories*. Department of English, University of Arizona. Tuscon, AZ. 25 August, 1997—8 December 1997.

Jarman, A. O. H. "The Merlin Legend and the Welsh Tradition of Prophecy." *The Arthur of the Welsh*. Eds. Rachel Bromwich, A. O. H. Jarman, and Brynley Roberts. Cardiff: U of Wales P, 1991. 117–46.

Jeffreys, M. D. W. "The Weird Sisters in *Macbeth*." *English Studies in Africa* 1 (1958): 43–54.

Jencson, Linda. "In Whose Image? Misogynist Trends in the Construction of Goddess and Woman." Reis 247–273.

Jewell, Helen. *Women in Medieval England*. Manchester: Manchester UP, 1996.

Jones, Claude E. "The Imperial Theme: 'Macbeth' on Television." *The Quarterly of Film Radio and Television* 9.3 (1955): 292–98.

Kaeuper, Richard. "The Societal Role of Chivalry in Romance: Northwestern Europe." *The Cambridge Companion to Medieval Romance*. Ed. Roberta L. Krueger. Cambridge: Cambridge UP, 2000. 97–114.

———. *War, Justice, and Public order: England and France in the Later Middle Ages*. New York: Clarendon Press, 1988. ACLS Humanities E-book. Kellogg Library, California State U, San Marcos. 20 October, 2008. <http://hdl.handle.net/2027/heb.01213>.

Kahn, Coppélia. *Man's Estate: Masculine Identity in Shakespeare*. 1981. Los Angeles: U of California P, 1999.

Karras, Ruth Mazo. "Sex and the Singlewoman." Bennett and Froide 127–45.

Kaske, R. E. "Sir Gawain and the Green Knight." *Medieval and Renaissance Studies*. Proceedings of the Southeastern Institute of Medieval and Renaissance Studies, Summer 1979. Ed. George Mallary Masters. Chapel Hill: U of North Carolina P, 1984. 24–44.

Katz, Leslie. "Rehearsing the Weird Sisters: The Word as Fetish in *Macbeth*." *Shakespeare Without Class: Misappropriations of Cultural Capital*. Ed. Donald Hedrick and Bryan Reynolds. New York: Palgrave, 2000. 229–39.

Kelly, Joan. "Did Women Have a Renaissance?" *Women, History, and Theory: The Essays of Joan Kelly*. Chicago: U of Chicago P, 1984.

Kieckhefer, Richard. "Avenging the Blood of Children: Anxiety Over Child Victims and the Origins of the European Witch Trials." *The Devil, Heresy, and Witchcraft in the Middle Ages*. Ed. Alberto Ferreiro. Leiden, Boston, and Koln: Brill, 1998. 91–109.

———. *Magic in the Middle Ages*. Cambridge Medieval Textbooks Series. Cambridge: Cambridge UP, 1989.

———. "Witch Trials in Medieval Europe." *The Witchcraft Reader*. Ed. Darren Oldridge. New York: Routledge, 2002. 25–35.

Kirschbaum, Leo. "Banquo and Edgar: Character or Function?" *Essays in Criticism* 7 (1957): 1–21.

Kiss the Girls. Dir. Gary Fleder. Perf. Morgan Freeman, Ashley Judd, and Cary Elwes. Paramount, 1998.

Knight, Stephen. "The Social Function of the Middle English Romances." *Medieval Literature: Criticism, Ideology, and History*. Ed. David Aers. New York: St. Martin's, 1986. 99–122.

Knights, L. C. "How Many Children Had Lady Macbeth? An Essay in the Theory and Practice of Shakespearean Criticism." 1933. *Explorations: Essays in*

Criticism Mainly on the Literature of the Seventeenth Century. Harmondsworth, UK: Penguin, 1964. 13–50.

Kowaleski, Maryanne. "The Demographic Perspective." Bennett and Froide 38–81.

———. "The History of Urban Families in Medieval England." *Journal of Medieval History* 14 (1988): 47–63.

Kowaleski, Maryanne and Judith Bennett. "Crafts, Gilds, and Women in the Middle Ages: Fifty Years After Marian K. Dale." *Signs* 14.2 (1989): 474–501.

Kristeva, Julia. *Powers of Horror: An Essay on Abjection.* New York: Columbia UP, 1982.

Krueger, Roberta L. "Beyond Debate: Gender in Play in Old French Courtly Fiction." *Gender in Debate from the Early Middle Ages to the Renaissance.* Ed. Thelma S. Fenster and Clare A. Lees. New York: Palgrave, 2002. 79–96.

———. "Questions of Gender in Old French Courtly Romances." *The Cambridge Companion to Medieval Romance.* Ed. Roberta L. Krueger. Cambridge: Cambridge UP, 2000. 132–49.

Labrynth. Dir. Jim Henson. Perf. David Bowie and Jennifer Connelly. Columbia/Tristar, 1986.

Lacan, Jacques. "The Meaning of the Phallus." Rose and Mitchell 74–85.

Lacnunga. Anglo-Saxon remedies, charms, and prayers from British Library MS Harley 585: The Lacnunga. Ed. and trans. Edward Pettit. Lewiston, NY: E. Mellen P, 2001.

Laȝamon. *Brut, or Historia Brutonum.* Ed. and trans. W. R. J. Barron and S. C. Weinberg. Essex: Longman Group, 1995.

Larner, Christina. *Enemies of God: The Witch-hunt in Scotland.* London: Chatto & Windus, 1981.

———. *Witchcraft and Religion: The Politics of Popular Belief.* Oxford: Basil Blackwell, 1984.

A Leechbook or Collection of Medical Recipes of the Fifteenth Century. Trans and ed. Warren R. Dawson. London: Macmillan, 1934.

Le Saux, Françoise H. M. *Laȝamon's Brut: The Poem and its Sources.* Cambridge: Brewer, 1989.

Levack, Brain P. *The Witchcraft Sourcebook.* New York: Routledge, 2004.

———. *The Witch-Hunt in Early Modern Europe.* 2nd ed. London and New York: Longman, 1987.

Lévi-Strauss, Claude. 1969. *The Elementary Structures of Kinship.* Ed. Rodney Neeham. Trans. James Harle Bell and John Richard von Sturmer. Boston: Beacon, 1969.

L'Hermite-Leclercq, Paulette. "The Feudal Order." *A History of Women in the West: Silences of the Middle Ages.* Vol. II. Ed. Christiane Klapish-Zuber. Cambridge, MS: Belknap P, 1992. 202–249.

The Little Mermaid. Dir. Ron Clements and John Musker. Disney, 1989.

Loraux, Nicole. *The Experiences of Tiresias: The Feminine and the Greek Man.* Trans. Paula Wissing. Princeton, NJ: Princeton UP, 1995.

Macbeth. Dir. Jack Gold. BBC Television. DVD. Ambrose Video Pub., 2001.

MacCulloch, Canon J. A. "The Mingling of Fairy and Witch Beliefs in Sixteenth and Seventeenth Century Scotland." *Folklore* 32.4 (1921): 227–244.

Macfarlane, Alan. *Witchcraft in Tudor and Stuart England: A Regional and Comparative Study.* 2nd ed. London: Routledge, 1991.

Maclain, Lee Tobin. "Gender Anxiety in Arthurian Romance." *Extrapolation: A Journal of Science Fiction and Fantasy* 38.3 (1997): 193–99.

Maid to Order. Dir. Amy Holden Jones. Perf. Ally Sheedy and Beverly D'Angelo. New Century Vista Film, 1987.

182 *Bibliography*

Malory, Thomas. *Morte Darthur. Malory Works*. Ed. Eugène Vinaver. 2nd ed. Oxford: Oxford UP, 1971.

Marie de France. *The Lais of Marie de France*. Trans. Glyn S. Burgess and Keith Busby. New York and London: Penguin, 1986.

"The Marriage of Sir Gawain." Hahn 359–372.

Masters, R. E. L. *Eros and Evil: The Sexual Psychopathology of Witchcraft*. New York: Julian, 1962.

Matossian, Mary. "Ergot and the Salem Witchcraft Affair." *American Scientist* 70 (1982): 355–57.

McCloskey, Susan. "Shakespeare, Orson Welles, And the 'Voodoo' Macbeth." *Shakespeare Quarterly* 36 (1985): 406–416.

Michelet, Jules. *Satanism and Witchcraft: A Study in Medieval Superstition*. Trans. A. R. Allinson. 1939. New York: Citadel, 1968.

Midelfort, H. C. Erik. "Were There Really Witches?" *Transition and Revolution: Problems and Issues of European Renaissance and Reformation History*. Ed. Robert M. Kingdon. Minneapolis, MN: Burgess, 1974. 189–205.

Miller, Naomi J., and Naomi Yavneh, eds. *Maternal Measures: Figuring Caregiving in the Early Modern Period*. Aldershot: Ashgate, 2000.

Milsom, S. F. C. "Inheritance by Women in the Twelfth and Early Thirteenth Centuries." *On the Laws and Customs of England: Essays in Honor of Samuel E. Thorne*. Ed. Morris S. Arnold, et al. Chapel Hill: U of North Carolina P, 1981. 60–89.

Mitchell, Linda E. *Portraits of Medieval Women: Family, Marriage, and Politics in England 1225–1350*. New York: Palgrave Macmillan, 2003.

Moranski, Karen R. "The *Prophetie Merlini*, Animal Symbolism, and the Development of Political Prophecy in Late Medieval England and Scotland." *Arthuriana* 8.4 (1998): 58–68.

Murray, Alexander. "Medieval Origins of the Witch Hunt." *The Cambridge Quarterly* 7.1 (1976): 63–74.

Murray, Margaret. *The Witch-Cult in Western Europe*. Oxford: Clarendon, 1921.

My Fair Lady. Dir. George Cukor. Perf. Audrey Hepburn and Rex Harrison. Warner Bros., 1964.

Neuendorf, Fiona Tolhurst. "Negotiating Feminist and Historicist Concerns: Guenevere in Geoffrey of Monmouth's *Historia Regum Brittanniae*." *Quondom et Futurus: A Journal of Arthurian Interpretations* 3.2 (1993): 26–44.

Notestein, Wallace. *A History of Witchcraft in England from 1558 to 1718*. New York: T. Y. Crowell Co., 1968.

One Hundred and One Dalmations. Dir. Clyde Geronimi, Hamilton Luske, and Wolfgang Reitherman. Disney, 1961.

Opitz, Claudia. "Life in the Late Middle Ages." *A History of Women in the West: Silences of the Middle Ages*. Vol. II. Ed. Christiane Klapish-Zuber. Cambridge, MS: Belknap P, 1992. 267–318.

Orgel, Stephen. "Shakespeare and the Antic Round." *Shakespeare Survey* 52 (1999): 143–53.

Pearsall, Derek. "Middle-English Romance and Its Audience." *Historical and Editorial Studies in Medieval and Early Modern English for Johan Gerritsen*. Ed. Mary-Jo Arn, Hanneke Wirtjes, and Hans Jansen. Groningen: Wolters-Noordhoff, 1985. 37–47.

Peters, Edward. *The Magician, the Witch, and the Law*. Philadelphia: U of Pennsylvania P, 1978.

Phillips, Kim M. *Medieval Maidens: Young Women and Gender in England, 1270–1540*. Manchester: Manchester UP, 2003.

Plato. *The Republic*. Trans. Richard Sterling and William C. Scott. New York: Norton, 1985.

Bibliography 183

Pollard, A. J. *Late Medieval England 1399–1509*. New York: Longman, 2000.

Postan, M. M. *The Medieval Economy and Society: An Economic History of Britain, 1100–1500*. Berkeley: U of California P, 1972.

Practical Magic. Dir. Griffin Dunne. Perf. Sandra Bullock and Nicole Kidman. Warner Bros., 1998.

Pretty Woman. Dir. Garry Marshall. Perf. Julia Roberts and Richard Gere. Touchstone, 1990.

Psycho. Dir. Alfred Hitchcock. Perf. Vivien Leigh, Anthony Perkins. Paramount, 1960.

Purkiss, Diane. *The Witch in History: Early Modern and Twentieth-Century Representations*. London and New York: Routledge, 1996.

Putter, Ad. "Arthurian Literature and the Rhetoric of 'Effeminacy.'" Wolfzettel 34–49.

———. "Transvestite Knights in Medieval Life and Literature." *Becoming Male in the Middle Ages*. Ed. Jeffrey Jerome Cohen and Bonnie Wheeler. New York and London: Garland, 1997. 279–302.

Reis, Elizabeth, ed. *Spellbound: Women and Witchcraft in America*. Wilmington, DE: Scholarly Resources, 1998.

Renehan, Robert. "The Staunching of Odysseus' Blood: The Healing Power of Magic." *The American Journal of Philology* 113.1 (1992): 1–4.

The Rescuers. Dir. John Lounsbury, Wolfgang Reitherman, and Art Stevens. Disney, 1977.

Rich, Adrienne. "Compulsory Heterosexuality and Lesbian Existence." *Journal of Women's History* 15.3 (2003): 11–48.

Rider, Jeff. "The Fictional Margin: The Merlin of the *Brut*." *Modern Philology* 87.1 (1989): 1–12.

Robbins, Rossell Hope. "Witchcraft: An Introduction to the Literature of Witchcraft." *Catalogue of the Witchcraft Collection in Cornell University Library*. Millwood, NY: KTO P, 1978.

Robinson, Ian. "The Witches and Macbeth." *Critical Review* 11 (1968): 101–105.

Rose, Elliot. *A Razor for a Goat: A Discussion of Certain Problems in the History of Witchcraft and Diabolism*. Toronto: U of Toronto P, 1962.

Rose, Jacqueline and Juliet Mitchell, eds. *Feminine Sexuality: Jacque Lacan and the école freudienne*. New York & London: Norton, 1982.

Rosen, G. "Psychopathology in the Social Process: A Study of the Persecution of Witches in Europe as a Contribution to the Understanding of Mass Delusion and Psychic Epidemics." *Journal of Health and Human Behavior* 1 (1960): 200–211.

Ross, Eric B. "Syphilis, Misogyny, and Witchcraft in 16th-Century Europe." *Current Anthropology* 36.2 (1995): 333–337.

Ross, Joe. "Hags Out of their Skins." *The Journal of American Folklore* 93.368 (1980): 183–86.

Rubin, Gayle. "The Traffic in Women: Notes on the 'Political Economy' of Sex." *The Second Wave: A Reader in Feminist Theory*. Ed. Linda Nicholson. New York: Routledge, 1997. 27–62.

Russell, Jeffrey Burton. *Lucifer: The Devil in the Middle Ages*. Ithaca, NY: Cornell UP, 1984.

———. *Witchcraft in the Middle Ages*. Ithaca and London: Cornell UP, 1972.

Rzepka, Charles J. "Checkhov's 'The Three Sisters,' Lear's Daughters, and the Weird Sisters: The Arcana of Archetypal Influence." *Modern Language Studies* 14.4 (1984): 18–27.

Savage, Henry. "The Significance of the Hunting Scenes in *Sir Gawain and the Green Knight*." *Journal of English and German Philology* 27 (1928): 1–15.

Schelling, Felix E. "Some Features of the Supernatural as Represented in Plays of the Reigns of Elizabeth and James." *Modern Philology* 1.1 (1903): 31–47.

Scream. Dir. Wes Craven. Perf. Neve Campbell, Courtney Cox, and David Arquette. Dimension, 1996.

184   Bibliography

Shakespeare, William. *Macbeth*. Evans 1306–42.
———. *A Midsummer Night's Dream*. Evans 217–49.
———. *The Tempest*. Evans 1606–38.
Shamas, Laura Annawyn. *"We Three": The Mythology of Shakespeare's Weird Sisters*. New York: Peter Lang, 2007.
Shorter Oxford English Dictionary. 5th ed. 2 vols. Oxford: Oxford UP, 2002.
Sidky, H. "Ergot, Demonic Possession, and Hallucinogenic Drugs." Breslaw 472–79.
"Sir Gawain and the Carle of Carlisle." Hahn 81–112.
Sir Gawain and the Green Knight: A Dual-Language Version. Ed. and trans. William Vantuono. New York and London: Garland, 1991.
Sleeping Beauty. Dir. Clyde Geronimi. Disney, 1959.
Snow White and the Seven Dwarves. Dir. David Hand. Disney, 1937.
Sparhawk. *The Spiral Dance: A Rebirth of the Ancient Religion of the Great Goddess*. San Francisco: Harper, 1979.
Spenser, Edmund. *The Faerie Queene*. Ed. Thomas P. Roche, Jr. London: Penguin, 1978.
Stallybrass, Peter. "Macbeth and Witchcraft." *Focus on Macbeth*. Ed. John Russell. New York: Routledge, 1982. 189–209.
Stallybrass, Peter, and Allon White. "Bourgeois Hysteria and the Carnivalesque." *The Cultural Studies Reader*. Ed. Simon During. London and New York: Routledge, 1993. 284–92.
Star Wars. Dir. George Lucas. Perf. Mark Hamill, Harrison Ford, and Carrie Fisher. Twentieth Century Fox, 1997.
Staub, Susan C. "Early Modern Medea: Representations of Child Murder in the Street Literature of Seventeenth-Century England." Miller and Yavneh 333–47.
Storms, G. *Anglo-Saxon Magic*. Norwood, PA: Norwood Editions, 1976.
The Student Bible: New International Version. Eds. Phillip Yancey and Tim Stafford. Grand Rapids, MI: Zondervan Bible Publishers, 1989.
Summerson, H. R. T. "The Structure of Law Enforcement in Thirteenth-Century England." *American Journal of Legal History* 23.4 (1979): 313–327.
Superman. Dir. Richard Donner. Perf. Christopher Reeve and Gene Hackman. Warner, 1978.
The Sword in the Stone. Dir. Wolfgang Reitherman. Disney, 1963.
Taussig, Michael. *Mimesis and Alterity: A Particular History of the Senses*. London & New York: Routledge, 1993.
Thomas, Keith. *Religion and the Decline of Magic*. London: Weidenfeld and Nicolson, 1971.
Throne of Blood. Dir. Akira Kurosawa. Janus Films. Public Media Home Video, 1993.
Tolman, Albert H. "Notes on Macbeth." *PMLA* 11.2 (1896): 200–219.
The Tragedy of Macbeth. Dir. Roman Polanski. 1971. Video. Columbia TriStar Home Video, 1987.
Trevor-Roper, H. R. *The European Witch Craze of the 16th and 17th Centuries, and Other Essays*. New York: Harper and Row, 1969.
"The Turke and Sir Gawain." Hahn 337–58.
Van Caenegem, R. C. *Legal History: A European Perspective*. London: Hambledon, 1991.
"The Wedding of Sir Gawain and Dame Ragnelle." Hahn 41–80.
Weisman, Richard. *Witchcraft, Magic, and Religion in 17th-Century Massachusetts*. Amherst, MA: U of Massachusetts P, 1984.
Weiss, Judith. "The Power and the Weakness of Women in Anglo-Norman Romance." *Women and Literature in Britain, 1150–1500*. Ed. Carol M. Meale. Cambridge: Cambridge UP, 1993. 7–23.

Wheatley, Henry B. "The Folklore of Shakespeare." *Folklore* 27.4 (1916): 378–407.

Willis, Deborah. *Malevolent Nurture: Witch-Hunting and Maternal Power in Early Modern England.* Ithaca and London: Cornell UP, 1995.

Wilson, J. Dover. *Macbeth.* Cambridge: Cambridge, 1951.

The Witches of Eastwick. Dir. George Miller. Perf. Cher, Jack Nicholson, Michelle Pfeifer, and Susan Sarandon. Warner Bros., 1987.

The Wizard of Oz. Dir. Jack Haley, Jr. Perf. Judy Garland, Frank Morgan, Ray Bolger, Bert Lahr, and Jack Haley. 1939. DVD. Turner Entertainment, 1999.

Wolf, Naomi. *The Beauty Myth: How Images of Beauty are Used Against Women.* New York: HarperCollins, 2002.

Wolfzettel, Friedrich, ed. *Arthurian Romance and Gender.* Amsterdam and Atlanta: Rodopi, 1995.

Zilboorg, G. *The Medical Man and the Witch During the Renaissance.* Baltimore: Johns Hopkins UP, 1935.

Index

A

abjection, 12, 47–49, 104, 110, 124–126
academic writing, theory of, ix
Achterberg, Jeanne, 22–23
agency: for subjects, 158–160; for women, 28, 54, 77–79, 86, 91–92, 94,144–146, 150, 152, 162
Alexander, Flora, 20
Alice in Wonderland, 148–150
Arden, Heather, 22
Arthurian romance, 2, 10–12; battle in, 30–36; carnivalesque imagery in, 57–63, 70–73, 83; economy and, *See* economy; gender conventions in, 15–21, 73–95, 98, 99–108, 111–129, 137; healing in, 21–30; in the fourteenth and fifteenth centuries, 52–95, 99–102, 110–114, 117–118, 137, 141–142; in the sixteenth century, 106–108, 110, 114–120, 122, 124–127, 137, 142; in the twelfth and thirteenth centuries,13–51, 117, 137, 140–141; love's function in, 20–21
Arthurian chronicle, 13–51, 113; gender conventions in, 15–21, 137, 140–141

B

Bailey, Michael, 141
Bakhtin, Mikhail, 57
Baum, L. Frank, 14, 148
Bennett, Judith, 92–93, 109
Bitel, Lisa, 93
Blacker, Jean, 49–50
Briggs, Robin, 132–133

Bruckner, Matilda Tomaryn, 16
Bullough, Vern L., 20
Butler, Judith, 5–6

C

"Carle of Carlisle, The," 11, 53, 55, 58, 62–69, 71, 73–75, 86–87
Cavanagh, Sheila, 125
Charmed, 152–154
Chaucer, Geoffrey, "The Wife of Bath's Tale," 53, 55, 60–62, 66–69, 73–82
chivalric code, 31–36, 62–74, 86
Chrétien de Troyes, 2, 10–11, 53–54; battle in, 30–36; *Cligés*, 15–16, 19, 20, 22, 25–30; *Erec and Enide*, 17, 19, 20; gender conventions in, 15–21; *Knight of the Cart, The*, 18; *Knight With the Lion, The*, 18, 32–34; *Story of the Grail, The*, 18; Thessela (from *Cligés*), 21–22, 25–28, 117, 121
churlish knight, 52–54, 56–58, 62–66, 73–75, 78, 82, 84–89
Cinderella, 52–53, 72, 95; Disney's film, 57, 96
Cixous, Hélène, 159
Cohen, Jeffrey Jerome, 34–35
Crane, Susan, 54
crises of the fourteenth century, 68–69, 89, 109, 141–142

D

Delaney, Sheila, 68–69
De Trafford, Claire, 28–29
discourse, 157–162
Disney. *See* witches, in Disney films
Duby, Georges, 35–36

188 Index

Dyer, Christopher, 68, 91

E

economy (in England): in the fourteenth and fifteenth centuries,
54–56, 68–69, 72–73, 89–94,
137, 141–142, 144–145; in the
sixteenth century, 108–110, 128,
137, 144–145; in the twelfth and
thirteenth centuries, 28–29, 50,
137, 144
Eller, Cynthia, 160
Emperor's New Groove, The, 148–150
estates, medieval, 54–73, 142
Ever After, 95

F

Feinstein, Sandy, 20
Ferguson, Gary, 20
Foucault, Michel, 157–158
Freud, Sigmund, 4–6, 75
Froide, Amy, 92, 109

G

Gadon, Elinor W., 159–160
Gardner, Gerald, 157
Gawain, 11, 32–33, 52–87, 111
gender: androgyny, 37–44; as performance, 2, 3–6; conventions in
fourteenth- and fifteenth-century
texts, 73–95, 137; conventions in
late-fifteenth- and sixteenth-century texts, 96–137; conventions
in twelfth- and thirteenth-
century texts, 15–21, 36–50,
137; conventions in twentieth-
and twenty-first-century texts,
143–162; division of labor and,
21–23, 50, 53, 73, 89–94, 97–98,
109–110, 128, 142, 144–145,
148; healing and, 21–30;
language and, 4; legal rights
and, 28–29, 35–36, 53, 89–94;
psychoanalytical models of, 2–6;
violence and, 30–36, 51, 141
Geoffrey of Monmouth, *The History
of the Kings of Britain*, 19, 34,
36–50; Arthur in, 18–19; battle
in, 30–36; gender conventions
in, 15–21; prophecy in, 36–50;
Prophetie Merlini and, 37, 43, 49
giants, 30–36, 65–66
Gies, Frances and Joseph, 35, 90, 93
Goldberg, P. J. P., 90, 109

Gower, John, "The Tale of Florent,"
53, 55, 58–62, 66–69, 73–82,
87–89
"Greene Knight, The," 53, 55, 58,
62–69, 73–75, 85–86
Greenwood, Susan, 157, 161
Griffin, Wendy, 160

H

Hall, Stuart, 158
Hansen, Bert, 8
Hudson, Harriet E., 54–55, 68, 72
Hughes, Pennethorne, 141

J

Jakobsen, Janet, 157
Jewell, Helen, 90, 91–92

K

Kaeuper, Richard, 35
Kelly, Joan, 110
Kieckhefer, Richard, 8–9, 128, 132–
133, 141–142
Knight, Stephen, 54
Kowaleski, Maryanne, 93
Kristeva, Julia, 47–48, 125
Krueger, Roberta, 16–17

L

Labrynth, 135–136
Lacan, Jacques, 4–6, 125
Laʒamon, *Brut*, 19, 36–50; Argante,
24–25; battle in, 30–36; gender
conventions in, 15–21
Larner, Christina, 143
Le Saux, Françoise H. M., 49
Levack, Brian, 99
L'Hermite-Leclercq, Paulette, 29
Little Mermaid, The, 148–150
loathly lady, 52–54, 56–62, 66–69,
73–85, 87–89, 97, 111
Loraux, Nicole, 37–38

M

magic: definition of, 7–9; demonology
and, 97–108, 142; divine vs.
natural, 8–9, 98–99; fourteenth-
and fifteenth-century representations of, 53–95; healing
and, 21–30; late fifteenth- and
sixteenth-century representations of, 96–136; prophecy and,
36–50, 141; twelfth- and thirteenth-century representations

Index 189

of, 15–50; twentieth- and twenty-first-century representations of, 1–3,13–15,137–162

Malory, Thomas, *Morte Darthur*, 2, 97–102; Brusen in, 117–118; Merlin in (*see* Merlin); Morgan le Fay in (*see* Morgan le Fay); Nineve/Nimue in, 101

Marie de France: "Bisclavret," 19; gender conventions in works of, 17–21; "Guigemar," 18; "Lanval," 17–18, 29–30; "Milun," 19; "Yonec," 38–39, 44

marriage: in fourteenth and fifteenth centuries, 59–62, 66–69, 74–81, 86–88, 90–94; in twelfth and thirteenth centuries, 25–26, 28–29; in the sixteenth century, 105–106, 108–110; in the twentieth and twenty-first centuries, 151–155

"Marriage of Sir Gawain, The," 53, 55, 60–62, 66–69, 73–82, 88–89

maternity: as monstrous, 124–129, 134–135; compulsory maternity, 151; sixteenth-century fascination with, 128–129; psychoanalysis and, 4–5; witchcraft and, 11–12, 53, 82–95, 96–98, 108–136, 145–157

McClain, Lee Tobin, 16

medicine. *See* magic, healing and

Merlin: in Chrétien's works, 37; in Disney's *The Sword in the Stone*, 150; in Geoffrey's *Historia*, 23, 36–37, 39–45, 47–50, 100; in Laȝamon's *Brut*, 38, 40–50, 100; in Malory's *Morte Darthur*, 99–102, 104, 105, 106, 113; in *Sir Gawain and the Green Knight*, 84–85

Milson, F. M., 28

Morgan le Fay: in Chretien's works, 23–24; in Geoffrey's *Historia*, 24; in Laȝamon's *Brut*, 24–25; in Malory's *Morte Darthur*, 100, 111–114,130; in *Sir Gawain and the Green Knight*, 82–85; transformation of, 2–3, 148, 161

Murray, Alexander, 141

Murray, Margaret, 157

N

Neuendorf, Fiona Tolhurst, 43

O

101 Dalmations, 148–150

Opitz, Claudia, 9

P

Phillips, Kim, 89–90, 109

Practical Magic, 50–51

Purkiss, Diane, 13, 94, 108–109, 133, 157, 160

R

rape, 79–82

representation, theory of, 5–6

Rescuers, The, 148–150

Rich, Adrienne, 151

Rose, Jacqueline, 4

S

Savage, Henry, 70

Shakespeare, William, 97–99; Lady Macbeth, 127–128; *Macbeth*, 102, 117–123, 127–128; *Midsummer Night's Dream, A*, 102–104; Sycorax, 123–124; *Tempest, The*, 102, 104–106, 123–124; Weird sisters, 1, 117–123

sexual difference. *See* gender

"Sir Gawain and the Carle of Carlisle," 53, 55, 58, 62–69, 73–75

Sir Gawain and the Green Knight, 53, 55, 56–58, 62–72, 73–75, 82–85

Sleeping Beauty, 148–150

Snow White and the Seven Dwarves: Wicked Queen, 96–97, 114, 116–117, 134, 148–150

Sparhawk, 160

Spenser, Edmund, *The Faerie Queene*, 97–99, 122, 124–127; Archimago, 106–108, 120; Duessa, 114–116, 126, 130; Errour, 124–126; hag-witch (of Book III), 117–120, 122; monstrous mothers in, 124–127

Staub, Susan C., 128

Sword in the Stone, The, 148–150

T

"Turke and Sir Gawain, The," 53, 55, 58, 62–69, 73–75

W

"Wedding of Sir Gawain and Dame Ragnelle, The," 53, 55, 58–62, 66–69, 73–82, 87–89

190 *Index*

Weiss, Judith, 28
Wicca,1, 8, 156–162
Willis, Deborah, 94, 110, 128–130
witches: Charmed Ones, The (from *Charmed*), 152–154; Cruella de Vil (from *101 Dalmations*), 148–150; Duessa (from Spenser's *Faerie Queene*), 114–116, 126, 130; feminist spirituality/witchcraft, 156–162; Glinda, 110–111, 146; hag-witch (of Spenser's *Faerie Queene*, Book III), 117–120, 122; Hindremstein, Dorothea, 132–133; in Disney films, 57, 96–97, 114, 116–117, 134, 148–151; in early medieval romances, 21–31, 137, 141; in late medieval romances, 53, 82–95, 137, 141–142; in Renaissance literature, 108–137, 142; in Renaissance theology, 129–131; in twentieth- and twenty-first-century film and television, 143–162; legislation against, 139–143; Mad Madame Mim (from *The Sword in the Stone*), 148–150; Madame Medusa (from *The Rescuers*), 148–150; maternity and, 82–95, 97–98, 108–136, 137–162; personal knowledge of, 1; Queen of Hearts (from *Alice in Wonderland*), 148–150; Sawyer, Elizabeth, 130–131; Stevens, Samantha (from *Bewitched*), 151–152; Sycorax (from Shakespeare's *The Tempest*), 123–124; Thessela (from Chrétien's *Cligés*), 21–22, 25–28, 117, 121;

Ursula (from *The Little Mermaid*), 148–150; Weird sisters (from Shakespeare's *Macbeth*), 1, 117–123; Wicked Witch of the East (from *Wizard of Oz*), 146; Wicked Witch of the West (from *Wizard of Oz*), 13–15, 117, 145–148; Wicked Queen (from *Snow White*), 96–97, 114, 116–117, 134, 148–150; Witches of Eastwick (from film), 154–156; witchcraft, 86–87, 108–136,137–143, 156–162; witchcraft trials, 129–131, 137–143; witches' sabbath, 129–130, 140; Yzma (from *The Emperor's New Groove*), 148–150
Witches of Eastwick, The, 154–156
Wizard of Oz, The, 13–15,145–148; Dorothy, 50, 110–111, 146–148; Glinda, 110–111, 146; Wicked Witch of the West/Elmira Gulch, 13–15, 117, 145–148; Wizard/Prof. Marvel, 14, 147
Wolfzettel, Friedrich, 16
Wolf, Naomi, 149
women: backlash against, 108–110, 145; beauty and, 96–97, 110–116, 148–149; in modern witchcraft movements, 157, 158–162; rights in Anglo-Norman England, 28–30, 51; rights in late medieval England, 89–95, 144–145; rights in Renaissance England, 109–110, 145; rights in twenty-first-century U.S., 145; single-women, 92–94, 109–110, 116, 145; widows, 91–94, 109–110, 116, 145